Rebel with
a Clause

Rebel with a Clause

· ·

Tales and Tips from a
Roving Grammarian

ELLEN JOVIN

MARINER BOOKS
Boston   New York

HarperCollins books may be purchased for educational, business, or sales promotional use. For information, please email the Special Markets Department at SPsales@harpercollins.com.

FIRST EDITION

Book design by Margaret Rosewitz
Map by Chrissy Kurpeski

Library of Congress Cataloging-in-Publication Data has been applied for.
ISBN 978-0-358-27815-3

22 23 24 25 26 LSC 10 9 8 7 6 5 4 3 2 1

To Brandt

Contents

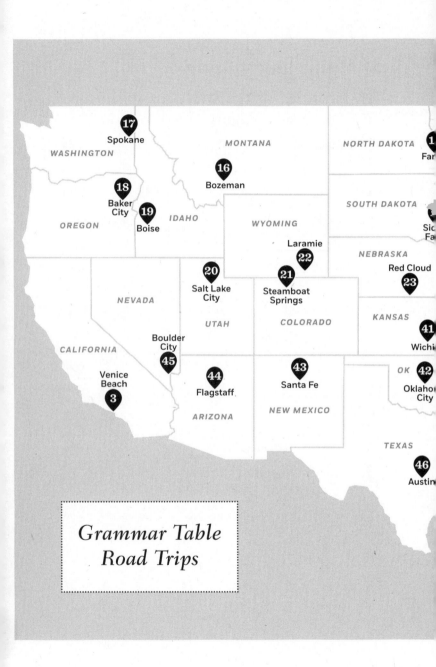

Grammar Table Road Trips

Introduction:
A Table Unfolded

In the late afternoon of September 21, 2018, I exited my New York apartment building carrying a folding table and a big sign reading GRAMMAR TABLE. I crossed Broadway to a little park called Verdi Square, found a spot at the northern entrance to the Seventy-Second Street subway station, propped up my sign, and prepared to answer grammar questions from passersby.

This might seem bizarre to some, but to me it felt like destiny. I've been teaching writing and grammar for decades. I love grammar. I've studied twenty-five languages for fun. My bookshelves are filled with grammar and usage books, carefully alphabetized by language from Albanian to Zulu. I majored in German in college and earned a master's degree in comparative literature, specializing in African American and German writers. One of the greatest pleasures of my life has been participating in a world of reading and literature and beautiful, varied words. I love exploring how they are put together, not just in English, which is the focus of this book, but in all the languages I have studied.

The Grammar Table idea originally came to me a couple of months before that inaugural fall afternoon. From the moment the whim first entered my head, I knew I had to make it happen. Waiting for the furnace days of summer to end, I took care of the practical details. I researched opaque city regulations before determining that dispensing free grammar advice qualified as free speech; I studied the folding table market and ordered my favorite and most grammar-friendly, a lightweight forty-eight by twenty inches; and I made a Grammar Table sign, adding to it what I thought were helpful discussion-inspiring suggestions, such as "capitalization complaints," "semicolonphobia," and "comma crisis."

That September day, it took me approximately thirty seconds to start getting visitors. One of the first questions involved a spousal apostrophe dispute. A woman came up to me with her husband, two kids, and a complaint. Handing me her cell phone, she told me her husband had sent her a text message with a misplaced apostrophe. The evidence was right there on the screen: "Another fun afternoon for the Benson's!" I told her she was right: no apostrophe. The husband laughed—he had no painful grammar sensitivities—and off went the apostrophe-free Bensons to enjoy their afternoon.

Some people just need someone to smile at them politely while they're complaining, and then they go home happier. I like listening to people, and I'm genuinely curious about them, which is why I included a "Vent!" option right on my Grammar Table sign. I've heard a lot of complaints—about apostrophes used for plurals, missing commas, extra commas, run-on sentences, spelling snafus, peripatetic participles, and more.

Sometimes my interventions soothe the insecurities of the questioner. A tiny Filipino woman—maybe five feet tall, about forty years old—approached the table holding the hand of a tinier girl. She wanted to know how to pronounce "finance." Did the word start out like "fine" and have the stress on the first syllable, or did it begin like "fin" and have the stress on the second? When she heard that her second-syllable stress was fine, even preferable in the opinion of one of the experts whose books lay on the Grammar Table, she started jumping up and down. This is neither hyperbole nor metaphor: she literally jumped up and down and made her smaller companion's arm sail in sync with her excitement. Someone had been telling her she was wrong, and now she knew she wasn't, and she felt better!

That turns out to be a common experience for people who approach me: teachers or co-workers or others in their lives have made them feel bad about their use of language. But mine is not the Grammar Judgment Table, and I will listen to whatever is on people's minds, even when they arrive with allegations rather than questions: "Millennials are ruining the language," or "No one knows how to write anymore because it's all text-speak." I have heard quite a few speeches about how young people are destroying English, but young people, even children, ask some of the best questions of all, so I remain profoundly unconcerned.

I know how deep people's relationship to grammar runs, because I've been teaching adults of all socioeconomic and educational backgrounds for thirty years. Language is connected to people's sense of self and their sense of power. There is a lot of grammar insecurity; people regularly wish they knew more about the building blocks of the words they use. Whoever the Grammar Table visitors are, I want them to feel good about the relationship they have with language today and, if they want to acquire new knowledge, hopeful about where they might end up.

In the beginning, I regularly sat out by the same Seventy-Second Street subway stop on Broadway. That station disgorges thousands of people every evening during rush hour. However, I was soon on the move to other locations around town. Language lovers are numerous and ubiquitous in New York. At Grand Central one day, I ended up surrounded by eight Metropolitan Transit Authority workers in uniform—five men and three women. At first I thought they were going to tell me I had to leave, but instead the encounter became an MTA grammar confessional.

One told me, "I can't tell the difference between 'your' and 'you're.'" Another complained, "I don't know what to do with the semicolon." A third MTA employee, a woman, confessed, "I can't pronounce 'ambulance' right. I keep saying ambilance!" Her co-workers agreed that yes, she did do that! Then a six-foot-seven employee jumped in. "I can do just two things," he said. "I can reach things and I can write. But you can't make money as a writer, so I work for the MTA instead!"

Within six months, I was answering grammar questions across state lines. That's because after the positive response to the Grammar Table in New York, my husband and I had the same thought: Road trip! And off we went. Brandt Johnson, my partner in life as well as in a communication skills training firm—and a language lover himself who is constantly making pronoun antecedent jokes around the home—has now filmed hundreds of Grammar Table encounters in forty-seven states, footage that he is turning into a Grammar Table documentary.

We were going for fifty, but the pandemic arrived in the US before we reached Hawaii, Alaska, and Connecticut.

Well, we did actually *reach* Connecticut, but Brandt and I were hungry and got pizza, which was delicious, so then we got more pizza, and then it got dark and cold, so we thought, "We can come back anytime," but then COVID-19 came first and we couldn't. As I write this, however, plans for the missing three states are in the works.

Because of the Grammar Table, I have met thousands of people I would never have known otherwise. A grandmother in Montana told us she had just been diagnosed that day with dementia, and Brandt and I each gave her a big hug and tried not to cry. A construction worker in Alabama revealed a secret fascination with fountain pens. In New York, a fashionably dressed young woman told me, "I am an obsessive lover of footnotes," then pulled out her phone and showed me a photo of her foot with [7] *ibid* tattooed on it. I had met my first footnote fetishist!

My visitors are diverse, and often really different from me in outlook and experience. We have conversations, however, that are filled with humor and feeling for the complex linguistic glue that binds us together as human beings and distinguishes us from other living creatures. Some of the experiences are so moving that I have to steady my voice when I reply.

It is important to me that people who don't speak English natively, or at all, feel welcome. That's why my sign says ANY LANGUAGE! I love and welcome discussions of *all* languages, and I treasure opportunities to exercise my skills in ones I speak or have studied. To date, Grammar Table conversations have extended well beyond English to cover topics in Spanish, German, Arabic, Polish,

French, Urdu, Chinese, Italian, Russian, Hebrew, Portuguese, Japanese, Tagalog, Turkish, Sinhalese, Armenian, Bengali, Lakota, Greek, Indonesian, Latin, Hindi, Korean, Dutch, and more.

In this book, I share some of my experiences at the Grammar Table, divided by topic, framed with guidance, and illustrated with real-life examples from around the country. You may recognize some of the questions as ones you have, too. Language is powerful: it enables large, organized collections of people to live together, to cooperate, to experience joy and wit, and to improve the human condition. It is a thing to celebrate.

At a time of deep divisions within the United States, my experiences have reminded me that it is still possible for strangers who disagree to talk instead of fight — and even if they do fight, to do so without hating. After all, how mad can one really get about a comma?* The quotidian is calming. We all poop, and we all punctuate.

Because† so many of the Grammar Table encounters were filmed, thanks to Brandt, I had a massive amount of documentation to use in writing this book. I have edited dialogue for clarity, length, and coherence, and have also altered identifying details, especially in cases where people told me something personal that they might find embarrassing. I changed most names. (To those who wanted to be publicly identified discussing their favorite grammar question, I apologize!) Finally, to avoid repetition

---

* Pretty mad.

† You *can* begin a sentence with "because." The notion that you can't is one of the most widespread and frankly wackadoodle myths oppressing American adults seeking to write like, well, adults.

and enhance explanations, I sometimes amended spur-of-the-moment sentence examples I used while chatting on city streets.

In each new city or town, we had to find the spots with the best grammar traffic. This was sometimes challenging. Our New York neighborhood has a population density of 110,000 people per square mile, as well as a pedestrian culture; most locations around the country did not provide the firehose of grammar questions I get outside our local subway station. Still, as long as there are places with people, there will always be places with people who want to talk about grammar.

Another consideration, a big one, was that we needed locations from which we wouldn't promptly be expelled by security or police. In Nevada, we drove around Boulder City for a while before we found an appealing spot outside a store called Sherman's House of Antiques. The store owner kindly let us set up the Grammar Table and camera equipment on the sidewalk in front of the store's entrance, amid antique chests of drawers and a life-size carving of the Blues Brothers.

People who like to browse antiques apparently also like discussing words, because I had a lot of visitors on that cold, gray afternoon. "We have to stop and talk to this woman about grammar," I heard a passing woman say to the man with her. She told me, "Do you know I was traumatized in sixth grade by all that sentence diagramming? I was so terrible at it. I didn't like grammar, but I do now, as an adult. I wish I could study it."

"There are options for that," I said.

"Yeah," said the woman. "So what do you do?" I explained the Grammar Table.

"Is this like a therapist, like for five cents?" she asked, alluding to the *Peanuts* character Lucy with her advice stand.

"I do like to think that I provide some therapeutic calm to people who are distraught about grammar," I said, and she laughed. "Everyone uses words, and everyone has a different relationship to language."

Now, please lie down on a nice couch with this book and let's have some grammar therapy.

*Rebel with
a Clause*

1

A National Obsession: The Oxford Comma

Whether I am sitting out there in the cold, the heat, the morning, the evening, a big city, or a tiny town, there is one thing I am approached about more than any other topic, by far, and that is the Oxford comma.

"Oxford comma, yes or no?"

"Oxford comma or bust!"

A woman in North Dakota told me, "Oh my god, I had somebody call me a coastal elite because I was talking about the Oxford comma!"

In case this term is unfamiliar to you, here is a sentence containing an Oxford comma:

A priest, a nun, and a sloth walked slowly into a bar.

The Oxford comma is the comma you see right before the "and" toward the end of that list. The term also applies to a comma before "or" in a list, though those are less common.

For her seventh birthday, my daughter is hoping for a stuffed brontosaurus, a Venus flytrap, or slime-eating monsters.

For something that could be mistaken for a speck of dirt on a page, the Oxford comma—known less snootily, but also less broadly, as a serial comma, and sometimes also as a series comma—inspires strong attachments. It is one of the emotional hot-button issues of our time.

"Tell us what the Oxford comma is," said a thirty-something man named Dan in Red Cloud, a dot of a Nebraska town best known for having been home to *O Pioneers!* and *My Ántonia* author Willa Cather. "I really want to know."

He was with his wife, Cori, whose straight brown hair hung far down her back, for a busy summer weekend of Willa Cather tourism. I was sitting in front of the National Willa Cather Center in the Main Street Historic District, next to a pickup truck from whose bed* a friendly woman was selling fresh corn.

"It appears in a list," I said, and began writing a sample sentence for them on a notepad. "I ordered books," I read aloud as I wrote, "from Willa Cather, Theodore Dreiser, and . . . Who should be my third?"

"Who's our favorite?" Cori asked her husband. "Oh, James Joyce!"

---

* I used "whose" to refer to a truck. Some people object to the use of "whose" with things. That is an unsupportable extension of the "Use 'who' for people" idea. English doesn't have a separate possessive form for "which"—"whose" is all we've got. To objectors, I offer this list of objects that have been referred to with "whose" in excellent literature: a tree in F. Scott Fitzgerald's *The Great Gatsby,* a game in Ralph Ellison's *Invisible Man,* streets in Virginia Woolf's *Mrs. Dalloway,* and an asylum in Evelyn Waugh's *Brideshead Revisited.* I won't go on, but I definitely could.

"James Joyce," I said, adding it to the end of my list. "You are hard-core!"

"We read *Finnegans Wake*," Cori told me. "Together, out loud, and it started the second day we knew each other. Our first date!"

"When I was in high school," said Dan, "there was an upperclassman I looked up to. He would brag about how he had read *Finnegans Wake*, and that was always a life goal for me. And so—"

"—we made it happen," Cori finished his sentence.

"We read it together out loud over three years," said Dan. "And it was hilarious—laughs on every page. And then I ran into this same guy, he was working in a grocery store, and I'm like, 'I did it! Remember when you told me you read *Finnegans Wake*? My girlfriend and I read it together!' And he said, 'Aw, man, I was just BS-ing, I never read that.' So now we're the only ones we know who have ever read it."

I was impressed. I showed Dan and Cori the finished sentence.

I ordered books by Willa Cather, Theodore Dreiser, and James Joyce.

"The comma after Dreiser is the one they call the Oxford comma," I said.

"I do it," Cori said. "I do it all the time!"

"Is that good?" asked Dan.

"You can do it either way," I said. "It's highly encouraged by *The Chicago Manual of Style*." I held up *Chicago* as a visual aid. "This book is used by a lot of people in the publishing industry. But *The Associated Press Style-*

book, which governs a lot of what you see in newspapers, doesn't advocate using it unless it's necessary for clarity."

"I'd be in the hard-core camp," said Cori.

While we were talking, an education specialist from the Willa Cather Foundation arrived, and the Willa Cather tourists caught her up on the critical details of our conversation.

"I heart the Oxford comma," said the specialist, Rebecca, forming a heart shape with her hands.

"Why?" asked Dan. "Why is it important to you?"

"Because there are contextual things that will potentially be misconstrued if you don't have that last comma," Rebecca explained.

"So you feel like it's lazy to leave it off," Dan said. "These people lack character."

"No, now you're putting words in my mouth," she replied.

To clarify Rebecca's point, I offer you these two sentences from what may be the most shared punctuation meme* in meme history:

We invited the strippers, JFK, and Stalin.

We invited the strippers, JFK and Stalin.

In the meme, the first sentence is applauded for its upstanding use of an Oxford comma, while the second

---

* An internet meme is a captioned picture or video that is shared by people online. In case you are wondering why I'm explaining such a well-known term, it's because there are plenty of people who are living along without knowing what a meme is. I have checked!

is illustrated with JFK and Stalin dressed as strippers. I am unimpressed. I do not feel concerned that anyone reading the second sentence will mistakenly think John F. Kennedy and Joseph Stalin were the invited strippers. Meme accuracy is not a prerequisite for meme popularity, however, and the American Oxford comma obsession rages on, even as plenty of people in other languages and countries keep right on functioning without one. That comma may be a national obsession, but it is surely not a global one.

"I think it's about the cadence," said Cori.

"I've started a brawl," Dan said.

"A grammar brawl!" said Cori.

"If you could have a brawl," I said excitedly, "that'd be great for the Grammar Table documentary!"

¶

It is fact that some people are reluctant to approach the Grammar Table. Perhaps they fear a quiz, or a hard sell, or a scolding, or—if Brandt is filming—the cameras. On a late December day in Verdi Square, a group of three young men and three young women were eyeing me and the Grammar Table from afar. They appeared to be discussing best next steps.

"Would you like to visit?" I semi-yelled, in the semi-yell I have perfected for Grammar Table use, so that I can sound welcoming while still being heard across parks and noisy subway stations. "Nothing bad will happen," I added as they headed over.

The ringleader, Tucker, was a cute, clean-cut guy with closely cropped light brown hair. "All right," he said as he approached, rubbing his hands together. "I have to vent about something. The Oxford comma I feel is an important part of grammar, and so many people don't use it, and it frustrates me."

As he spoke, he looked up at the sky and clapped in time to his words. "What"—*clap*—"is your"—*clap*—"opinion"—*clap*—"on that?" he asked.

"Do your friends all share your point of view?" I asked.

"Yes," said Kim, a young woman in a maroon shirt—sternly, with her arms crossed.

"I believe they do," said Tucker, the Oxford comma ringleader.

"Is that why you're friends?" I asked. "You're friends because you're in sync about the Oxford comma? My feelings about it are not as strong as yours."

"Okay," said Tucker, eyeing me suspiciously.

"I've gone through multiple Oxford comma phases in my life," I said. "When I worked as a freelance reporter, I had to follow Associated Press style, and that typically leaves it out, unless the comma is needed for clarity. So I wrote article after article without it. But then about a year after I stopped freelancing, it went back into my writing. And I'm still using it. Do you use it even in simple lists?"

"All the time," said Tucker. "One hundred percent of the time."

"Do *all* of you use the Oxford comma?" I asked.

"Yes, every second," said Kim, the woman in maroon. The other two women nodded. They formed an intimidating all-girl punctuation posse. A man in a Superman T-shirt silently raised his hand to indicate agreement. That left one holdout—and Tucker, the ringleader, pointed accusingly at him.

"It depends on my mood," said Oxford-Ambivalent

Guy. "I don't have a rule. If I feel it's right, I use the Oxford."

The Oxford? He didn't even bother with the word "comma." This was a man who could truly take the Oxford comma or leave the Oxford comma. His friends looked at him aghast.

"Are you going to be ostracized after this?" I asked, and everyone laughed.

"You know, this is the kind of thing I would expect from you," Tucker told him.

I learned that this (mostly) punctuation-passionate crowd had all gone to high school together in Florida. They were now sophomores at different colleges but were reuniting in New York City during their winter holidays for the second year in a row.

"We're trying to make it an annual thing," said Kim.

"You must really like each other," I said. "Although you"—I indicated the holdout—"are probably going to be on the outs now because of your erratic Oxford comma use." Oxford-Ambivalent Guy nodded philosophically.

"What are you going to do for the rest of your time here?" I asked.

"We're about to go catch an opera," said Kim. "At the Met: *The Magic Flute*."

"Wow," I said. "You're a really cultured group. I'm impressed. The opera thing, the Oxford comma thing—"

"It's really just him," said Oxford-Ambivalent Guy, pointing to the ringleader. "He's the biggest one about the Oxford comma."

"No!" said Tucker.

"No!" said Kim, accompanied by protests from her other friends. "I have great passion about this."

"You do?" asked Oxford-Ambivalent Guy.

"We are *all* passionate about this!" said Tucker.

"Okay," said Oxford-Ambivalent Guy.

"You just wouldn't understand," said Tucker.

¶

One thing became clear early on in the travels of the Grammar Table: If people took the time to ask me how I felt about the Oxford comma, they were unlikely to be indifferent to it themselves.

I met a man in Utah, however, who was an exception. On an August day that would later reach a hundred degrees, I spoke to him while sweatily stationed across the street from Temple Square, a ten-acre Mormon complex in the middle of downtown Salt Lake City. An ID tag hanging from his shirt identified him as Charles.

Charles told me that the Oxford comma had been a source of friction between him and a friend. "My friend didn't want them," he said.

"Yes, people can get very upset about the Oxford comma," I said. "Do you use them?"

"Well, my friend and I were having a knock-down-drag-out fight about this, so I did some research," he said. "And I was right: either way is fine. She was not open to the idea that both were acceptable. That fight has served me well, though, because every time I argue with her, every time we come to an impasse, I say to her, 'Remember the comma!'"

"I approve of your open-mindedness about the Oxford comma," I said.

"Open-minded grammar is my business," he replied.

¶

In the Bozeman Public Library in Bozeman, Montana, I met a man in a gray hoodie who apparently had *not* been encountering open-minded grammar.

"Hey, how ya doin'?" said the man, thirtyish, with sunglasses atop his head.

"Welcome to Grammar Table," I said.

"What's up?" he asked. "I'm a rappa." He leaned over to the Grammar Table microphone (yes, there is one!). "I got gramma. I got lyrics, I got ad libs, what you need, what's goin' on?"

"This is the mobile Grammar Table," I said. "It originated in New York City. It's on the road, and the Bozeman Public Library is part of the road."

"Nice," said Rapping Man. He was on the road himself, he told me.

"What are you doing at the library today?" I asked.

"Just taking care of some business," said Rapping Man. "You know, what you do when you're on the road. You're like, I gotta sit in the library so I can use the internet."

"It's a good library," I said. "Do you have any grammar comments or questions?"

"What's up with that Oxford comma?" asked Rapping Man. "Is that correct?"

"I am a user," I said, "but I'm not a fierce advocate. I can take it or leave it. What do you prefer?"

"I say just do away with it completely so there's no confusion," said Rapping Man.

"Well, some people get very attached," I said. "They're adamant about their Oxford commas. So you have to watch it."

"What's up with that?" said Rapping Man. "English teachers."

"No," I said. "A lot of people."

"Yeah," said Rapping Man. "Callouts on Facebook: 'You forgot the comma, dude!' Don't you have anything better to do? Fires are burning in the Amazon. Are you going to Area 51? Do something good!"

¶

We were in Flagstaff, Arizona, not far from where my wonderful, witty great-aunt Lenore lived when I was a child, and it was snowing. She had once been a high school librarian, and perhaps that is why, once I saw that it was going to be too cold and snowy to set up outside, I thought of emailing the local library for permission to set up in one of their branches. They said yes, so the next morning Brandt and I headed over to East Flagstaff Community Library.

Soon a young librarian named Bethany came over to talk. "What is your opinion on the Oxford comma?" she asked.

"I'm guessing that you like it," I said.

"Oh, yes!" said Bethany.

"You sighed when you said that," I said.

"I needed to get it off my chest," said Bethany.

"So this isn't just a mild affection," I said. "You really like to have it in there."

"Yeah," said Bethany.

"Have you always been drawn to it?" I asked.

"Yes, definitely," said Bethany.

"This a lifelong attraction?" I asked.

"I definitely have a lifelong attraction," said Bethany.

"Good to know," I said. "You feel a lack without it?"

"Yes," said Bethany. "I just always think of . . . I don't know if you've seen the meme of the eggs, toast, and orange juice."

"Yes, I have," I said. That particular meme failed to convince me that if I wrote "eggs, toast and orange juice" without the Oxford comma rather than "eggs, toast, and orange juice" with the Oxford comma, someone would mistakenly think there was orange juice on the toast.

"I've also seen the Stalin and JFK meme with the strippers," I told her.

"I haven't seen that one, but I can maybe piece it together," said Bethany. "I'll just google that and see what comes up."

"Just google strippers," suggested Brandt helpfully. "You'll get all sorts of hits."

"I'll google strippers and see what happens," said Bethany. "I'm sure it will talk about grammar. I'm sure that's what I'll get. I don't even know. But yeah, I just feel like it's too easy for it to take on a different meaning if you don't explicitly separate it out."

"I feel it's not really likely to take on a different meaning," I said, "but I am attracted to it at this stage of my life because it keeps the rhythm of the list. You know: this, this, and this—so it just feels more musically appropriate."

"Yeah," said Bethany. "I like that!"

"You do?" I asked. "Okay. But for things like marketing or advertising writing for our business, like on our website, although I do put it in, I feel it can look a little heavy. It's not as sleek."

"That makes sense," said Bethany. "But I'm very fond of it."

"Well, I do put it," I said, "so in that sense we are kindred spirits, although you may be more . . . more . . . I can't think of the word . . ."

"Maybe a little more loyal," she said.

¶

Some people simply find life too gross without the Oxford comma. I met one of them in downtown Starkville, Mississippi.

"Do you believe in the Oxford comma?" asked a young man there. His name was Joseph, and he was a college student majoring in chemical engineering.

"I personally use it right now," I said, "but I've gone through long stretches of life not using it."

"It freaks me out to not use it," said Joseph. "It doesn't seem right."

"What if it's just three words, though?" I asked. "Like 'I ordered salad, spaghetti, and soda.' You still use it there? I'm testing the depths of your dedication."

"Yeah, definitely," said Joseph. "It just sounds weird otherwise, because if you say 'I ordered salad comma, spaghetti and soda,' it's like spaghetti and soda are one entity. What is that?" He made a face. "That's nasty."

"You make a good point," I said. "We want to keep the food delicious."

"Amen," said Joseph. "We want to keep the items separate. And food is separate on one plate. It's like keeping it separate with a comma."

¶

In Chicago I set up the Grammar Table not far from the famous Bean sculpture in Millennium Park, but far enough that I wouldn't be expelled. Some places are vigilantly patrolled for grammar advice stands and other interlopers. The Bean is one of those places; you cannot mess with the Bean.

I was glad I persisted, because it was there that I met a man of real commitment: his position on the Oxford comma had cost him his livelihood. His name was Samuel, and he was a retired copy editor from Massachusetts.

"I was fired from a job once, partly because of my stern defense of the serial comma," said Samuel. "I really think it's necessary. There are many sentences where the sense will change without the comma. I had this job, and there was a new head of production, and he called a meeting to make some pronouncements. One of them was, 'We're no longer going to use the serial comma.' I said, 'I think there are many uses for the serial comma. I propose that we retain it.' That didn't sit well with him."

And that was that for his job.

Beat that, you Oxford comma lovers.

Quizlet

....

Is there an Oxford comma in the following sentences?

1. My horse is a good judge of character, and my cat is a good judge of tuna.
2. A noun is a person, place, thing, or idea.

Answers: *(1) No, there's no list. This is a compound sentence consisting of two independent clauses* combined with the word "and." (2) Yes. An Oxford comma can precede an "and" or an "or" before the last item in a list.*

----

* An independent clause is a group of words that (a) contains a subject and a verb and (b) can stand alone as a sentence. "You have now finished Chapter 1" is an independent clause.

2

The Joy of Grammar Vocabulary

One Halloween night in Manhattan, I wore a pink wig, a grammar T-shirt of my own design, and a silver cape. Glowing atop the Grammar Table, next to my reference books, was a plastic orange pumpkin with a gaping mouth full of candy.

A woman walked up to the Grammar Table and yelled, "Boo!"

"Interjection!" I yelled back.

I've always loved knowing the names of the bits and pieces that make up sentences. I often encounter people who wish they had been taught those things in more detail. I meet others who were taught them but who wish they remembered better what they learned.

"I feel like I've started to forget a lot of grammar, like terminology and things about grammar, that I learned in middle school," confessed a blond college freshman and teacher-to-be. That day the Grammar Table was at the side of a trail in Zilker Park in Austin, Texas, not far from the popular Barton Springs Pool, where people were swimming but I was not, because I was conjugating at the Grammar Table.

"Does that bother you?" I asked.

"Yes!" said the teacher, whose name was Susan. "So

much." For someone so young, she had an impressively, luminously maternal encouraging air.

"We learned those names to help us follow explanations of general principles of language use," I said, "but the names aren't as important if you retain the instinct. I happen to like knowing the vocabulary, so I can relate to your comment, because I just think it's fun."

"It *is* fun," said Susan. "I think so, too. And I found myself kind of wanting to understand grammar more. I found that whenever I would be speaking, I would try to focus too much on making sure my grammar was correct, and I would kind of get flustered in what I was actually trying to say, just because I was so focused on being grammatically correct. And I couldn't really articulate my words the way that I wanted to because of that."

"Well, I think it's important not to let that get in your way when you're speaking, because the most important thing is the ideas," I said. "Also, you sound great."

"Thank you!" said Susan. She gave me a big smile.

¶

In Morgantown, West Virginia, sixty-two-year-old Gary at first seemed taken aback to encounter a Grammar Table on the streets of his city. I was stationed across the street from a statue of the actor Don Knotts, who grew up there and whom I grew up watching on television, first on *The Andy Griffith Show* and later on *Three's Company*. Behind me was an empty storefront with a For Rent sign in the window.

"Do I have to speak right?" asked Gary.

"You don't have to do anything," I said. "Do you have any grammar questions?"

"Nah," said Gary, but instead of leaving, he stayed to chat. He told me he was originally from Baltimore but had lived in West Virginia for twenty-four years.

"You said this is your Grammar Table," he said. "What's an adjective?"

"An adjective," I said, "is a word that can modify a noun or a pronoun. 'Modify' means describe or limit in some way. For example, 'a red apple.' 'Apple' is the noun and then 'red' is the adjective; it describes the noun. And you can heap them up, like you could say 'a shiny red apple.'"

"Like 'a black train,'" said Gary.

"Exactly," I said. "Or 'a fast train,' or 'an angry woman.'"

"I've run into a few of them," said Gary. "More than I'd care to tell about." He laughed heartily.

"Why did you want to know what an adjective was?" I asked. "It just popped into your head?"

"Yeah," he said. "And I'm trying to think of some other things, like I know what a noun is: a person, place, or thing."

"That's right!" I said.

"What's a pronoun?" he asked. Smoke from the cigarette in his hand enveloped him.

"A pronoun is like a vague noun," I said. "They work the same way; they also describe people and places and things, but in a vaguer way. Like 'everyone' is a pronoun, but it's not as specific as a noun like 'boy' or 'girl.'"

Next Gary wanted to know what a conjunction was.

"A conjunction," I said, "is a combining word like 'and,' 'or,' 'but,' or 'because.'"

"Oh, okay," said Gary, nodding with apparent interest.

"There are dozens and dozens of those," I explained. "And the punctuation rules vary depending on which type of conjunction you use, so that's sometimes why they teach them. You remember stuff, though! You're pulling these terms out of your head."

"Yeah, I remember them," he said, "but I just don't know what they are."

"It's like you went to high school yesterday," I said.

"Nah, it's been about forty-five years since I've been in high school," said Gary. "I have trouble with English."

"I'm understanding you perfectly," I said. "What do you think your trouble is?"

"I don't understand it," he said. "It's so easy to speak, but when they put it down on paper and make you work it out, it's like, really? Like business English? You gotta have your commas and your periods and your question marks and everything right, and I failed the pre-test for the GED because of business English."

"Did you try taking it recently, or was that a while ago?" I asked.

"Oh, it was a while ago," said Gary.

"Do you ever think of taking it again?" I asked.

"No," he said. "I'm sixty-two years old. I don't need no high school diploma. I'm allowed to make up to seventeen thousand a year, I get six hundred and thirty-three dollars a month, and I'm happy with that. And I'm smarter than most high school graduates anyway!"

¶

Pleasure is a powerful motivation in student learning—and life. In Red Cloud, Nebraska, a woman named Gale reminisced about the grammar games she played in eighth grade.

"Every Friday afternoon in Mrs. Macavay's class, we'd play grammar baseball," she said. "I geared up for it all week. She would divide the class into two teams and the room into three bases. We'd open up a book, and every person had to take a sentence, and if you got through the sentence—"

"Wait, what would you have to do with the sentence?" I asked.

"You had to say the parts of speech,"* said Gale. "Linking verb,† prepositional phrase,‡ and so on. The game started off with a student naming the part of speech for the first word in the sentence. If they got it right, they would go to first base. The next student would continue on with the same sentence and the next word. If you answered incorrectly or you weren't keeping track of where we were in the sentence, that counted as an out."

I was impressed by this classroom ingenuity. Gale continued: "Once the bases were loaded, the player coming up to bat had the option of hitting a home run. In order to hit a home run, the student had to name all the parts of speech in a sentence and identify the complete subject and predicate. When that happened, the team went wild!"

"And did you like it?" I asked.

---

* The parts of speech include nouns, pronouns, adjectives, verbs, adverbs, prepositions, conjunctions, and interjections.

† A linking verb describes a state or condition. Here are some examples, with the linking verb underlined: "I <u>am</u> tall," "He <u>feels</u> hungry," "They <u>became</u> greedy," and "Gertrude <u>looked</u> authoritative."

‡ Examples of prepositional phrases include "at the train station," "of the people," "for the community," and "in the grammar book."

"Oh, I loved it," said Gale. "I couldn't wait for Fridays!"

Gale grew up to become a first-grade teacher.

I never played grammar baseball in school, but when I taught comprehensive grammar classes for adults, I would often teach—or more often, reteach—them the names of different grammatical elements: independent clauses, adverbs, and so on. It's difficult to discuss punctuation rules, for example, or grammar principles in other languages, without some basic terminology.

To reinforce the definitions, I sometimes gave students sentence models and asked them to create sentences based on those models. For example:

[noun]	[verb]	[prepositional phrase]
Karen	doodled	behind the sofa.
Dogs	bark	at household appliances.
Chocolate	is	in the safe.

This may not sound quite as exciting as grammar baseball, but it can take people past the point of reflexively reciting definitions and help them connect the terms with actual examples from their stores of vocabulary and their lives. Once you get the hang of it, you can go wild! Composing fresh sentences to fit various patterns allows for creativity and whimsy along with a growing sense of grammatical elements.

For example:

[adjective][adjective][noun][prepositional phrase]
[verb][verb][verb][adverb][prepositional phrase]*

Knowing the word ingredients in what I write gives me joy and a sense of control. It demystifies sentences for me. If something is structurally awry in one, I can identify the problem and fix it.

When an activity is pleasurable and rewarding, children as well as adults are much more likely to pursue it.

---

* For the purpose of this exercise, students should be allowed to use articles ("a," "an," and "the") as adjectives. Some readers will have been taught to view articles that way, and some readers will regard the conflation of those two things as an abomination, but putting them in the same bucket makes this sentence-creation exercise more fun and flexible.

Whoever you are, I sincerely hope you are enjoying yourself so far in this book.

Quizlet

••

What part of speech is each underlined word below?

> Yesterday Vladi canceled the grammar gala.

Answer: *"Yesterday" = adverb, "canceled" = verb, "gala" = noun. In case you are troubled by the spelling of "canceled": there will be a discussion of that in Chapter 10.*

3

"Affect" and "Effect" Are Mean Spelling Trolls

I have answered questions about "affect" and "effect" in dozens of states: New York, South Dakota, Louisiana, Virginia, and anywhere else there's been a need. I often draw "affect"/"effect" tables — like the one shown here — for grammar customers.

	affect	effect
verb (Here.)	Your lack of commas affects my mood.	Dara effected change in the workplace napping guidelines.
noun	He had a flat affect.	Ice cream has a positive effect on my productivity.

This spelling topic came up once again on a street corner in downtown Decatur, Alabama. Brandt and I were packing up after a Grammar Table session when a businessman named Hal stopped to talk. He was curious about what we were doing, so I gave him a brief summary.

"Well, you will find that the great state of Alabama and

the King's English are not necessarily compatible with each other," he said, laughing.

"My English isn't really the King's English," I said. "Is this where you're from?"

"Yes," said Hal.

"Thank you for making us feel welcome in our forty-seventh state," I said. "We're going to all fifty states, and then I'm writing a book, and my husband's making a Grammar Table documentary."*

"Wow," said Hal. "That's the husband?"

"That's the husband," I said, and Brandt confirmed the accuracy of that statement.

"I just figured you picked up some random guy," said Hal.

"I mean, I do think he's cute," I said. "If I were single, I would definitely go for it."

"Do you have any grammar questions or complaints?" Brandt asked. "Or comments?"

"Uh," said Hal, who was elegantly dressed in a jacket and tie. I suddenly noticed we were standing next to a garbage can. "Now it's going to bother me until I remember that word that I never get right. It's not 'accept' and 'except.'"

"'Affect' and 'effect'?" I offered.

"Yes!" said Hal. "That's it. 'Affect' and 'effect.' That's always a hard one for me."

"It's a bit more complicated than a lot of people think," I said, "which is probably why there are so many errors.

---

* This conversation took place on January 13, 2020. When I said this, I didn't know that COVID-19 had already reached the US and that this would be the last Grammar Table stop for many months.

But in general, in their most common usage, one is a verb and one is a noun. Do you know which is which?"

"'Effect' is a verb, like 'I have to effect something,' and 'affect' is a noun," said Hal. He emphasized the initial vowel sounds on "effect" and "affect" so that I could tell which was which.

"You know what your problem is?" I said. "You know too much. I think what you need is a quick Grammar Table grammar table." He laughed.

"See?" said Hal. "What'd I tell you? I was afraid to ask. Now I know why."

"You came to the right place," said Brandt, reassuringly pointing a camera at him.

"You're going to give me the easy way to remember, right?" asked Hal.

"Yes," I said. "So 'affect' as a verb . . ." I began writing down examples for him. Cars and trucks whizzed by.

"'Effect' and 'affect,'" said Hal. "Yeah." He seemed committed now, or perhaps resigned.

I was writing and speaking simultaneously. "'His actions affect me,'" I said as a loud FedEx truck passed. "Then 'effect' with an *e*— Uh, I'm not keeping you from work or anything, am I?"

"Well, I'm the boss," said Hal.

"Okay," I said, continuing to write standing up on the street corner. "'He effected change.' This is 'effect' as a verb. And then here's an example for 'effect' as a noun: 'The effect on me was significant.' This is the final frontier here; I'm leaving off the very specialized one."

"Yep," said Hal, as he stood on the corner watching me write. "So 'affect' is never a noun?"

"It is," I said.

"Oh lord, that was the extra-special one," said Hal, laughing. "I shouldn't have asked. It serves me right."

• •

"Affect" in the Wild

Since "to affect" is a verb, you will find it lurking in different tenses with different forms.

Your indifference to paragraphing _____ (to affect) my mood.

future	will affect
present	affects
present continuous	is affecting
past	affected
present perfect	has affected
past continuous	was affecting
past perfect	had affected

• •

"No, but this is good," I said, "because then it will be complete. That one is a psychological term."

"Oh, 'affect,' yeah, I understand that," said Hal. "Like 'His affect was flat.'"

"Now you have a summary," I said, handing him the page. "And aside from the messy writing, I hope you will find it helpful."

"I do a lot of writing," said Hal, "so I'll probably tape that up somewhere in my office so that I can remember."

"It would be such an honor if that happened," I said. "Would you be willing to sign a release if we wanted to use this footage in our documentary?"

"Uh, I guess," said Hal.

"You were very nice," I told him encouragingly.

"How will that affect me?" he asked.

"Spell!" I commanded.

"*A f f e c t,*" said Hal.

"Yes!" I said. "This is so great. I feel so happy with this outcome!"

"Can you get Robert Redford to play me?" asked Hal.

"We wouldn't want anyone but you to play you," I said.

¶

Even on a dark night on a nearly abandoned stretch of California beach, I encountered people who wanted to know about these two words.

"What's the difference between 'affect' and 'effect'?" asked Tara, towering over her companion, Alicia. They had been equally enthusiastic producers of language questions for the past half hour.

"Ooooh!" said Alicia.

I laughed. The Venice Beach Boardwalk was almost deserted, and I had been out there since noon, but my lingering Grammar Table guests had questions, and I wasn't going anywhere until I had answered them.

"I feel like 'effect' is the verb," Tara said as a harmonica played in the background. "Am I totally wrong?"

"It can be, but not in its most common use," I said.

"Okay," said Tara. "Wrong!"

"You're such a good teacher," Alicia told me. Invisibly I preened.

I gave them this example: "He had a big effect on my writing."

"So that's a noun," said Alicia.

"Or I could say 'His class affected my writing,'" I said, writing as I spoke. "Here it's a verb, right?"

"Oh," said Tara. She made a hand gesture of an explosion by her face, complete with sound effects. I began drawing a Grammar Table table for them.

"The thing that confuses people," I said, "is that each can be used as both a noun and a verb. Have you studied psychology?"

"You use 'affect' in psychology, in the mental status exam," said Alicia. "Which is not a verb, though!"

"A term for someone's mood, right?" said Tara.

"Right," confirmed Alicia.

"You are absolutely right," I said happily. "You are on a roll. And then there's one other specialized use: 'effect' as a verb."

"Ooh, what's that one?" asked Alicia.

I wrote, "The group effected change in the community," and this time they oohed in unison.

"Oh, man," said Alicia.

"I like the sound effects!" I said. "'Effect' as a verb

means 'bring about.' That's the one that people get confused about a lot, I think."

"So if something affects you—" said Tara.

"Oh, yeah," said Alicia. "How about 'I was really affected by this Grammar Table in a positive way'?"

"That would be *a f f e c t*," said Tara.

"Perfect," I said.

"And 'This Grammar Table really effected change in my grammar,'" said Alicia.

"In the community of Venice!" added Tara.

"Yes," said Alicia. "Which would that one be?"

"*E f f e c t*," said Tara.

"I don't know if that's right," Alicia replied. "We have to ask her." She looked at me.

"It's right!" I said. "That one is *e*."

"*E*!" said Alicia. "The effect of this discussion was victory!"

Quizlet

....

Identify the part of speech underlined in each sentence.

1. The constant scratching sounds in the wall <u>affect</u> my sleep.
2. The constant scratching sounds in the wall have an <u>effect</u> on my sleep.
3. We need to <u>effect</u> change in our family's vacuuming and toilet-cleaning schedules.
4. Roger's behavior <u>affects</u> the other hamsters.

Answers: *1. verb 2. noun 3. verb 4. verb*

4

Corrections, Humility, and Etiquette

"I hate when people correct my speech," said Tamara, an elegant woman dressed in cool white. We were on Martha's Vineyard, an island twenty miles long in southeastern Massachusetts.

"Well, it's rude to correct people's speech," I said. "But what are they correcting?"

"If I say 'he' or 'him'—" Tamara started.

"Oh, they'll try to fix your pronouns," I said. "You know what? I could write a whole book on the etiquette of grammar. You're not allowed to do that."

"Noooo, see, thank you!" said Tamara. "Sometimes I feel like telling people, 'I know the difference. I'm talking casually! I'm talking with friends.' I don't want to sound stilted—which happens."

"Also, sometimes they don't know what they're talking about," I said.

"True that," said Tamara.

"People get miscorrected," I said.

"See, *you* would get into a discussion with them," said Tamara. "I was like, 'Okay, thank you.'"

"It's gracious of you not to escalate," I said.

"No," said Tamara. "It's because I'm on vacation. I'm

on an island! In fact, it usually happens on *this* island!" I looked around me, taking in the island vibes.

Aside from being annoying, correctors of other people's grammar are often wrong. Telling someone at a party that they* have just used an incorrect verb form does not make you a superior person. It might make you a boor, however, and if you are wrong at the same time that you are a boor, that escalates the boorishness.

Often I hear, as justifications for grammatical positions, things like "We were always taught to do it that way," or "That's not what my grammar book from seventh grade said." People remain remarkably impervious to new information and updated ideas from writers, editors, linguists, lexicographers, and an array of excellent modern reference works. When they cite the authority of their seventh-grade grammar book, they often do not have the seventh-grade grammar book in their possession, nor do they know the name of the seventh-grade grammar book, which means it is unlikely that they know the details of the explanation contained within the pages of that seventh-grade grammar book.

How well do we really remember what we learned in fifth, sixth, seventh grades? People often don't remember the contents of yesterday's lunch, so why do so many believe they can accurately recall what they were told when they were different people in a different age? Sometimes

---

* What I was taught back in the day: Don't use "they" when the antecedent (meaning the noun or pronoun it refers back to) is a singular word such as "someone." What happens today: I ignore that when I don't see an obvious alternative that is natural and mellifluous. More on this point in Chapter 37.

children misunderstand things they are told. Alternatively, people may retain a general point but forget all the special cases and caveats associated with it. It is also fact that teachers, even well-intentioned teachers, have on occasion said untrue things.

There is no reason to privilege your memory of what you think your teacher told you in, say, 1981 over adult discussions well into the twenty-first century. There is no reason to be more skeptical about something you encounter in a reliable source as an adult than you are about your fading memory of a middle school teacher from a time when your brain was still developing. If you are applying far stricter standards to reliable modern inputs than to half-remembered memories from when you were ten—which I regularly observe people doing—then you are going to end up with a skewed and outdated perspective on language, its varieties, and its evolution, not to mention plenty of other types of information.

Nonetheless, what we are told when we are too tiny to argue has a tenacious hold on our minds and emotions. My grammar interactions have taught me a lot about why advertisers want to get to children young.

It is also common for people to measure the violation of what they perceive to be grammar by the distance between (a) what they learned in school, or think they learned in school, and (b) the way children and young adults are speaking and writing in the present. For instance, I encounter quite a few adults who still insist that splitting an infinitive is a word crime.

Split infinitives can sometimes be inelegant, but they *are* acceptable grammatically in English, and sometimes even desirable. Like this: "To boldly go where no grammarian has gone before!" The verb "to go" is the infinitive, and the adverb "boldly" intervenes. "To boldly go" is exactly the kind of thing generations of schoolkids were taught to avoid, starting in the nineteenth century—but English was already old by then, and infinitives already had a long history of being split, including by literary giants. I *delight* in the ability to split for effect: I love toboldlygo places!

Despite the acres that have been written across decades about the fallaciousness of this prohibition, smart people still insist on turning straightforward, natural sentences such as "They need to more than double their lemonade-stand sales" into tortured constructions such as "They need to increase their lemonade-stand sales by more than one hundred percent" or "They need to increase their lemonade-stand sales more than two-fold." Since there's nothing wrong with the original, there's no point in pumping out confusing second- and third-rate alternatives—but memory is sticky.

"I've had hilarious conversations, and also sometimes very moving ones, because language is so tied up with people's identity," I told a couple named Beth and Mitchell in The Villages, Florida.

"And fluid—it does evolve," said Beth, who wore flowing peach.

"Yep," I agreed. "That's right. You appreciate that; not everyone does. Sometimes I get people who are a bit cranky about that."

"It shouldn't change!" Beth acted out the role of an annoyed person and pounded her fist in the air.

I replied, "Well, if that were true, then they would have sounded just like their great-grandparents."

"Or we'd still be speaking Middle English," said Beth. "I never could get 'thee' and 'thou.' I'm glad we dropped those!"

¶

"I'm a complete and utter grammar scold," said a writer I met on Martha's Vineyard. At the time he uttered these words, I was sitting at the Grammar Table in front of a building where a conference called Islanders Write was underway.

"You are?" I asked skeptically. He did not seem like a scold.

"Somewhat." He moderated the claim. "I mean inwardly. I don't actually scold people. I think, *Aghhhh,* but I don't say anything."

"Right," I replied. "Because you're congenial, so you keep it to yourself."

"What's the point of lording it over someone, you know what I mean?" said the man. "It's silly."

"Right," I said. "You never know how people arrive at their state of language skill."

"I always assume they did the best they could," said the man.

"I don't necessarily assume that, but that is often the case," I said.

"Or perhaps they weren't exposed to a love of language at any point, and that helps a lot," said the man. "To care."

"It's almost everything," I said.

¶

Back in Verdi Square, a man in an orange coat and his forties told me, "I'm not a grammarian by any stretch, but I find that when I'm reading things now, like on my news feed, I just have to write a letter."

"You get bothered?" I asked.

"It's the anger of the moment," replied the man. "It's channeled into something that bothers me, and why should it even bother me, you know? Language is so fluid."

"That's nice," I said. "See, that's a very flexible philosophical point you just made."

I added, "I do also think that a lot of the criticism leveled at news organizations for missing a typo or something like that is unfair given the pressures of daily publication."

"Plus they've reduced all their copy editors," said the man, "so it's really not about the writers. It's like, you can't write and risk your life every day *and* eliminate every dangling participle."

Quizlet

You hear someone make a grammatical error. Should you correct that person?

Answer: *You are allowed to correct your students, children, grandchildren, and employees. You are not allowed to point out the errors of random strangers. If you correct the errors of friends, plan to stay home on Saturday nights.*

5

Adverbial Antics

One summer day in Spokane, Washington, I was sitting at the Grammar Table in Riverfront Park, not far from a semi-famous garbage-eating metal goat sculpture, when a young man named Julian arrived wanting to talk about adverbs.

"What is the adverb form of 'silly'?" he asked. "Because too often, I'll end up just coming out with 'sillily.' Sillily!"

"The convention is to not form *ly* adverbs for certain adjectives," I said.

"That's no fun," said Julian.

"I know," I said. "I'm with you on that, and if I'm just hanging out, I will absolutely say 'sillily.' I like to invent words for fun in my spare time."

There are limits even for word playtime, though, and this sentence exceeds them:

He greeted her friendlily and exclaimed livelily, "You dance so lovelily!"

Even though adverbs are the most famous *ly* words, there are also adjectives that end in *ly*. These include "friendly," "lively," "lovely," "silly," and so on. When you already have one concluding *ly* in a word, the conventions of English bar you from adding another, even if you are craving an adverb.

There are lots of words to use instead, though, so you can avoid the ungraceful "You move in a lovely manner" or "You move in a lovely way." That's what "gracefully" and its numerous friends and acquaintances are for.*

Many people know adverbs can modify verbs, but often they don't know or remember that they can also modify two other parts of speech. Do you know what they are?

This drawing shows three adverbs modifying three different types of words: a verb, an adjective, and another adverb.

---

* Yes, I ended my sentence in a preposition. See how natural that sounds? More on this point in Chapter 36.

"Intellectually" modifies the adjective "curious," "quickly" modifies the verb "finished," and "extremely" modifies the adverb "quickly."

Adverbs were more popular than average in Spokane. Another visitor there, a woman named Christine, told me, "I like the 'Vent!' option on your sign. I think of grammar as venting, because my sister and I, well, we just like to correct people."

"True. True statement," said her husband, smiling.

"My thing lately has been adverbs," said Christine. "People don't use them properly, you know what I mean?"

"I think you're talking about adjectives used for adverbs," I said.

"Yes, like 'Run quick!'" she said. "Or any command and then an adjective. And if I correct them, I get in trouble."

• •

Sly Adverbs

Not all adverbs end in *ly*. These are just a few I have enjoyed over the years.

already	also	never
now	often	quite
soon	too	very

• •

Christine's point was that if you are modifying a verb such as "run," you should opt for "quickly" rather than "quick." "Quickly" is the standard adverb form of the adjective "quick." Even though "quick" is also regularly used as an adverb by many Americans (which is what is happening in "Run quick"), many people find it objectionable. I've heard it plenty of times in my life, I'm used to seeing adjectives double as adverbs in another Germanic language (German), and Merriam-Webster's website even includes an adverbial definition for "quick." I don't use "quick" as an adverb myself, though.

It's also common in the US to hear "real" used adverbially. Many Americans do things real quick. Others do them real slow. What is acceptable to your audience varies based on context. If you decide to write something for a local paper, unless it's a work of fiction or an informal personal essay, "real quick" is almost surely going to be turned into "really quickly" really quickly.

Christine and her husband, a jazz musician, were accompanied by their young son, James, and a seven-month-old baby girl. "She doesn't say anything yet," said Christine, "but I'm hoping that she will speak well and that her first word will be 'Mama.'"

"The chances of that seem pretty high," I said.

"Well, his was 'blueberry,'" Christine said, gesturing at her little boy.

"Come on," I said.

"'Blueberry' was *one* of the first," said her husband.

"'Mama,' 'Dada,' 'moo,' and 'blueberry,'" said Christine.

"Yeah," said her husband. "After 'moo' it was 'blueberry.'"

"James speaks a lot, but he's just being shy here and

not talking," said Christine. She told me that they read together all the time.

"It's literally what I do almost all day every day," she said. "Like, the dishes are kind of dirty and there's dust, and I don't care, because it's not going to last."

"You have a good sense of priorities," I said.

"He's almost three now, but not long ago he was just this size," said Christine, indicating her baby daughter. "So we read books."

¶

On the streets of Baker City, Oregon, which has just under ten thousand residents and a chic tumbleweed vibe, I met a couple who had transcended adverbial obstacles. Irene, a stylish Canadian woman, was passing through town with her Texan husband, Ed, who had a big voice and a big white beard.

"When we first met, because he's from Texas, we spent a lot of time on language differences," said Irene.

"That's fun, isn't it?" I said.

"Oh yeah, it was totally fun," she replied. "When he came to Canada, I gave him a box of *ly*'s, because Canadians have adverbs, and Americans no longer have adverbs."

"I have a lot of adverbs," I said.

"But your countrypeople do not," said Irene.

"I say, 'That burger was real good,'" said Ed.

"And I would never say that," said Irene.

"She says, 'That burger was really good,'" said Ed.

"And see, you two still seem to get along," I said.

"Yeah," said Irene.

"On Thursdays and Sundays," said Ed.

Quizlet

••

How many adverbs are there in the following sentence, and what part of speech does each modify?

> While I would like to have good table manners, I am often inclined to move too swiftly to dessert.

Answer: *There are three adverbs: "often," "too," and "swiftly." "Often" modifies the adjective "inclined," "too" modifies the adverb "swiftly," and "swiftly" modifies the verb "move."*

6

How Are You?

So, how are you at this point in the book? Are you well? Are you good? Or are you both well *and* good?

In South Bend, Indiana, a young blond woman in beige told me, "One of my friends, whenever someone asks, 'How are you doing?' he always corrects the people who answer 'I'm doing good.' He tells them, 'I'm not doing good, I'm doing well.' When I saw your table, it kind of made me think of him."

"What would your friend say if the person answered 'Fine, thank you'?" I asked. "Would that be acceptable?"

"That would," said the woman. "That's okay."

"I could say 'I'm doing well,'" I said. "But I don't usually say 'I'm well,' and I also can't say 'I'm doing good.'"

"It bothers me now," said Lee. "He has trained me not to say 'I'm doing good.'"

"Really?" I asked, laughing. "Does he get invited to parties?"

"Yes," she said. "He's a bartender, and he's very social. He usually *has* the parties!"

"Well," by the way, can be multiple parts of speech. In the sentence "You sang well," "well" is an adverb explaining how you sang, but in the sentence "I am well,"

"well" is an adjective describing the person's condition: good health, good spirits, good whatevers.

I regularly said "I'm well" when I was younger, because that's what I was taught to do. I recall being told that saying "I'm good" was like proclaiming you were morally good. How embarrassing it would be to unintentionally end up bragging about your moral goodness! Nonetheless, for most of my life, "I'm well" has sounded a bit outdated to me. I'm perfectly happy for other people to say "I'm well," but when I say it, I sometimes feel as though I am reporting on, say, the alignment of my spine and the function of my liver.

On Venice Beach, I encountered a person with similar "I'm well" concerns. Seth had salt-and-pepper hair and wore a stylish black shirt. He was visiting from Arkansas with his wife, Laura, whose polka-dot top matched her buoyant personality.

Seth told me, "When people say 'How are you?' I know 'Well' is the appropriate way to reply, but I always just say 'Good.' I don't care."

"I understand why people say 'I'm good,'" I said. "'I'm well' sounds a little prissy, I think, to most modern speakers."

Seth agreed. "It's like, oh, I've got something to prove — that I know the right way to say it," he said.

"There's a whole subtext!" I said.

"It actually gives me a little bit of angst every time somebody asks me how I'm doing," said Seth. "Because I'm consciously going to say 'I'm good' even though —"

"Okay, so that's where we differ," interrupted his wife.

"— even though I know that's not the right way to do this," finished Seth. He put "the right way" in air quotes.

"You could try 'I'm doing well,'" said Brandt, who was filming. "It sounds a little less prissy. 'How are you?' 'I'm doing well.'"

"Okay, that's good," said Seth.

"But do you never say 'Fine'?" I asked. "If someone says, 'How are you?' would you not say 'Fine, thanks'?"

"'Fine' seems a little harsh," said Laura.

"'Fine' to me seems like you've given up," said Seth.

"What?" I said. "How?"

Seth adopted a tone of extreme indifference: "I'm fine."

"I don't say it like that, though!" I replied, laughing.

"What do you say?" asked Seth. "I'm *fine!*" He delivered the sentence with exaggerated peppiness and a rising pitch.

The two of them consulted privately on this matter for a moment, then turned back to me.

"I'm doing reasonably well," offered Laura as a compromise.

"I could say that," said Seth. "I could say 'reasonably well' or also 'I'm doing well.'"

"Okay, ask me how I am," I said.

"How are you?" Seth asked.

"Fine, how are you?" I replied perkily.

"Okay," conceded Seth.

"That's nice," said Laura. "But it's hard to be that bubbly."

¶

In Concord, New Hampshire, a woman with flame-red hair and a male companion came up to the Grammar

Table and said, "You were on TV. You set up in various places and correct those who don't understand."

"I don't think of it as going around correcting," I said. "If people come up and ask a question, then I'll answer it."

"I am a grammar freak," said the woman, whose name was Jane. "My children—I mean, they're grown—still say, 'Don't mess with grammar! Because Mom will get in your face!'"

"That's very cute," I said. "I feel that's sort of the function of a parent. People aren't allowed to go around correcting strangers' grammar, because that would be rude. But you can certainly correct family members' grammar, right?"

"And my friend's," she said, looking pointedly at her companion, who wore a red jacket and a placid expression.

"She corrects mine," said the man, whose name was Joseph. "But it's very infrequent that I need correction."

"So he says," replied Jane. "I had to teach my ex-husband the difference between 'well' and 'good.' And I should have known that very minute that it would be ex someday."

"Ah, there you go," said Joseph amiably.

"I do online dating," said Jane, "and if there's a grammar misstep, it is absolutely a no-go."

"The last time I did one of these," Joseph told me, "a woman stopped me on the street, and they were doing a survey about toilet paper."

"This is better, right?" I asked.

"Not necessarily," he said. "The question was, 'Are you over or under with toilet paper?' So we had some fun with that, and then they sent me a check for two hundred bucks."

"For answering that question?" I asked.

"Yes," he said. "We had a little chitchat."

"Are you sending me two hundred bucks?" asked Jane.

"Sorry," I said.

"When I first started seeing Joseph," said Jane, "he was an under man. And I'm an over, so every time I used his bathroom, I'd switch the roll until he finally caught on that he was an over person now, too."

"Well," said Joseph, and left it at that.

"I would not mess with you, I think," I told her. "I'm over, but I don't care."

"Oh, it's one of those things for me," she said. "Grating fingernails on the chalkboard. I've been known to change it in public restrooms. No wonder my boys talk smack on me."

"I don't understand why anyone would want under," said Brandt.

"Do you know what the problem is?" said Jane. "You pull it and you get half the roll, whereas if it's over, it kind of stops. I mean, I have my toilet paper down like I do my grammar."

Quizlet

••

You are helping your nineteen-year-old niece prepare for a job interview for a summer office job. She asks you what she should say if the interviewer—a forty-five-year-old manager—asks, "How are you?" She wants to use one of these two options because they are familiar to her:

(a) I'm good, thank you.
(b) I'm well, thank you.

Which would you be more likely to recommend?

Answer: *In a professional US context, I'd normally advise her to pick (b) rather than (a), but managers and regional dialects vary, and no matter what anyone tells you, it is impossible to predict with certainty—unless you know the interviewer's predilections—what will work best. If you live with other family members, consider comparing answers to this question over dinner. You are welcome to message me on Twitter @GrammarTable if you'd like to report on the outcome of the dinner conversation!*

7

Bookzuberance

I like to keep reference books on the Grammar Table. They represent the importance of (a) books and (b) looking things up in books. What I talk about with Grammar Table visitors is often documented in the reference works I keep on the table. Although I consider myself trustworthy and conscientious, one should not generally trust random strangers on the street, and I think it is important to model what I do when I'm alone at home: look things up in reliable sources whenever I don't know something, and often even when I do.

Also, proof in bound form comes in handy for skeptics.

There has been more than a little visitor sentimentality about some of the books I bring out with me. I am a heavy user of style guides. Style guides are not grammar books, but they do offer advice on grammar as well as on usage, format, and various other writing ingredients to help create more professional, consistent, readable writing. In descending order of emotional attachment, visitors seem most attached to these books: *The Elements of Style, The Associated Press Stylebook,* and *The Chicago Manual of Style.*

Initially I didn't bring out *The Elements of Style,* also

known as Strunk & White for the authors' last names. It's not a comprehensive reference book, it's dated, and I don't use it anymore. But so many people used it in school—as did I—and I can see that they enjoy reminiscing about it. In case you didn't already know this, the White of Strunk & White is E. B. White, author of *Charlotte's Web*.

At first I didn't bring out a dictionary either, but people often ask about word origins and pronunciations, so I decided it would be helpful to have something with me for that category of word emergency. I used to bring out my *American Heritage Dictionary,* which I find visually appealing, but most days now I prefer *Merriam-Webster's Collegiate Dictionary.* I often use their website at home.

Physical books inspire conversation. Julia from Virginia, whom I encountered while at the Grammar Table in the Bozeman Public Library, was clearly a bibliophile. Bozeman is in the Rocky Mountains and has a population of about fifty thousand people, as well as a gorgeous, stylish library to feed local residents books. Julia and her husband were in town dropping off their son for his fall semester at the local university, and stopping by the library was apparently their idea of fun.

Julia, an editor, was a *Chicago Manual of Style* enthusiast. Julia's husband, Dean—an English professor at a university in the South—was a regular witness to this enthusiasm.

"I sometimes tell my students what it's like in a household of English teachers," he said. "I tell them how sometimes at night, I'll read poetry to Julia. Julia's not a huge poetry fan."

"Not a big poetry fan," confirmed Julia.

"But she'll sort of sit there reading, and she'll listen

to me read a poem aloud," said Dean. "And I remember one night, she had the new *Chicago Manual of Style* sixteenth—"

"It was when the sixteenth edition came out," said Julia.

"And she was like, 'Listen to this,' right?" said Dean. "And so she read a long stretch of *The Chicago Manual of Style,* and I was like, That *is* kind of awesome."

"He turns his light off and I stay up reading," said Julia.

He continued: "I'm telling my class about this, and then all my students have this glazed look over their faces. Some of them don't even know what *The Chicago Manual of Style* is, so I explain it to them. And then there's always one or two, they're leaning forward in their chair, right? Like 'I want to know about those rules,' and I say, 'Okay, we should talk after class—'"

"You italicize an artificial satellite, but not a natural satellite!" said Julia exuberantly.

"'—because you might be one of those rare, strange creatures called proofreaders or copy editors,'" concluded Dean.

I held up *Chicago* like a spokesmodel. That's what users call it: *Chicago.* Like the city, but italicized, because it's part of a book title.

"Isn't it beautiful?" said Julia, gazing at it adoringly. "It's like, in this crazy world, here's one of the places where answers are clear. And they're hilarious."

Chicago is deeply satisfying to people who like detail, and for that reason, it was alluring to the quirky Florida family I met at the Grammar Table in downtown Savannah, Georgia. It was Black Friday, and I was sitting on the perimeter of Ellis Square chatting with passing post–Thanksgiving Day shoppers.

"So you take questions?" asked the mom, Larissa.

"Yes," I said.

"I don't have any right now," Larissa said.

"Yeah, I find that people can't necessarily think of them in the moment —" I began.

"It's mostly because I'm usually right," interrupted Larissa. "So I don't have questions. I just want to report other people. I need backup."

"I believe you," I said, and she laughed.

"Thank you," said Larissa. "But my punctuation is atrocious."

"She doesn't know when to use a comma or when to use a semicolon," said her husband.

Behind me I heard a girl's voice say, "She doesn't know what an Oxford comma *is*."

It was then that I realized a large group spanning three generations was curling around the Grammar Table like a giant comma.

"These are all your family members?" I asked.

But Larissa was occupied. She was stabbing an index finger at her accuser. "I know what an Oxford comma is!" she said. "I know what an Oxford comma is! Don't talk about me!"

To me, she said, "These are my children and my mom and my husband. But I think I have like a — oh, and I had a concussion too, and I forget words! — but I think I have a problem, like a learning disability, with punctuation. And I think he does, too." She pointed to an older son over my shoulder. "Do you?"

"I don't know," he said.

She pointed to a teenage girl and said, "It's not you."

"I definitely don't," said the teenage girl. "Don't even talk to me."

"So what's *The Chicago Manual of Style* about?" asked the father, who was wearing a jaunty hat.

"This is a very detailed book," I said. "It's used heavily in the publishing industry and by various language nerds. It covers everything you'd ever want to know for editing and writing all kinds of things."

"Oh, wow!" said Larissa as her husband hugged their young son, who was nine and, they told me, autistic.

"And the index alone!" I flipped through it for them. The seventeenth edition contains 1,144 pages. The index alone is the size of a small book: 130 pages.

"Look at that," said Larissa.

"It's crazy," I said.

"Can I take a picture of it?" asked Larissa, as though we were standing in front of Machu Picchu.

"Of course!" I said.

"It might be on the Christmas list," said Larissa. "Because we are dorks."

"I know a lot of words that are hard to speak," said Jacob, another son, also nine.

"You do?" I asked. "Can you give me an example?"

"Anemone," said Jacob. "Onomatopoeia. Antidisestablishmentarianism. Floccinaucinihilipilification."* His mother laughed and ruffled his hair.

---

* Floccinaucinihilipilification: "the estimation of something as valueless (encountered mainly as an example of one of the longest words in the English language)," according to Dictionary.com.

8

Going Farther and Further

There was a trumpet playing, it was January, and Brandt and I were in New Orleans. Unlike in our hometown of New York, it was sunny and sixty-five degrees where I was sitting—at the Grammar Table in front of the Louisiana Supreme Court building on Royal Street. Trucks with supplies kept rumbling by, because this was the French Quarter, and things were going to be hopping that night, as on all nights.

I was on the sidewalk awaiting grammar questions from passersby, and also responding to the questions of a New Orleans reporter doing a story on the Grammar Table. He asked, "'Further' or 'farther'?"

"You aren't going to like my answer to this," I said. "If you're asking about that, you probably care about the distinction, and I don't care very much."

"What do you care about?" asked the reporter. "What is grammar if it's not distinction?"

That seemed like a can of worms, maybe even a can of snakes, so I sidestepped it.

"'Further' or 'farther'?" repeated the reporter.

He wanted something he could use in a TV piece, so

I replied with this example: "I looked *farther* down the page for something that would discuss the matter *further*." I then added, "However, this is not a distinction I always observe."

It definitely isn't. And I'm not alone. Merriam-Webster confirms that others are up to the same thing. "As adverbs they continue to be used interchangeably whenever spatial, temporal, or metaphorical distance is involved," says the dictionary's website. "But where there is no notion of distance, 'further' is used."

I would love to audit the actual speech of people who are positive that for physical distance, they use only "farther." If you are one of them, would you mind if I followed you around with a recording device for a couple of weeks? I'll be really quiet, and you'll hardly even notice I'm there.

In the meantime, I can't get excited about a tiny variable vowel sound in the middle of such a thrilling combination of consonants.

A few months earlier and about a thousand miles to the northeast of New Orleans, Brandt and I had just set up near the Kunta Kinte–Alex Haley Memorial, located at the City Dock in historic Annapolis, Maryland, when a woman in a black knit hat showed up mad about "further" and "farther."

"So you distinguish between them?" I asked.

"It makes me so angry," said the woman, whose name was Joan. "You don't go further away; you go farther away."

"If you were talking about a page and looking for something on that page, and someone said, 'It's blank down the page,' would you want 'farther' or 'further'?" I asked.

"It's 'farther,'" Joan said bitterly. "It's distance, so it's 'farther.' Have you had people complain about that?"

"A little bit," I said. "Not a huge amount, but sometimes. We're making a Grammar Table documentary. Would you be willing to sign a release in case we want to use that bit?"

She agreed and signed. "How far will this documentary go?" she asked.

From behind the camera, Brandt piped up: "Don't you mean how *fur* will it go?"

Further away, in downtown Asheville, North Carolina, around Thanksgiving— Oops, wait, did that "further" at the beginning of the sentence bother you? I will begin again just in case. *Farther* away, in downtown Asheville, North Carolina, I was sitting there at the Grammar Table, halfway between a singer and a juggler, when up walked a friend of ours from New York. I had never been to Asheville before that day and we live hundreds of miles from there, so I was flabbergasted to see him.

One great thing about sitting on street corners is that the chance of random encounters with not just nice strangers, but also preexisting acquaintances, increases dramatically.

This particular friend, whose name was Steve, happened to be in town for Thanksgiving, and he was with two friends. We all chatted a while, and then Steve told me, "I was talking to somebody recently about the difference between 'further' and 'farther.' The person I was talking to said that 'farther' refers to distance and 'further' is a more abstract progression."

"It's a common distinction," I said. "I don't really care about that one. Here's an example that I don't have strong feelings about: 'farther down the page' if you're talking about a book, or 'further down the page'?"

"Well, it is distance, so I guess 'farther,'" said Steve.

"But is that what you would say naturally?" I asked.

"I would almost never say 'farther,' I don't think," said Steve.

"Yeah," agreed one of his friends. "I would say 'further.'"

"I don't read books, so it doesn't matter," said Steve. We all laughed. Steve is a writer. Steve went to Harvard. Steve has read books.

"I think I'm inclined to say 'further,'" I said. "In Annapolis, there was a woman who came up and asked about this distinction, and she found my habits very offensive."

"It's one of those things that I never actually stopped to think about," said Steve, "and if I've done it, I've probably done it wrong."

"I feel 'farther' requires more physical energy to pronounce," I said.

"Yeah, it does seem like more of a specialty choice somehow," said Steve.

"I mean, how much energy should we put into one word like that when we have so many other words we have to say?" I said.

"It's exhausting to talk," said Steve. "We could just brrrrrrrrrrghhhhhhh."

Quizlet

••

Dr. Campos wants to talk _____
(farther, further) about the five students
who live _____ (farthest, furthest)
from the school.

Answer: *"Further" and "farthest," according to the people who main-
tain strict distinctions. The reality, though, is that plenty of people
would say "furthest" for the second one, including probably me, so I will
support your ways.*

9

Texting Grammar

"Texting in complete sentences gets me nothing but ridicule," said Matthew, a man about my age whom I met on Martha's Vineyard. "I also feel less and less sure that my way is the right way, you know what I mean? Language is very plastic, very flexible."

Still—and contrary to stereotype—there are plenty of young people who prefer fully spelled-out words and ideas. I met one of them on a cold December afternoon in Wichita, Kansas, when the Grammar Table was at the place where the Kansas and Arkansas* rivers meet. From where I was sitting, I could see the *Keeper of the Plains,* a forty-four-foot-tall sculpture by a local Native American artist.

"I don't like abbreviations in texts," said Maddie, a college softball player who rode up to the table on an electric scooter. "At all! It's confusing. Like, okay, I know 'wyd,' which is 'What are you doing?' but I'd rather just spell it out so it's clear. I know 'omg,' that's 'oh my god.' Like a

---

* In Kansas, you pronounce the name of the Arkansas River not like the state of Arkansas, but like the state of Kansas with an Ar stuck on front.

couple of people might get 'lol' mixed up. It's 'laugh out loud,' but they think it's 'lots of love.'"

"Yes," I said, lol-ing.

"When I told my grandmother my cat died, she goes, 'Oh, lol,'" said Maddie. "And I was like, Wait, are you laughing or telling me you have lots of love? Oh, you mean lots of love? Okay, that makes more sense, so just spell it out, please."

If I tell you I laughed at this familial cat grief, I hope you won't judge me too harshly.

"It's just confusing," continued Maddie. "Like, people get mad at me because I use too many words in my texts. And I'm like, 'Well, you're not confused, are you?'"

"For deaths of living creatures, full words are probably a good idea," I said.

Maddie laughed. "Yeah, I'm like, I have no idea," she said. "It goes over my head, always." She indicated the spot over her head where it went.

"All right, well, thank you for this," she said. "I never knew this existed." And she rode off into the frigid night.

I met a second youthful abbreviation-shunner in Decatur, Alabama, who zipped over as soon as he saw us setting up in front of Moe's Original Bar B Que on Moulton Street. "How long have y'all been doing this?" asked the man, who was accompanied by a lanky friend in a baseball cap.

I was distracted by our unloading process. "I'll give you a postcard so you can see the origin," I said.

"Please do," said the man, whose name was Jason. He was twenty-three. "I'm interested in this because I love the English language, like I really love grammar."

I eyed him. He was wearing a black leather jacket, was clearly drunk (it was noon), and was standing in a cloud of his own cigarette smoke. "You do?" I asked. "Are you being serious?"

"Honestly, I text with like commas and apostrophes," said Jason. "It drives people crazy. Like, my dad says *k* still, and it drives me nuts."

"He says *k*?" I asked, confused.

"Yeah, *k*," said Jason. "He'll text *k*." He imaginary-texted on an imaginary phone.

"Oh, for 'okay'?" I asked.

"Yes," said Jason. "And I'm like, Man, do you save that much time not typing those extra three letters?* Just type 'okay'!"

"This sounds like generation reversal," I said.

"I think so," said Jason.

"How did that happen?" I said. "Let's go back to your childhood."

"Personally, I think I was born in the wrong generation," said Jason. "We'll go all the way back if y'all want to."

A family in Charleston, South Carolina, conformed more to age-based expectations for texting. On Thanksgiving there, I met a bearded dad, a blond mom, and four blond children. They had just finished the Turkey Day Run & Gobble Wobble five-kilometer race.

"Hi, everyone!" I said. "Happy Thanksgiving!"

"Happy Thanksgiving!" said the mom, whose name was Ariana.

"Do you have a question?" her husband, Ron, asked her. "Or a complaint? The sign says you can vent!"

---

* If you normally write "OK" rather than "okay," *k* saves you only one letter.

"I don't have a grammar question," said Ariana, "but I love grammar, and I love to proof papers and stuff. Can I get my photo with you?"

"I would be honored," I said.

"I love this!" said Ron. "We were just having a grammar conversation on the way here. We were literally—"

"I knew it," I said. "That's why we showed up."

"My grandmother was a teacher in a one-room schoolhouse in rural, rural Wyoming," said Ron. "She would always correct your English. Always."

"Did you enjoy it?" I asked.

"No, but it wasn't mean," said Ron. "We just had to stop and do it correctly—so I was used to that. But now with texts and things like that, it's awful. It is awful. That's why my vent is texting. No one says 'Dear blank.'"

As soon as I heard the word "dear," I knew what was coming. I turned to the right, where their oldest child, a teenage girl, was standing, in time to see her make a face and a "tch" sound.

"It's 'Yo dude!'" Ron said.

"You text people with 'dear'?" his daughter asked incredulously.

"Oh look, he's texting," said the mom, Ariana, pointing to her teenage son, tall and topped with an explosion of curly hair. "He wasn't even listening."

"No, I was," said the son. "But I'm using correct grammar. That's what matters."

"What's even worse is Snapchat," said the dad. "There's no English. No. One hundred percent. You guys are like this—" He put his fingers on his chin and posed. "Do your face," he told his two older children.

His two older children did not do their faces.

"They take a picture of like half their face on the edge
of the camera," said a younger boy, maybe ten years old
and the third of the child four-pack.

"What does it convey?" said Ron. "What does your elbow convey to your friends? Like, I'm here. I'm present.
Here's my elbow. It's bizarre." He shook his head. "Is it
not bizarre?"

"Dad!" said the teenage girl.

"I do love grammar, though, and I love, like —" said
Ariana, the mom.

"It says you can rant," interrupted Ron. "Vent, I mean.
I was venting! An appropriate place. It even has a sign!"

Quizlet

....

Do you know what the abbreviation in this auto-reply work email means?

> Thank you for your message. I will be
> OOO until July 5. Please contact Henry
> Hapenny regarding any urgent matters.

Answer: *OOO means "out of office," but when I first saw it, I thought,
"Oooooooh"? I can't recommend it for general use, as too many people won't recognize it and it may prompt them to think of things they
would say "Oooooooh" to. Besides, how long does it really take to type
three words totaling eleven letters?*

10

Sentimental Speller

I was trying to talk to a nice woman on Venice Beach when a tall young man approached and asked me, "Do you spell words?" He wore his curly brown hair in a ponytail, and he did not seem entirely sober.

"Do you want to test me?" I asked.

"How do you spell 'minute'?" asked the man. He did not mean an amount of time equivalent to sixty seconds; he pronounced it my-*newt*, as in tiny.

"*M i n u t e,*" I said. "Unless you're saying *m y* space *n e w t,* for your pet newt."

"How do you spell 'pondersous'?" asked the ponytailed man, ignoring my wit.

"Ponderous," I said, repronouncing it without the extra *s.* "*P o n d e r o u s.*"

"Can you spell 'proton'?" he asked.

"*P r o t o n,*" I said. "I love spelling. I did an—"

"Electron," he interrupted me.

"*E l e c t r o n,*" I said.

"Atom," said the ponytailed man.

"You're going to have to make them harder," I complained.

"Let's go," said the spelling quizzer. "Aardvark."

"*A a r d v a r k,*" I said.

"Asinine," he said.

"Do you know how to spell all of these?" I asked. "Are you sure I'm doing them right? Or could I just be saying random things? What did you just say?"

"Asinine," he repeated.

"That's a good one," I said, and proceeded to spell it wrong: *a s s i n i n e.* He didn't even notice.

"I'm interested that you're able to pull these words out of your head," I said. "It's like you have a random word generator in there. Do you read dictionaries for fun?"

"I have a set of encyclopedias," he said. "Can you spell 'syntax'?"

"Yes," I said. The name of the company Brandt and I run together is Syntaxis, so I can definitely spell "syntax."

"Spell 'syntax,'" he demanded.

"*S y n t a x,*" I said. "Unless it's a sin tax. Like on alcohol and cigarettes." My wit once again went unappreciated.

¶

Spelling tasks are complicated when words arrive from other languages bearing letters that are not part of the standard English alphabet.

This point came up in Richmond, Virginia, on a street corner in a busy outdoor shopping district called Carytown. There I met Logan, who had on a black baseball cap and looked contemplatively into the distance for some moments before speaking.

"There's a couple of words that pop out," he said, "but I don't know if they're worthy of the Grammar Table."

"I think they're worthy of it," I said. "There are no judgments at Grammar Table. It's part of the philosophy here."

"'Façade' and 'fuckade,'" said Logan. He had a conspicuously southern accent and pronounced the word "façade" in two ways for me: once correctly, with an *s* sound, and once with a *k* sound. For the sake of clarity in this discussion, I am writing them as "façade" and "fuckade," okay? Also, please stress the second syllable of "fuckade" when you say it in your head and rhyme it with "parade."

"Down in Charlotte," continued Logan, "somebody said that the movie star Canoe Reeves"—he laughed and continued with the correct pronunciation—"Keanu Reeves was just a big fuckade, and that's why a lot of his movies weren't so popular."

I explained that "façade" came from French and opened the dictionary to show him.

"It really bothers me that he actually believes that the word is pronounced fuckade," said Logan, leaning over to look at the dictionary with me. "But why do we pronounce it with an *s* sound? Are we that much more pompous than he is?"

In French, I told him, "façade" is written with a cedilla, which is what you call that little hook on the ç. "That makes it an *s* sound," I said.

"But I thought this was where I could voice my complaint," complained Logan.

"I take complaints and I lodge them with the appropriate authorities," I said. He laughed.

In French, when the letter *c* appears before *a, o, u,* or a consonant, it is always pronounced with a *k* sound, as in *cadeau* (gift), but the ç with a hook makes an *s* sound no matter where it appears.

In English, we don't have the letter ç in our twenty-six-letter alphabet. For that reason, many people write "façade" with a plain *c*: "facade." It's an accepted spelling too, though I like putting the ç because how often do we get to put cute little doohickeys on our letters in English? I mean, let the good times roll!

In general, letters that are not part of our alphabet are not consistently preserved in English spelling, even when we preserve the original pronunciation associated with those letters. You see this with *piñata* in Spanish. In the English alphabet, we don't have an *ñ*—pronounced roughly like the *ny* sound in "canyon"—so it is common for people to write "pinata" with a plain old *n* even though they still say it like *pinyata*. "Façade," "facade," "piñata," and "pinata" all appear in *Merriam-Webster's*.

When I finished my spelling explanation, Logan pointed a finger at me. "That is a hundred percent helpful," he said, "because this guy, I'm going to give him the business when I get back down there and tell him the ç with that little thing is not a *k* like in 'fuck.'"

He solicited my opinion on the best order of events. "Should I start with the fact that he thought his name was Canoe Reeves," he asked, "or should I just get him with the fuckade?"

"I personally think Keanu Reeves is cute, so I would pronounce his name right," I said, sidestepping the question.

"I learned a lot today," said Logan. "A hundred percent clarification."

¶

A little bit later that day, on the same Richmond street corner, a woman named Alyssa came up with a little girl to talk about spelling.

"What's one of your spelling words that has to do with grammar?" Alyssa asked the girl. "Do you remember?"

The girl, Skye, was in fourth grade, I learned, but doing sixth-grade spelling.

"No," said Skye. But then she thought a bit more and came up with a word.

"Punctuate," she said.

"Punctuate?" I asked. "Oh! That just reminded me. There are two words that people misspell a lot that are kind of funny. Do you want to know what they are?"

She said she did.

"One, 'grammar,'" I said.

"Really?" asked Skye.

"Yes, people misspell 'grammar' all the time," I said. "Do you know how they misspell it? Can you guess what they do?"

"Like graham cracker?" said Skye.

"No, they put an *e* and spell it like this," I said, showing her "grammer" where I had written it on my notepad.

"Oh," said Skye.

"You know what else they do?" I said. "They misspell 'misspelling.'"

"That's awesome," said Alyssa. "You know what word stumped me in the second-grade spelling bee? 'Penguin.'"

"Aw, how'd you spell it?" I asked.

"I don't even remember," said Alyssa. "But not correctly, clearly. I say penguins are my nemesis."

"That's so cute," I said. "My husband still remembers his mistake."

"I got knocked out on 'symphony,'" said Brandt. "S *y m p h* — and I thought, I've got this: *a n y.*"

"Oh no," said Alyssa. "Oh no."

"Yes," said Brandt.

As he and Alyssa relived their personal spelling tragedies, I told the little girl, "I think it's very impressive that you know this much spelling, and I wish you a lot of luck, and keep up the good work!"

¶

Grammer with an *e* came up in The Villages, Florida, where I was eating Kilwins ice cream at the Grammar Table right in front of the Kilwins in which the ice cream had been acquired. (In case you're wondering which villages I mean and why I'm capitalizing those villages, The Villages is the actual name of the place. The Villages is* famous for its customized golf carts, used in place of cars, and prolific senior sex. I can verify the existence of the former but not the latter.)

An older man in a dark sweatshirt passed me, walked a bit down the sidewalk, turned around, and came back.

He told me, "I was in Japan for a long time teaching part-time at a university. They put out a new catalog, and I looked at the director and said, 'You know you got a course here on grammar and you spelled "grammar" wrong?'"

"No," I said. "Really?"

"He spelled it with an *-er,*" said the man. "And you

---

* It's unnerving, but The Villages is the name of a singular entity and therefore takes a singular verb.

know what he said? He said, well, it was just no problem."

"Really?" I asked.

"He was later fired," said the man.

¶

On the streets of downtown Starkville, Mississippi, a pleasant woman named Nora asked me, "Has anyone mentioned to you this texting phenomenon of people when they say 'aw' and they put *a w e*?"

"No, I don't think so," I said.

"It drives me nuts!" said Nora. She smashed a fist against her thigh to indicate the amount of nuttiness it produced.

A soothing *mmmmm* sound emerged from her husband, Ben.

"I have about three people that I text, and they'll say, 'Awe, thank you so much' and I say, 'But—'" said Nora.

"You're not in awe," said Ben.

"When I mean 'aw,' I often do this," I said, showing her my standard "awww" stocked with extra *w*'s.

"Yes!" said Nora.

"To draw it out," I said.

"Because you're not in awe," said Nora.

"Maybe your friends are actually in awe of you," said Brandt from behind the Grammar Table.

"Yeah, maybe they're in awe of you!" echoed Ben, touching her shoulder.

"And they're just trying to let you know!" said Brandt.

"It's because you're too humble that you haven't realized this," I told her.

"Maybe," said Nora, meaning not maybe.

¶

In Chicago I talked about spelling with a nice family of five. I told them about a store sign Brandt and I had seen in Wisconsin that said WAGIN' TAILS instead of WAG-GIN' TAILS.

"It's for dogs," I said, writing it out to show them.

"Oh yeah," said Annie, the mom, explaining it to her children. "One *g* where it should be two *g*'s, so it looks like 'waging tail' as opposed to 'wagging tail.'"

The children gigled.

Just kidding. They giggled.

"I haven't done this yet," said Annie, "but I have a Sharpie with me, and if I had to fix something, I would."

"You're the person I've read about in the newspaper!" I said. I had seen articles about a grammar vigilante who would go out at night with a tricked-out stick, surreptitiously fixing apostrophe errors and other grammatical problems on signs.

"It wasn't me," said Annie.* "But I admire that person. Spelling isn't so much emphasized in schools anymore because of, I guess, spellcheck. I cannot handle spelling mistakes. Like, as a person, I cannot handle them. My children all know that if I'm reading anything they're going to turn into a teacher or write to someone, it's like, Let's just do it. Let's just spell correctly. Why not? It feels like anarchy otherwise."

"Sometimes when I teach writing," I said, "I point out

_____

* Or me!

that there's no spellcheck on flipcharts, whiteboards, or Post-its."

"That's right," said Annie. "I remember in the fifth-grade spelling bee, the word I went out on was, ironically, 'competition.' I'm not competitive in sports, but I'm competitive in spelling."

"It stays with you forever," I said.

"I just did it too fast," said Annie, proving my point. "I skipped the *e*. I went straight to *t i t i o n*. I missed one syllable."

"I feel you should forgive yourself for this," I said.

"I should," said Annie. "It was thirty years ago."

¶

In Ohio, one of my two Grammar Table locations was at the Toledo Mud Hens game. I had never heard of mud hens, capitalized or uncapitalized, but the day I was there I learned that lowercase mud hens are birds fond of swamps and marshes, and capitalized Mud Hens are a minor league baseball team.

It was a warm and muggy evening. A boy of about thirteen, dressed sportily in gray, came up and told me, "I'm going to ask you a grammar question." He had a shy, sweet smile.

"You are?" I said encouragingly.

"Like what kind of grammar question?" he asked.

"Oh!" I said. "Well, it could be anything. People ask about spelling, pronunciation, punctuation—anything to do with words."

"All right," said the boy. "Can you spell 'supercalifragilisticexpialidocious'?"

"What do *you* think?" I said, oh so full of Grammar Table bravado. He shrugged.

Of course I could! This was the Grammar Table! What kind of Grammar Table could not spell *s u p e r c a l i f r a g*— Oops.

There was pride, and there was a fall. As I began fumbling letters, his family rescued me by calling for him from the stadium entrance.

"I gotta go," said the boy, and he left me there alone, shaken by my newly discovered intellectual attrition. Last I knew, I could spell that word at high speed with about the same amount of mental energy it took me to tie my shoelaces.

"Bye!" I called out as he walked away. "I tried!"

P.S. I checked later and at least I can still spell it on paper.

¶

Will, who looked like Santa Claus might on a low-cal diet, was a repeat Grammar Table visitor in Verdi Square. He stopped by one cold March afternoon wearing a pointy red wool hat, his long, flowy, snowy hair and beard spilling out over his shoulders and down his shirt.

"When you do suffixes," Will told me, "you should always be using a double consonant. And people are using single consonants. Like in 'canceled.'"

"That's a good one," I said, writing "canceled" and "cancelled," "canceling" and "cancelling" on my notepad. "I use one *l*. But it's more common in the UK to see it with two."

"Actually, that's the proper way to be doing it: two *l*'s," said Will. "One *l* has become the common form of doing it, but two is the proper way of doing it."

"I'm going to have to disagree with you on that, because both are accepted," I said. "I have looked into this extensively. But what's funny is that on 'cancellation,' you have no choice: it has two *l*'s."

"That is true," said Will. "But 'cancelling' would be the same thing: *c a n c e l l i n g*."

"What do you do with 'traveling'?" I asked. "Do you double the *l*?"

"Yes, and 'traveller,' too," he said.

Besides "cancellation," I personally don't double the *l* in any of these words, just because I go with the more common American English spellings. But I *like* all the spellings, so there is no emotional cost to me no matter what people choose to do.

"Think of all the time I'm saving by not doubling the *l*," I told Will. "I could probably walk back and forth to the grocery store in the time I save over the course of a year."

He laughed. "Well, you may, but I'm sorry, I was raised on the other."

"Okay, what I'm going to do now is, I'm going to pull out the big guns here," I said. By big guns, I meant a big dictionary. "Let's see what we have happening for 'cancel.' I think that they're going to give us both spellings. I'm going into this pretty confident, you know."

"Yup," he said, looking at the dictionary with me.

"Here we go: 'cancel,'" I said. I rotated my *American Heritage Dictionary* for him to look at.

"Right," said Will.

"They give you the different forms," I said, "and the

first ones *American Heritage* gives you are the single-*l* versions, 'canceled' and 'canceling.' Then they add 'cancelled' and 'cancelling' with two *l*'s. So I regret to inform you that mine comes before yours, at least in *American Heritage*."

"I was raised on the double," said Will. "I mean, I'm past my Medicare age and my Social Security age, so—"

"So you probably won't be changing it anytime soon," I said.

He laughed. "Right!"

"All right," I said. "I think we can get along, though."

"Oh, yes," said Will, thanking me politely for the consonant chat. "The only thing I can offer you in return would be some green jelly beans," he said, pulling out a purple bag.*

I declined, but Will was full of good will, and I dug that.

¶

Like Will, many people seem to dislike contending with multiple spellings of a familiar word.

"I love spelling, and I love vocabulary, and I love words," said Kara, "but there are some things, like double consonants, that I'm never sure of." This conversation took place on Martha's Vineyard under a tree.

After we briefly addressed "traveled" and "travelled," Kara said, "This brings me to a dilemma I have. I have a

---

* Besides jelly beans, the Grammar Table has been offered payment in the form of cash, coffee, and even a doggie bag of leftover lunch. While appreciative, the Grammar Table has declined all such payments.

daughter. Her name is Pammella, with two *m*'s and two *l*'s, because when I was pregnant with her, I thought, Pamela does not look right to me. It doesn't look balanced. I have to double the *m*, I have to double the *l*, because those are two strong sounds in the name. So when I was in the labor room, I'm like, Okay, I've got to spell it *P a m m e l l a*. Don't you know that's come to bite me in the ass."

"Did you really do that?" I asked.

"I did," said Kara.

"And what does Pammella have to say about this?" I asked.

"Pammella does not like it," said Kara. "She can never get anything with her name spelled correctly. Our last name isn't easy either. And I said, 'Pammie, I have two words for you: Scarlett Johansson. People will get it.' And she's like, 'Mom, what did you do to me?'"

¶

There is a massive amount of information in dictionaries. Not just definitions, but also information on word origins; comments on usage; audio files of pronunciations, if you are online; and helpful guidance on whether something is best written as one word, as two words, or hyphenated.

"Mind if I take your picture?" asked Joanna, a blonde in purple who came across the Grammar Table one day when I was back in Verdi Square in New York.

"Not at all," I said.

"You know what?" said her brunette friend. "I have to tell you, she could probably dethrone you."

"No, I could not," said Joanna, looking embarrassed. "I'm a retired copy editor." She held out her hand, and we shook. She had read about the Grammar Table in the *New York Times*.

"My last job was at *Parents* magazine," she told me. "I think it's the only magazine with a style sheet that has the word 'poopyhead' in it."

"That is so perfect and funny," I said. "I think I might die of happiness right now."

"'Peekaboo' is also one word," said Joanna.

"Well, that seems obvious to me," I said. "But 'poopyhead' I was a little bit less sure about, because I don't have a lot of experience using that." The two women laughed.

"Nor had I until I got a job at *Parents* magazine," said Joanna.

"Why, you don't call your friends 'poopyheads'?" her friend asked me.

"No," I said, "but now that I know how to write it, according to *Parents* magazine, I might!"

I enjoy specialized spelling topics like that. I had another specialized spelling discussion in the same location on another day.

"Hello!" I said to a lively approaching couple. It was a cold afternoon, and I was all fluffed out in a tall fluffy fake fur hat and a wide fluffy fake fur coat. According to multiple visitors that day, my outfit made the Grammar Table look like the Russian Table.

"Hello, are you the grammar lady?" inquired the man.

"She's the Grammar Table lady," his wife corrected him, then turned to me. "I just want to tell you I think you're a wonderful lady. I don't have a question at this moment, but believe me, I'm going to make my list."

Her husband, however, was ready with one. "There's a word 'tendinitis.' Is it *t e n d o n i t i s*? Or *t e n d i n i t i s*?"

"Isn't that one of those weird ones that's not spelled as you think?" I asked. "Are you a doctor?"

"Yes," said the doctor. His name was Melvin.

"Is this a quiz?" I asked.

"No!" said Melvin, shaking his head. "I've looked it up. I was at a big meeting of august authorities where they disagreed."

"A bunch of doctors disagreed?" I asked.

"That is right," he said placidly.

"Surely the dictionary must have an answer," said his wife, whose name was Meryl.

"Wait, you don't say 'My ten-*dins* hurt,'" complained a man standing nearby in a cap.

"But the thing is, I think this is one of the ones—" I said.

"That's 'ten-*don*,'" said Melvin, the doctor. "But 'tendinitis' is different."

"Which is the inflammation of the tendons," said the man in the cap.

"You don't say 'my appendectis,' but you do say 'appendectomy,'" said Melvin.

"This sounds vaguely familiar, as though it's something I looked up because it surprised me," I said.

Melvin smiled. "Uh-huh."

"Because normally I would just say t e n d o n," I said. "But I'm thinking that there was a spelling idiosyncrasy with this one."

"There often are in Latin and in medicine," said Melvin.

"Yeah," I said. "My guess is, I'm going to just go with the *i*."

"Okay," said Melvin. "But you're saying that as a sort of surmise rather than as a—"

"I don't know for sure off the top of my head," I said.

"She doesn't have a dictionary," said his wife protectively. "She doesn't have a dictionary, because she's the *grammar* lady." I liked Meryl. Meryl was nice to the Grammar Table.*

"I don't think it's going to be in this book," I said, picking up *Garner's Modern English Usage,* "but every once in a while I'm surprised, so I think we should just double-check, because there might be something weird happening here."

And there it was, right under *t.* "Tendinitis!" I said. "It is spelled 'tendinitis' with an *i,* according to this."

That proclamation caused a hullabaloo.

"I am such a country bumpkin," said the bystander in the cap, disappointed in himself.

"That's the one I like, too," said Melvin.

"I can't believe it was in there," said Meryl.

"Oh, I can," said Melvin.

"It's wonderful that it was in there," said Meryl.

"Of course, it's possible we could consult three encyclopedias and get three opinions," said Melvin.

"What happened with tendinitis?" asked a woman perched on her bicycle.

"The *i*'s have it!" declared Melvin.

"It seems like it should be *o n,* right?" I said.

"It did to me," said the man in the cap.

"There could be alternative spellings," I said.

"But still, it could be that one is more accepted than the other," said Melvin. "How old is that?" he asked, pointing to *Garner's.*

---

* She was right. That day I did not have a dictionary, but after this incident, I made sure I always had one with me.

"It's quite current," I told him. I try to be an up-to-date Grammar Table.

"I have never seen it with an *i*," complained the woman on her bike. "It's a ten-*don*. It's not a ten-*din*. It's a ten-*don*. They also say 'dilitation' instead of 'dilation' because they think it's more correct." I was not sure who "they" were, but I could see she was irritated. Melvin was not. Melvin had a calm Grammar Table–side manner.

"When you correct us, are you covered by insurance?" Melvin asked me. I laughed.

"Next time I want to tell you about 'lie,' 'lain,' and doctors," I said.

"Oh, 'lie' and 'lay,'" said Melvin. "I know — doctors get it wrong all the time. 'Lay' is a transitive verb, like you lay down the book."

"You just really dazzled me," I said, dazzled.

¶

In Alabama, I negotiated a "y'all" spelling situation, despite my amateur northerner relationship with this handy second-person plural pronoun.

It happened in Decatur while I was talking to Jason, the leather-jacket-wearing twenty-three-year-old visitor frustrated in an earlier chapter by his father's use of abbreviations. He and his friend, Jack, talked to me for a long time. It turned out that they were playing hooky from their construction job.

"'Y'all,'" said Jason. "The proper way to use 'y'all.' Tell me, does the apostrophe go before or after the *a*?"

"It doesn't go at all," said Jack, who was tall and wore his baseball cap backwards. "What are you talking about?"

"Before," I said.

"Ooof," said Jack.

"Thank you!" said Jason. "I agree with that. I hate motherfuckers that use it after the *a*! I can't stand it! It is *y* apostrophe *a l l:* 'y'all.'"

Jack bent down to see what I was writing.

Jason repeated loudly, "Y apostrophe *a l l.* That is how you spell 'y'all.'"

"Whoooo," Jack hooted.

"That is right," said Jason.

"But a lot of people do put the apostrophe after the *a*, right?" I said.

"They do, and I cannot stand it," said Jason.

"Does this give me any southern cred?" I asked.

"I think it does," said Jason. "I have to say it does."

Quizlet

....

How many of the three words shown below are spelled correctly?

- pastime
- responsible
- tendinitis

Answer: *All of them!*

11

Please _____
(Lie, Lay) Down*
and Read This

One day a young doctor with brown hair appeared in front of me where I was stationed in Verdi Square. He seemed excited that there was a Grammar Table outside his subway exit where he could ask grammar questions.

"There is no grammar-checker in the program I use to type my patient notes!" he told me. "I'm always getting confused about the different forms of 'lie' and 'lay.' Sometimes I just say 'Fuck it!' and pick a different verb so I don't have to deal with it!"

"I can draw you a chart," I told him. I did draw it. It looked something like the one on the next page.

He was delighted. He took the chart and put it in his bag. "I'm going to put it up right next to my computer at work!" he exclaimed. "And I'm going to tell all my doctor friends about you!"

Some months later in Salt Lake City, while sitting at the Grammar Table in front of Temple Square, I met another doctor and told him about this verb experience. He was unimpressed.

"I worry more about whether people are having a heart attack," he said.

---

* Answer: "lie." If you're not sure why, please read this chapter!

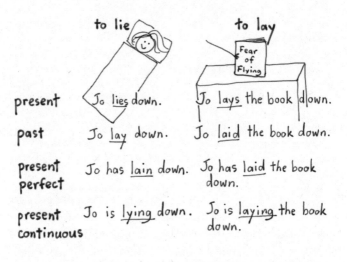

	to lie	to lay
present	Jo lies down.	Jo lays the book down.
past	Jo lay down.	Jo laid the book down.
present perfect	Jo has lain down.	Jo has laid the book down.
present continuous	Jo is lying down.	Jo is laying the book down.

¶

Now, let's take care of one *l*-word spelling detail right away. In Detroit, I had been chatting with a woman named Anne for a while when she showed me a piece of paper on which she had written "laid" and "layed."

"Never use this," I said, crossing out "layed" on her paper.

"Oh!" she exclaimed.

"That one was easy," I said.

"Oh my goodness, you crossed it out!" she said.

"It doesn't exist except as a misspelling," I said.

"That was strong!" said Anne.

"Yeah, I'm all done!" I said cheerfully.

Anne laughed. "I will never use *l a y e d* again," she promised.

In Richmond, Virginia, a woman with dark, romantically curly hair arrived to discuss the obstreperous "lie"/"lay" pair. "It makes me crazy," said the woman, whose name was Tina.

"Do you want me to make you a little table?" I asked.

"Yes!" said Tina.

I was happy to hear that, because I love making tables. "First of all, do you know what a direct object is?" I asked. "Is that familiar to you?"

She said it was, but in case it's not to you, here are three quick examples with the direct object underlined:

My daughter drew a <u>piglet</u>.

Hail damages <u>cars</u>.

Marsupials pocket their <u>children</u>.

In each case, the direct object receives the action of the verb.

"I'm bringing this up because it helps you pick the correct infinitive," I told Tina. "'To lie' cannot take a direct object. That's the mistake some people make: they pick 'to lay' as their starting point when they instead need the verb 'to lie.'" I wrote down this example for her:

He lies down.

"There's no object for it," I said. "You have an entity—it could be a person or an animal or whatever—that lies down. And then an example for 'lay' would be 'She lays the feather on the ground.' The verb 'to lay' always takes a direct object, and in that sentence, the direct object is the feather."

"Got it," said Tina.

"Now this is where it gets hairy," I said, continuing to draw. "The past tense of 'to lie' is the one that people get wrong a lot. It begins *l a*— Do you want to guess the rest?"

Tina paused, then guessed "laid."

"Lay," I said.

"Lay!" exclaimed Tina.

The fact that "lay," an infinitive for one verb,* works a double shift as the past tense of another verb—"to lie"—is confusing and a source of annoyance to people. Not Tina, though. Tina was calm.

"I almost said 'lay,'" she said. "And then I changed it."

"Maybe you're overthinking it," I said.

"Yeah, I'm really bad about that," said Tina. "I'm always rethinking things."

"Well, it's confusing," I said.

Next I gave her sentences for "lay" containing past tense and what is known as the present perfect.

past: *She <u>laid</u> the feather down.*

present perfect: *She <u>has laid</u> the feather down.*

In the example with present perfect, "laid" is a past participle. Combine it with a present-tense form of "have" and you get present perfect: "has laid." Explaining

---

* Some people have the impression that infinitives in English always include a "to"—for example, "to conjugate," "to diagram," "to parse"— but infinitives can still be infinitives without a "to." A "to"-free infinitive is often referred to as a "bare infinitive," as underlined in this sentence: "I would <u>conjugate</u> those verbs for you, but I am too busy eating these chocolate chip cranberry nut cookies."

that to Tina, I asked, "Do you remember that from school?"

"Sort of," said Tina. "A little. It's been a while."

"You can go to parties and say, 'So what's your favorite past participle?'" I suggested. She laughed politely.

"It's a real conversation starter," I added. "And then the past participle of 'lie': 'He has blank.' Do you want to guess what goes in the blank?"

"Lain?" she said.

"Yes!" I was excited.

Tina was not excited. "Yeah," she said. "That just doesn't sound right."

¶

"Which side do I sit on?" asked a man with a woman and three children on the Venice Beach Boardwalk. "That side or this side?"

Oh my goodness! By "that side," he meant *my* side! I laughed externally while internally preparing to protect my Grammar Table from his chutzpah.

"We talk about grammar all the time, don't we, kids?" he said to the kids.

Okay, never mind. This man was willing to talk grammar. He would immediately be forgiven by the Grammar Table.

The oldest boy, whose name was Adam, was ready with a question. "Is it 'to lie down' or 'to lay down'?" he asked.

"Give me a sentence," I said. "I need a context."

"I was tired, so I went to my bed and laid down," offered Adam. "Or lied down?"

"What do you say?" I said, looking at the rest of the group. "Do you all want to vote? Are you all related?"

"Yes," said the woman, laughing.

"This is all one family?" I asked.

"We all came here together," said the man, Peter. "We're leaving together."

"No matter what happens here?" I asked.

Peter walked over to the Grammar Table microphone and leaned in. "We're leaving together," he confirmed into it.

Their continuing family unity assured, I returned to the son's sentence:

I was tired, so I went to my bed and <u>*laid*</u> *down.*

The thing about "laid down" is that hearing it doesn't tell you how people would write it. The speaker could be picturing "*l a i d* down," "*l a y e d* down," or even "*l a y* down"—because all of those sound more or less the same in speech.

"How are you spelling the verb?" I asked Adam.

"*L a y e d,*" he said. Oops!

"Okay," I said, setting down my apple. "Does anyone else want to guess?"

"Whoa!" said Peter. "She's puttin' down the fruit! We are bona fide!"

"Yeah," I said. "So *l a y e d.*" I looked at the son.

"Mm-hmm," he said.

"That is not the spelling if you do want this form; it's *l a i d,*" I said. But that wasn't the right form anyway.

Reader, do you know what it should have been? Think about this a moment before going to the next paragraph.

There's no direct object, so you start with the infinitive "to lie," and then you need the past tense. That means "lay"—*l a y*—as discussed previously with Tina of Richmond, Virginia.

"I'm going to have to make a table," I said. "This won't take long, and it won't hurt." I noticed that Peter, the dad, was laughing.

"Why are you laughing?" I asked.

"He's charmed by this whole idea," said Peter's wife.

"I think it's great!" confirmed Peter. "I want to do it, too!"

I made the son a grammar table and finished off our grammar chat with The Tale of the Grammatical Dog.

"I met someone in Texas once," I said, "who told me that before he trained his dog to lie down, he looked up whether it was 'to lie' or 'to lay.' Everyone around him said 'Lay down' to their dogs, and he had a feeling that was wrong. When he looked it up, he discovered that his instinct had been correct, so he taught his dog to respond to 'Lie down.' After that, his dog would not respond to 'Lay down.' It was a grammatical dog."

"I'm trained the same way," said Peter. "With my wife. Ten o'clock at night, I'm waiting!"

¶

Wherever I went, I kept getting questions about these verbs. Nationwide there is quite a bit of impatience with the difficulty of keeping these two *l*-verbs straight.

"You know what I would like to do?" said a woman named Lisa in South Bend, Indiana. "I would like to take 'lay' and 'lie' and unify them. Because why do we continually fight this generation after generation? Let's just blend them and make it all one."

"I think your wife is really smart," I told her husband, who nodded. "She's right on top of the key issues." I turned back to Lisa and said, "I actually enjoy the 'lie'/'lay' thing because I don't have any trouble remembering it; there's just something about that one that locks into my brain."

"Yeah," said Lisa, "but see, I have to stop and figure out the sentence, and where's the direct object, and is it there, and then I do this, and which is 'lay' and which is 'laid,' and which is 'lie.'"

"A lot of people don't know this form at all," I said. I held up the notepad to show her what I had written.

"Lain," she said. "No."

"They think it doesn't exist," I said.

"No," said Lisa. "I have a friend. Her name is Lain."

"Her name is what?" I asked.

"Lain," said Lisa.

"Oh, but not like that," I said, pointing to the word.

"Yes," said Lisa.

"Spelled like that?" I asked.

"Yes," she confirmed.

"That's amazing," I said. "That's astonishing. So she's a past participle of 'to lie.'"

"I've never told her that," said Lisa. "I'm not going there."

¶

Not everyone wanted to change their "lie"/"lay" situation, and that is their grammar-given right.

On President Clinton Avenue in Little Rock, Arkansas, a buxom middle-aged woman with red hair yelled at me as she was crossing the street, "Hey, what's going on at this Grammar Table, girl?"

"Answering grammar questions," I said. "Do you have any grammar questions?"

"Do I have any?" she asked. "It's always the 'lie' and the 'lay.' I need the 'lie' and the 'lay.'"

"Yes," I said empathetically. "I could make you a quick table of it if you wanted!"

"A table?" said the woman. "No, I'm good. You are hilarious. What is going on? Y'all are so cute." Then to Brandt behind the camera: "And *you* are precious back there. Nice smile!"

"This is my husband," I pointed out. "Didn't I do well?"

"Thank you!" said Brandt, to her, not me.

"He's precious," she said. "You did do well! Look at that smile on him!"

"I'm very happy with myself," I said.

"Good!" said the woman. "I'm happy for you! Absolutely! So you break it all down over here, do ya?"

"Whatever people come up and want to know, I'm ready," I said.

"All right, Morgan!" she yelled to a young woman who appeared to be her daughter. "Come on, Morgan!"

"I'm good," replied Morgan from a safe distance down the sidewalk.

"You can come up with something," the woman insisted, telling me, "I'm good on the 'there,' thank god. We're good on that."

"That's good," I said.

"Thank the lord," she said.

"I'm enjoying your grammar confidence," I said.

"Are you?" she asked. "I am pretty confident, aren't I?"

I confirmed that she was.

"Sometimes I am," she said. "Oops! But my mom used to drill! my! ass!" She punctuated the last three words with her right hand.

"I mean till she died," she continued. "She would correct me. And then, after she died, she still haunts me. I still think, ooh, is that 'lie' or 'lay'? Fuck!"

I laughed.

"Yes, ma'am," she said.

"Did you enjoy the drilling when it happened?" I asked.

"No," she said. "And let me tell you what I would tell her. I'm fifty-two now, so in my forties, I would say, 'Honey, if I haven't caught on by now, it's not gonna happen. It's not that it's not important, but do you know what I mean when I say "Blah blah blah"?' And she did. But still, I was wrong."

She paused. Briefly. "Go ahead, get me, Grammar Woman!" she said. "It's all right. I can take it. I can take it."

Her name was Cora. She shook hands with Brandt and me.*

"Hi, Cora!" said Brandt.

"Hi, sugar, how are you?" Cora said to Brandt, winking at him. "Nice smile you got there!" She looked at Brandt, laughed, and touched me. "And honey, I've got a man. I'm not even lookin' for a man."

Then she realized Brandt was filming. "Oh Jesus," she said. "Y'all gonna do a couple of them bleepouts, I hope."

---

* "Me" is the correct pronoun because it is the object of the preposition "with." More on this soon!

"Are you two related?" I asked.

"Yes, I'm her daughter," said Morgan.

"I embarrass the hell out of her," said Cora.

"I see she's standing quite far from you," I observed.

"We're used to it," said Morgan. "I let her do her little thing."

"Her little thang," twanged Cora. "Hey, Morgan, has your momma gotten on to you about your English?"

Morgan confirmed that she had.

"So it's passed on from generation to generation," I said.

"Come on up to the table," called Cora to her daughter. "Don't be afraid. Do not be afraid, baby." She told us, "Well, she did manage to get through college, so that's a plus."

"What sorts of things does she get on you about?" Brandt asked Morgan.

"Same thing," said Morgan, still from a safe distance. "It's the same."

"So you're saying I'm like your grandma," said Cora.

"No, but she would get on me about it, too," said Morgan.

"It's a family thing," said Cora. "My aunt, God love her soul, was a teacher. So you know, that was important in our family. But all the way around, yeah, English is important. Good grammar is even more important. Yes!" She gave us a thumbs-up.

"You guys are really cute together," I said. "You seem to love each other."

"We do!" said Cora.

"Of course!" said Morgan.

"And also just have fun with it," I said.

"There are moments," said Morgan.

"Yeah," I said. "Well, what would life be without moments?"

"Hey, ain't that the truth?" said Cora. "We have a good time."

As a trolley rolled past down the street, she added, "My mother would say, 'We're not here for a long time, we're here for a good time.'"

Quizlet

1. After reading this chapter, I need to _____ (lie, lay) down for a bit.
2. Rover _____ (laid, lay) under the covers with his head on my pillow.
3. She wordlessly _____ (laid, lay) thirty dollars on top of my trigonometry notes.

Answers: *1. lie (infinitive) 2. lay (past tense of "to lie") 3. laid (past tense of "to lay")*

12

The Life, Times, and Punctuation of the Appositive

I was in Verdi Square one day when I was approached by a man wearing a gray coat and gray cap.

"What's an appositive?" asked the man, who appeared to be in his sixties.

"An appositive is— Wait, is this a quiz?" I asked. "Are you testing me?"

"Yes," he said. "I'm looking at your, uh, skill set."

I began writing on my pad.

"So you have to write it down?" he asked.

I stopped and looked up at him. "I think it's easier with examples," I said. "Do you object?"

"I know what an appositive is," he said.

"Well, I'm showing you the way I would normally explain it," I said.

"All right," he said. "But do you know restrictive versus nonrestrictive appositives?"

"Yes," I replied. "Okay, I see you want the efficient version. An appositive is a kind of renaming. You have a noun or a noun phrase, and then you offer an alternative way to refer to the same thing."

"Good, good, good," said the man in gray.

"And if it's restrictive, then you don't put commas, and if it's nonrestrictive, you do," I said. "Did I pass?"

"Absolutely," said the man in gray.

I'll show *him* a restrictive appositive or two. Sheesh. Anyway, let's take a few steps back. Here is a sentence with an appositive (underlined) for you:

> *My boss, <u>Margie Whittlefish</u>, just lent me her copy of* Middlemarch.

"Margie Whittlefish" and "my boss" refer to the same person. "Margie Whittlefish" is an appositive for "my boss." This type of appositive, which is set off with commas, is called a nonrestrictive appositive. The idea is that Margie's name is not necessary to the sentence, because I have only one boss. I'm just telling you her name for kicks—and I think you can see why.

Here is a different type of appositive, this one comma-free:

> *My colleague <u>Lena</u> lent me her copy of* Soul on Ice.

"Lena" is a restrictive appositive. Her name is being used to *restrict* the larger category of colleagues to this one individual. You need the name to clarify which colleague you mean, because there are other colleagues floating around out there. Do not use commas with restrictive appositives.

Do people know the difference between restrictive and nonrestrictive appositives? The reality is, many do not. Therefore, unless you are reading reliably edited writing, it is hard to know what you will find floating about in the appositive-punctuation universe. You cannot always count on correct punctuation in what you read at work, but you can surely strive for it yourself.

Here are two more examples for you:

nonrestrictive: Her favorite book, Clarissa, *is long.*

restrictive: The book Clarissa *is long.*

In the first sentence, *Clarissa* is the appositive for "her favorite book." You could remove it and the sentence would still make sense. It's kind of like saying, "My favorite book is long, and oh, by the way, that book happens to be *Clarissa*."

In the second sentence, you cannot remove the appositive: it is essential to the meaning of the sentence. It identifies which book of all books you are talking about. It's a restrictive appositive, so no commas.

¶

One of my counterarguments to Oxford comma partisans involves a relatively rare appositive case. This topic came up in Santa Fe, New Mexico, where a woman named Dina asked, "The Oxford comma is always right, right?"

"It is—I mean—" I stammered. It was morning, and I was not emotionally prepared for such direct comma confrontation.

"It avoids confusion," declared Dina.

"It does," I said, "except I just want to be difficult and show you one place where I think it can create a little confusion."

"Okay," said Dina.

I wrote down this sentence and showed it to her and her companion, a man named Bernie:

*I invited my mother, my first Spanish teacher, and
my sister.*

"So I'm going to an event, and I invite three people," I
said. "And I'm an Oxford comma user. Let's say you don't
know the context when you see the sentence. You don't
know how many people it is."

"No, I know it's three people," said Dina.

"But let's say you don't know," I said.

"That could be an appositive in there," said Bernie.

"You're fancy," I said. "'My first Spanish teacher' could
be an appositive in that sentence—an alternative way to
describe my mother."

"But I would never assume an appositive," said Dina.
"For clarity, I would say 'I invited my mother, who was my
first Spanish teacher, and my sister.'"

"I'm just saying," I said. "Because if I were a no-
Oxford-comma-user here, then it would be totally clear,
right?" I showed them this:

*I invited my mother, my first Spanish teacher and
my sister.*

"No, because your mother could also be your sister,"
said Dina.

"You know what?" I said. "You're taking it to a different
plane than I had in mind."

"She's a lawyer," said Bernie.

¶

Back in Alabama on that Decatur street corner, Jason and
Jack lingered a long time. You have seen them before:

they are the hooky players. At one point I said, "Should I ask you a question?"

"Yes, ma'am," said Jack, the tall wearer of the backwards baseball cap. "Please ask me about grammar."

"Oh my god, please do," said Jason, the leather-jacket-wearing grammar enthusiast. "Tell me that I'm wrong on something because, god, I want to fix it."

"I'm going to give you a little mini-quiz," I said, and began writing.

"Oh my goodness," said Jack.

"God, your handwriting just . . ." said Jason.

"Dude, it's beautiful, man," said Jack.

Amid effusions of flattery, I wrote:

I invited Rona Jackson, my former roommate, and my boss to the party.

"That sounds awful," said Jason. "I would never invite my boss to a party."

"Okay," I said. "How many people did I invite? That's the quiz."

"One," said Jason, then quickly changed his mind: "Two. At least. No. 'I invited Rona Jackson, my former roommate, and my boss.' That's at least two people, I don't know how many more."

"Is it two or is it three?" I asked.

"It's two," said Jack, holding up two fingers.

"No, it's at least two," said Jason. "Or more."

"How could it be three?" I asked.

"Because you invited her and your boss and . . ." said Jason.

"Yeah, she's right," said Jack. "She got you by the balls there, son."

"I did this one for you because you like commas," I told Jason.

"God, you guys are so cool," said Jason. "I've never loved English grammar this much."

"I don't know," I said. "You seem like a grammar nerd to me."

"I absolutely am," said Jason.

"He is a nerd," said Jack. He was clearly delighted to confirm that.

"So Rona Jackson is the former roommate," said Jason, looking at the sentence.

"Or is she?" I asked.

"Or is she?" echoed Jason.

"That's the question," I said.

"Or is she!" said Jason, excitedly.

"Oooooooh!" said Jack.

"It could have been three people," I said. "It could have been two."

"It could have been two," said Jason, who was now dancing around. "It could have been three. It could have been more. You never know."

Well. You do actually know. I mean, yes, the party might have had a hundred people, but there were not more than three in that sentence. Two or three was up for grabs, though.

"With this punctuation, those commas, you can't tell which it is," I said. "This is a comma question!"

"God, it gives me a chubby, dude!" said Jason. "I love fucking English!" He giggled as he took the page I held out to him.

"Dude," said Jack. "Yeah."

"Like, I will seriously hold on to this shit," said Jason.

Quizlet

....

Is the punctuation in the second sentence below correct?

> Grant has many creative friends. His friend, Mariela Snodgrass, is a talented animator.

Answer: *No, because "Mariela Snodgrass" is a restrictive appositive. Remove the commas.*

13

Weird Plurals: Your Data ____ (Is/Are) Giving Me a Headache

On a sunny fall day in Vermont, a woman pushing a stroller on the Middlebury College campus wanted to know whether "data" was singular or plural. I gave her my usual answer, which is that I use plural if the context underscores the individual data points and singular if it doesn't.

"If it's in scientific analysis, I would expect it to be 'are,'" I said.

"What about a report on scientific analysis?" she asked.

"There I would probably use plural," I said. "I've seen sentences where I think that the more natural usage is 'is,' but I've actually done both, with full consciousness."

"This is a debate we have at work all the time," she said. "I'm a social scientist."

"I would think that for you it would pretty much be 'data are,'" I said.

"Yeah," she said.

"But often people are just talking very loosely," I said, "and there's not really any kind of detailed analysis. They're referring to a collection of information in a different kind of way."

A lumpy kind of way. And yes, *I know*: the word

arrived in English as a Latin plural. That does not mean that it needs to stay that way once it has loitered here awhile. This is not a battle that might go a different way anytime soon: "Data" is used singularly all over the place. "Spaghetti" is a plural in Italian, conjugated with a plural verb, but in English do you ever hear people saying "These spaghetti are delicious"?

Origin is not destiny. We don't necessarily import the same singular and plural noun formation practices across language lines.

The data suggest(s) the word "data" is going to keep living a complicated life in English, and regardless of any one person's wishes, "data is" will continue to swirl around us, sent through the keyboards of educated, thoughtful purveyors of both data and English. It's definitely time to get over this one and let the two options coexist.

And now let us travel to Chicago for the next datum.

¶

In Millennium Park in downtown Chicago, a Marine told me that when he was stationed on the North Shore of Oahu, he and a number of his Marine colleagues had spent a healthy portion of an evening debating the plural of "mongoose." Apparently there were quite a few multi-mongoose situations on the island.

They argued about it for three hours, he said. "All of a sudden, everyone was a scholar. But no one looked it up."

If you do look up "mongoose" on, say, Merriam-Webster's website, you will see "mongooses" listed as the first plural. "Also 'mongeese,'" it adds.

A couple of weeks later, in Montana, a man in a beige

fishing hat at the Bozeman Public Library had just taught me some hunting idioms, and in exchange, he wanted me to give him some grammar tips.

"Okay, I have one for you," I said. "What is the plural of 'mongoose'?"

"That's a hard question to answer," said Jim. "It can't be 'mongooses.'"

"Why can't it be, though?" I asked.

"Well, because would you put an *s* on the end?" asked Jim.

I said, "That's what's interesting, is that people think because there's a goose in it that it should be 'mongeese,' but really, the preferred plural is 'mongooses,' which sounds funny to a lot of people. On the other hand, not that many people need the plural of 'mongoose.'"

"Yeah, because if you see more than one, I'd run," said Jim. "I really would. That would be a problem. That means there's snakes comin'."

¶

Back in Chicago, a girl with a wavy blond ponytail wanted to discuss the plural of "octopus." "It's 'octopuses,' right?" she asked. She was with a group of about fifteen young people, which to this day remains my Grammar Table simultaneous-visitor record.

"That's what I do," I said—but talking about more than one octopus at a time is just asking for trouble.

"Or 'octopodes,'" said one boy.

"No, 'octopi,'" said a second boy.

Then came a positively cephalopodic explosion of octopuses, octopodes, and octopi.

"I'm a Latin student," said the second boy. "Octopi."

A girl in the group disagreed, recited a bunch of endings, covered her mouth, and said, "I— Wait."

"No, no, there's a book," said the girl with the blond ponytail. "There's a book about the spelling of 'octopuses.'"

"A whole book?" asked the Latin student.

"And it's not supposed to be 'octopi,'" said the girl.

"'Octopi' sounds better," said the Latin student.

"I tend to go with the regular anglicized plurals of a lot of things," I said. "Which is typically not what I learned growing up."

A new girl chimed in. "A lot of people say 'one bacteria,' and that annoys me so much. It's, like, 'bacterium'!"

"Oh, here's one for you," I said. "Do you use 'data' with a plural or a singular verb?"

"Data are," said a girl in a miniskirt.

"'Datum' is the singular," said a boy.

"Datum!" said most of the rest of the group simultaneously.

"But do you really do that in real life?" I asked.

"No," said a tall boy in the back of the crowd.

"All the people in the University of Chicago lecture we were just in did," said the girl in the miniskirt.

"Did what?" asked multiple students at once.

"Data are," she said.

"Yes," I said, "but it's often also used to mean, rather than a collection of data points, a bunch of information, and then you'll see it with the singular. Plenty of writers will switch back and forth. Let's go to *Garner's Modern English Usage* and see what he has to say on 'octopus.' Are you guys bored?"

"No, this is fascinating," said a boy in stripes. "We're just all such nerds."

"That's why we're here," said another girl. There was a murmur of agreement from the group.

"This is pretty spectacular for me," I told them. "I could not have picked a better group of people to talk to. Seriously, this is exciting for me!"

"Aw," said the boy in stripes. "We should go on a road trip together."

"We totally should!" I said.

"We can be your table," said the girl in the miniskirt. "I'll hold books!"

"Okay!" I said. Then I read aloud to them from *Garner's*: "Because this word is actually of Greek origin — not Latin — the classical plural is 'octopodes,' ok-*top*-o-deez, not 'octopi.'"

"Ohhh," said the boy in stripes.

"I'm going to go out and say, 'Do you see those ok-*top*-o-deez in the aquarium?'" announced a girl in a gray cap.

I continued reading from *Garner's*: "But the standard plural in American English and British English alike is 'octopuses,' which has vastly predominated in print sources since the early twentieth century. Still, some writers mistakenly use the supposed Latin plural." I looked up and added, "Meaning 'octopi.'"

"Also 'panini' is a plural," said a boy on the left of the group. "One is 'panino.'"

"Is it really?" someone asked.

"Yeah, it's two panini but one panino," said the panini counter.

That is sort of true. "Panini," like "spaghetti," is plural in the original Italian, but once words make their way into English, the plurals often end up conforming to English plural-formation patterns. Many people use "panini" as the singular in English, and "paninis" and "panini" coex-

ist as English plurals. These are things that happen naturally as languages commingle and evolve over time.

"See, you guys know so much," I said. "That's just going to mess with your heads when you're trying to make
editing decisions." A boy giggled.

As for me, I like my syllabuses like I like my octopuses.

Quizlet

....

**When should you correct random strangers on
their noun plurals?**

Answer: *When you are on a grammar reality show competing for, say,
ten thousand dollars' worth of language books. Otherwise never, especially if you're wrong.*

14

Yes, Ma'am!

"You know what you do that I almost never hear in New York?" I asked a man named Jerry in Little Rock. He was tall, bearded, and in his early twenties.

"What?" asked Jerry.

"You say, 'Yes, ma'am,'" I said.

"Really?" he asked. "They don't say 'Yes, ma'am,' 'No, sir,' 'Yes, sir' in New York?"

"Every once in a while someone will say 'Yes, ma'am' there," I said, "but here it's just part of the conversational flow. Would you say it to me if I were eighteen, or would you say something different?"

"I would say it to someone to recognize their experience and authority over me," said Jerry.

"I was just going to say that!" said his friend, a radiant redhead named Julia. "We're the same age, but anything older than me, I'll definitely say 'ma'am' or 'sir.'"

Not saying "ma'am" or "sir" doesn't tend to read as rude where I live in New York. In fact, I told them, "Women are sometimes bothered by 'ma'am' because once they hit 'ma'am' age, they may feel like that means they're old."

The man exhaled and smiled.

"But I like it," I said. "I think it's charming. And I noticed as soon as we passed a certain latitude, we started hearing it more."

Julia laughed. "You got to the South?" she asked.

I nodded. "It's like, I'm a ma'am now," I said. "It's nice. I like it."

"I usually try to say it for authority reasons, though— not by, like, age," said Julia.

"I say age," said Jerry.

We chatted a bit longer. "It's been very enjoyable to talk to you," I said.

"Yes, ma'am," said Julia.

¶

"You're very polite," I told Jack, the taller, backwards-cap-wearing man of my two boisterous new friends in Decatur, Alabama. "Aside from the part where you ate my apple." During our long grammar conversation, he and Jason had decided to help themselves to the lunch apple that I had placed atop the Grammar Table.

"I'm sorry," said Jack.

"I'm now going to be starving with no food," I said.

"No, you got like two bites left," said Jack.

"Okay, that's great," I said. "But you know how you say 'Yes, ma'am'? Would you say that to me if I were twenty, or is it only because I'm older?"

"I would say that out of respect because you're older than me, and if you was younger than me, I'd still say it," said Jack.

"You would?" I asked, confused.

"You would really have to correct me to not do that," said Jack. "It's just ingrained in me to be respectful to elders because—No disrespect, ma'am, but you've been on this earth longer than I have, you know how it works better than I do."

He added, "You've had your experiences."

"Yes," I said.

"I've had mine," said Jack.

At this point Jason returned from a trip to the bathroom of a nearby restaurant. He contributed some words to the conversation—words that an editor politely requested I cut from this book—in response to which Jack requested that he shut his mouth.

Jason then turned his attention to me. "I think in the South, I would say we are more polite," he concluded. "To a degree. You piss us off to a degree, we like to brawl. We'll brawl. We will throw down. We step heavily away from the subject at hand, however." He bent down toward the Grammar Table. "So, tell me something about English," he said.

15

Accents Keep Things Fresh

In late December in downtown Little Rock, Arkansas, two high school students from Little Rock Central High School stopped to chat. Their school is a major civil rights landmark in this country: the site of forced desegregation in 1957 following the US Supreme Court *Brown v. Board of Education* decision. They were in tenth grade, and school was going to be starting up again soon.

"Do I sound country to you?" asked Lily, who had red hair.

"You don't sound country to me," I said. "You sound like you're from the southern part of the country, which is different. When you say 'country,' what does that mean to you?"

"Country," Lily said. "It's like a country accent. I get told I have a country accent a lot. But I also get told I don't."

"It just sounds southern to me," I said. "The association I have with your accent is that it feels kind of warm and friendly. The New York accent, the one you hear on TV shows, is a little bit rougher and sort of like 'Get out my way because I'm trying to get on the subway,' or that kind of thing."

"Y'all do that for real?" asked Hazel, her friend, who

had on a headband that reminded me of ones I had worn in the 1970s.

"I mean, *I* don't," I said.*

"But they do?" asked Hazel.

"Well, there are a lot of people and not much space, so it can be like this," I said, demoing elbowing someone. "But mostly people are very friendly. It's just that it reads a little differently. It sounds a little different. You should come visit sometime!"

¶

"When I lived in Colorado," said a man named Ken on the streets of Starkville, Mississippi, "people would make fun of my accent."

"I love your accent," I said. "I think it sounds amazing."

"I don't feel like I have one, but that's me," said Ken.

"Do you feel like I have one?" I asked.

"I feel like you have a lack of one," said Ken. "Does that make sense? And, to be honest, if I hung around you more, I'd talk like you more. I can't help it. I pick up who I am around. If I worked all day with a bunch of farmers, by five o'clock that afternoon, I'd sound like a farmer."

"Some people do that more than others, I have found," I said.

"I don't know why I do it, but I catch myself doing it," said Ken.

---

* I think I said this because I didn't want to alarm those nice tenth graders, but the reality is, I have at times been grumpy getting on subways. Now, if people would simply *move over a little instead of blocking the doors,* we wouldn't have to have this conversation.

"Maybe it's a sign of friendliness," I said. "Like group camaraderie."

"Maybe," said Ken. "Yeah, wantin' to fit in a little bit."

"That's funny," I said, then added, "The accent in this region feels like hospitality to me."

"Everything's kind of shorted," said Ken. "In the southern dialect, everybody tries to make things come out easier without as much difficulty, and I don't see how that makes a lot of difference, because how hard is it to say a word? Why would you have to shortcut it?"

"I feel some of your vowels take longer, though," I said. "How about *c a n*?"

"Cayan," said Ken.

"See, to me it sounds almost like two syllables," I said.

"Yep," said Ken. "Well, the nut that people make pies with: *p e c a n*. Say it."

"Peh-*kahn*," I said.

"You said peh-*kahn*," said Ken. "Most people not from the South say *pee*-can. And it drives us insane, because it's peh-*kahn*."

"Is there anything that's annoying about the way I speak?" I asked.

"No!" said Ken. "Not to me."

"You're not just being polite?" I asked.

"No no no no," said Ken.

"Okay," I said. "Because I kind of put you on the spot."

"No," said Ken. "Well, for somebody who's never been out from around here, they'd say, 'She talks like a damn Yankee.' They'll never say it to your face, but it'd be like, 'Did you hear that Yankee again?' That's what they'll say."

"Really?" I asked.

"Absolutely," said Ken. "Yankee. Which is a terrible

term. But that's what they'll say, because you don't talk like them. I've lived other places, and I've experienced other accents."

"Traveling around is a very quick way to learn a lot of things about other human beings," I said.

"Here's another example," said Ken. "My name is spelled *K e n*. Say it."

"Ken," I said.

"Here we say Kyin," said Ken, throwing open his arms. "Not Ken but Kyin. Almost like *K i n*, but they stretch the *i* out. Kyin."

"Kyin," I said, practicing. "It sounds almost like there's a *y* stuck in there."

"Uh-huh," he said. "Yep. Kyiiin. That's exactly right. I have family members in Austin, they say Ken. They've shortened it to Ken—or, not shortened it; they say it the proper way. And so the first time I heard them say my name, I was like, 'That's not my name! I'm Kyin!' My relative said, 'That's what I said: Ken!' I was like, 'No, I'm Kyiin.' He thought that was hilarious."

"Well, it *is* kind of funny," I said.

We chatted a bit longer and talked about later stops. Of Alabama, which would be our next destination, Ken said, "The smaller the town, the more exaggerated the accents. Promise."

"Okay," I said. "I believe you."

"You may need a translator," he said. "I don't know."

"That would be fantastic to get to a point where we needed that," I told him.

"You say that until you really need some information and you can't figure it out," he said. "It's like, 'Man, where did he say the hospital was?'"

¶

We did make it to Alabama right after that, and we didn't need to go to the hospital, and I understood everyone we talked to in Alabama, perfectly, but I did consult Jason and Jack in Decatur about my accent.

"Does the way I speak sound funny to you?" I asked them.

"It does, yes," said Jason.

"What does it sound like to you?" I asked.

"You sound very proper," said Jack. "You sound like you're from the North."

"Yeah," said Jason. "You know, you can tell. We can tell somebody that's a Yankee. No offense to that. Anything above the Mason-Dixon line—honestly, that's the way it is. I'm just sayin'."

"Ma'am, you got very nice teeth, and you speak very well," said Jack.

"So you must not be from around here," added Jason.

16

The Great American Spacing War

When some people arrive at the Grammar Table, they say hello. Other people dispense with any question-delaying niceties, and I confess I enjoy it. It tickles me to be interpreted as a kind of public utility.

"Two spaces or one space?" That was an actual greeting from a man with glasses propped on his shaved head. We were on the Middlebury College campus in Vermont.

"Well, I grew up with two, but I do one now," I said. The man made a guttural sound of disapproval. "If you still do two, I'm not going to call it wrong, but it pegs you to a certain time period."

"I know," he said, then added, "Over what? Over forty?"

I hesitated.

"Over forty-five?" he asked.

"Definitely over forty," I said. "But I think we can all get along. Except, you know, the one-spacers will often sneak into two-spacers' documents and edit the second spaces out. They'll do a global replace."

"I get some of that at work," said the man, "but I just change it back to two spaces."*

---

* When the copy editor for this book saw this sentence, she wrote

People often want to know why things changed. You can read detailed explanations of this spacing shift on oodles of websites all over the internet, but the simple answer is this: conventions sometimes change.

In Verdi Square in Manhattan, a woman in her fifties told me that her "somewhat older" husband insisted on two spaces after periods. She herself preferred one. "Who's right?" she asked.

"Well, there is not an absolute right or wrong," I replied cautiously, "but momentum is clearly toward one space, and when we are all dead and gone, it will be a one-space world."

I added, "Older people applying for jobs are often advised to delete the second spaces from their résumés. Otherwise they risk dating themselves."

She burst out laughing and said, "Oh my god, I can't wait to go home and tell my husband that part about 'older people.'"

¶

This spacing topic also came up on a Michigan train—specifically the Detroit People Mover, which loops through downtown Detroit. I was sitting on it at my mini–Grammar Table with my mini–Grammar Table sign, which together ensure that I do not take up more than the single space I've paid for on public transportation. Brandt was filming, and our only companions on the car were several young women who told us they were in town for a church program.

"How do you feel about spaces after periods?" asked

"<scream emoji>" in the margin. I think she speaks for many of us.

one of the women. She had long blond hair and seemed to find the Grammar Table a more natural and reasonable fellow commuter than her friends did.

"Are you a one-spacer?" I asked. "Not to stereotype, but I just figured you for a one-spacer."

"Yeah," said the woman. "I used to work at the writing center at my college, and everyone did two spaces, and I had never heard of that before."

"Were they older?" I asked. "I teach adults, and I sometimes have adults in my classes who enforce it with their children. And I always tell them, 'Don't do that! You can do what you want, but don't do that with your child.'"

She laughed. "That's so funny."

"I switched over in the nineties," I said. "It was perfectly easy to switch, it was no big deal, but many people my age still do two spaces."

"Really?" she said. "Why?"

"Because it's one of those things you were taught you were supposed to do back in the typewriter era," I said. "And they say that one space looks funny to them. But the thing is, almost every publication we've read in our entire lives—magazines, newspapers, books—has always been one space. So they often don't know what they've been looking at."

"This is the Millender Center," announced the automated train voice, and the doors opened.

I told my new one-spacing friend, "I wanted to make a T-shirt that would say TWO SPACES AFTER A PERIOD IS THE MOM JEANS OF PUNCTUATION. But I thought it would seem mean."

"I think you should make it," she said.

"You do?" I said. "All right, but maybe I'll sell it under a pseudonym."*

¶

In Bozeman, Montana, I chatted for a while with Lynn, a part-time employee at the library. "For decades when I typed, we always did two spaces," she told me. "It was just habit. It took me a while to switch. I was extremely resistant and had to read several articles about why we don't need to do that anymore before I gave in."

"Did you stop then?" I asked. "You actually stopped?"

"Yes," said Lynn.

"I think this is a really good sign about you," I said. Lynn laughed.

"Do you do astrology readings too?" she asked.

"Because lots of people are permanently resistant to making that change," I said.

"I'm a very logical person," said Lynn. "When I actually started reading people who were knowledgeable about typesetting and all that stuff, I kind of went, All right, I guess I see. I understand."

"I'm impressed!" I asked. "This is what libraries represent: facts! I'm going to congratulate both of us right now for making that change."

She put out her hand and we shook on it.

¶

---

* I did not write this book in order to sell T-shirts, but just in case you are interested, the mom jeans shirt now exists in the Grammar Table store at grammartable.com.

A gray-haired tourist I met in St. Louis violated my demographic expectations by telling me, "When I was taught to type, it was one space."

Her name was Naomi, and she was a small woman with a big personality. Naomi was visiting St. Louis with her cousin and their respective husbands. "If you were in the college prep corps," she said, "you had to take one semester of typing. And I flunked because I got arrested during the final." She whacked her husband to punctuate this point, and everyone laughed.

"We went to this creek to go swimming," she continued, "and there were badasses from the west side of Columbus with machetes and chains, and the sheriff came, and we got arrested."

"Your childhood was like a combination of *West Side Story* and *American Graffiti*," her husband told her.

"And the sheriff just told our parents, 'Yeah, they were in the wrong place at the wrong time,'" said Naomi.

"You don't seem like a hardened criminal," I told her.

"No," said Naomi.

"Don't let her pull that on you," said her cousin's husband.

"I got an F because I didn't take the exam because I was in jail," said Naomi.

¶

In Santa Fe, Dina—an Oxford comma lover you met in an earlier chapter—had spacing concerns. "There are still two spaces after a period, yeah?" she asked. "I've tried the one, and it just looks like a sea of words." She waved her hand to indicate the sea-like state of the words, and her companion, Bernie, smilingly shook his head.

"When you read a newspaper, how many spaces are after the periods?" I asked.

"I don't read newspapers in printed form," said Dina.

"What if you read a news website?" I asked.

"It looks like two," said Dina.

"It's not," I said. "It's one." Bernie tried unsuccessfully to conceal a guffaw with his right hand. "Everything that you read, if you pick up a book, if you pick up a newspaper, a magazine, if you read a website, it's one," I added.

"Interesting," said Dina. "But it's like muscle memory at this point."

"I am so happy that I stopped doing it," I told her, "because it is fewer keystrokes, which is good."

"I do like efficiency," Dina conceded.

"Twenty years ago," I told her, "half of my adult students were doing two spaces, and the other half were doing one. It's now down to like a quarter or a third. It depends on what you do. If you're a lawyer, there are a lot of two-spacers."

Bernie's face lit up, and he touched her. "I'm a lawyer and I'm a two-spacer," admitted Dina.

"She's good," said Bernie. "She is good."*

"Are you seriously a lawyer?" I asked Dina. "That's funny. In law there seems to be a lot more resistance to the single space."

Bernie was smiling and nodding at her. He appeared to be enjoying this. A lot. "So I think you could get away with preserving the two spaces longer there," I said.

"When she writes something, it begins, 'Come here, all ye,'" said Bernie.

"It does not," said Dina, rolling her eyes.

---

* The antecedent for "she" is clearly the Grammar Table!

Quizlet

· ·

How many spaces appear after each sentence in this brief message?

> Olive, I will pick you up from your skydiving lesson at noon. Could you please wait for me by the barrel cactus? If you finish early, message me and I will try to arrive sooner. Thank you! I'm looking forward to seeing you soon.

Answer: *2, 1, 2, 1*

cAPiTaLizAtiON CHAoS

To film on the Venice Beach Boardwalk, we were required to obtain a permit and have someone there to supervise the shoot. The man assigned to us, Al, hung out with us all day to ensure that we didn't do anything forbidden. In exchange for Al's supervisory services, I acted as his capitalization confessor.

He told me, "I have a tendency to always capitalize the first letter, which I know is wrong."

That didn't sound bad. "The first letter of what?" I asked.

"Everything!" Al said. Al was a manly kind of man, but he suddenly got gushy: "I just *looooove* writing in caps. I don't know why!"

I personally am a low-capitalization person. By low capitalization, all I mean is that I capitalize appropriately in public: I don't capitalize with abandon.*

In Buffalo, New York, I met a writer named Neil, a former army officer, who wanted to talk about New York City mayor Bill de Blasio—not about his politics, but about his name. More specifically, Neil wanted to talk about the

---

* In private texts with friends and relatives, I cannot guarantee there will be any capitalization at all.

capitalization of the "de" in de Blasio when it appeared at the beginning of a sentence.

"I've seen it done two different ways," said Neil. "His last name is de Blasio but it's a small *d*. And then if you were to begin the sentence with de Blasio, I've seen it small *d,* and then I've also seen it with a large *D*."

In other words:

De Blasio was the 109th mayor of New York City.

or

de Blasio was the 109th mayor of New York City.

"Small *d* starting a sentence is weird," I said, using my most advanced grammar words.

"That's his name, though," said Neil.

"I know, but any word at the beginning of a sentence is capitalized," I said.

"But that's his name," he repeated. "So when you're starting a sentence 'de Blasio did this,' do you then change his name to be a capital *D*?"

"Yes," I said. "It's just a conventional lowercase. There's nothing idiosyncratic about capitalizing it at the start of a sentence. Do you want to lowercase it?"

"Well, say your name is Ben and your last name begins with a lowercase," said Neil. "Who am I to change that simply because it's the beginning of a sentence?"

"You're not changing the name," I said. "It just falls under the normal rules of word capitalization at the beginning of a sentence."

I love discussing names and their treatment in print. In fact, Neil's question reminded me of one of my favorite grammar topics: plural possessives of names in English. I can hardly wait for us to get to Chapter 28!

¶

I read a lot of books as a child, but I also hungered to read any text I could find on any product package I encountered in the kitchen or bathroom.

Cereal boxes and Kleenex boxes were my main targets. I read and reread every bit of text on all six sides of every Kleenex box that ever passed through our home. I even learned some American history from the bottom of those Kleenex boxes.

At the kitchen table, no ingredient or percentage of RDA (recommended dietary allowance) on a cereal box was ever too lowly to be read by me for the six hundredth time at breakfast. I had unbounded energy for lists of additives.

Outside the Milwaukee Art Museum, where we set up on the boardwalk along Lake Michigan, I met a boy of about eleven, Ricky, who was apparently a label reader too, because he wanted to know about capitalization choices on a car interior.

"There was a little tag on the inside of her car," Ricky told me, referring to the woman with him, who I think was his aunt. "It said, 'This is equipped with Advanced Airbags.' The Advanced Airbags part was capitalized. Why was it?"

"One possibility," I said, "is that there's actually some sort of official product whose actual name is Advanced Airbags, which I don't know about. But the other possibility is that someone is capitalizing to make the airbags look more important. Without knowing more, I really can't tell which one it is, but I find it remarkable that you made such a close and careful observation."

"I was kind of just looking at it and thinking, That doesn't make sense," said Ricky.

In the adult world, capitalization often doesn't. People learn moderate, sensible capitalization rules in school, grow up, enter the workforce, and suddenly go on capitalization rampages. That day in Milwaukee, I could have told Ricky what lay ahead, but I did not. He will know soon enough.

¶

Back on Venice Beach, a professor named Eva told me, "I just learned something, and I was very ashamed that I didn't already know it—that you don't capitalize fall and spring when they refer to seasons. Is that correct?"

"That's right," I said. "Are you sure that you've always been capitalizing them? Did you change habits at some point when you didn't notice?"

"No, I always capitalized them," said Eva.

"But are you supposed to capitalize summer and winter?" asked another professor who was accompanying her. He was a native Urdu speaker, and capital letters don't exist in Urdu.

"No, none of them," said Eva. "But the problem with 'fall' and 'spring' is that they mean other things, whereas summer and winter are clearly seasons."

"Ah, good point," said her colleague.

"But to indicate that you're not talking about falling down, or springing," continued Eva, "I always thought I should capitalize them, and I had a terrible fight with my partner. She's always right, and I looked it up, and she was right. And that's from somebody who got an eight hundred on my English college boards because I was such grammar perfection!"

¶

Not all capitalization crises involve overcapitalization. On Martha's Vineyard, I met Evelyn, who taught government and was the director of paralegal studies at a community college.

She told me, "We have students who've already gone to school who come back to community college for things, and when they walk through the doors of this college, they don't capitalize anything. It's like anti-capitalism."

I laughed. "I mean, we have PhDs that come in to take courses," said Evelyn, "and I've had people in my paralegal program from other countries who want to take paralegal courses, and we have people here who were English majors, but as soon as they walk in, it's like a disease."

"In their papers, they don't capitalize?" I asked.

"It's like you walk through the door, and you don't even know each other, but everyone just stops capitalizing things," she said.

¶

In Buffalo, Jennifer—an elegant bank executive in an elegant dress—had strong capitalization preferences for email.

"It drives me crazy when people capitalize both the *b*

and the *r* in 'Best regards,'" she said. "Shouldn't it just be the capital *B* and then a small *r*?"

I agreed that it should.

"Yeah!" she said. "And I try to correct people and they say, 'Oh, it can be either.' Or 'All My Best' with all initial caps. No! Capital *A,* small *m,* small *b.*"

Here, look at them next to each other:

All My Best,   All my best,
Gregor   Gregor

Which do you like better? I much prefer the one on the right, but if you want to sign off your emails "All My Best" with three capital letters, I will still receive your emails with pleasure.

"How often do you see 'All my best'?" I asked. "Is that common here?"

"Lately more," said Jennifer. "It's getting more common. Whenever a closing is more than one word, I think you should capitalize the first word, not the other ones."

"That's what I do," I said. "But the one that bugs me more is 'Good morning' with a capital *m.*"

Good Morning, Hermione!   ⇦ ugh
Good morning, Hermione!   ⇦ much nicer

Jennifer agreed with me. "Oh, yeah," she said. "Only the first word capital *G,* and then a small *m.*"

She thanked me for the capitalization commiseration. "I'm going to go into my office now," she said, "but I'm going to let them know that you're out here, and I hope that they will come out and use your services. I'll bring you out water and snacks."

And she did! Buffalo was our first cross-country stop, and this boded well for the hospitality to come.

> All my best,
> Ellen

Quizlet

••

How many additional words should be capitalized in the following sentence?

> In the summer of 1982, I worked for the general manager of a footed-pajama company.

Answer: *None! Don't capitalize seasons, and don't capitalize ordinary business titles in standard prose. Stop leaning on that Shift key, over-capitalizers!*

18

Contract with Confidence!

In Verdi Square one day, a young woman stopped by the Grammar Table with her mother and younger sister. We all chatted about writing for a bit, and she told me she was a college student.

"How's college going?" I asked.

"It's good!" she said. "Speaking of writing, when we're freshmen, we have to take college writing. And something that really surprised me when I got to college was that we were able to use contractions. Like 'I'd.'"

"That surprised you?" I asked.

"Yes!" she said. "I had a very good English teacher when I was a junior and senior in high school. She always drilled it into us that we couldn't use contractions, but then in college, they were like, no, you can do that. I was like, what?"

"You can," I said. "You really can. And in fact, I find some adults are still hobbled by that, and they end up sounding like robots."

I don't usually notice people's contraction-usage rates, but every once in a while someone will sound extra stiff to me in writing. Please compare:

Contractionless	Tastefully Contracted
I will see you at five.	I'll see you at five.
No, I do not hear anything.	No, I don't hear anything.
I am not a robot.	I'm not a robot.

Either way is fine, but compulsive contraction evasion is unnecessary. Still, you do need to do the contractions right. On Venice Beach, a thirtyish man named Arthur arrived at the Grammar Table with a complaint. "I don't know if you have this problem in the States," he said, "but it's a huge problem where I'm from."

"Where are you from?" I asked.

"Sydney, Australia," said Arthur. "And I'm an English teacher, and it really pisses me off. I'm in my third year teaching, and I find it amazing how in grade eleven, some students still write, 'I would of done this' with an 'of.' It's like, you learned contractions in primary school, and you somehow forgot about it."

"When you write, do you contract 'would've'?" I asked.

"Yes," said Arthur, "but I write the apostrophe *v e,* and I do it in informal writing. I wouldn't do it in an essay."

"It's a contraction that I write only in texting," I said, "whereas I contract up the wazoo with everything else. Even in formal writing, I'm a contractor. Like 'isn't,' 'doesn't,' 'wouldn't.' I don't want to sound stilted. If I would contract something speaking to a group, I often contract it in writing, too."

A fire truck squeezed carefully between us and the row of stores on the other side of the Venice Beach Boardwalk.

"'Would of' happens because of the sound, right?" asked Arthur.

"Yes," I said, "but they're different parts of speech, so it suggests you aren't aware of apostrophe *v e* as the verb 'have.'"

The word "of" is a preposition. "Would've" definitely sounds like "would of." But we have no use for "would of." You can't put those two words together to form a real idea in English.*

"This was a small thing," said Arthur, "but it pissed me off recently, because I just finished marking papers."

Teachers often need catharsis after grading, I pointed out. "Yeah," said Arthur, smiling. He mock-addressed his students: "Kids! Read more! Stop reading texts! Stop reading YouTube videos! Wait, you can't even read YouTube videos! You've got to read novels and newspaper articles!"

Quizlet

....

How many different things can "aren't" mean?

Answer: *Two. It stands for "are not," of course, but here's another option: "Aren't I the best blueberry pancake maker in the entire family?" There it substitutes for "am not."*

---

* Okay, smart alecks, things like this don't count: "Gia <u>would, of</u> all the townspeople, be the most capable of capturing the vampire."

19

The Pleasure of Pronunciation

In Boise, Idaho, a woman stopped at the table with her husband and their nine-year-old triplets.

"She is a grammar pro, you guys," she told the children—two boys and a girl. "This is homeschool work, right? We're going to have a field trip with this lady."

As a child, I went on numerous field trips, but this was the first time I had ever *been* the field trip. I was honored.

The parents wanted to talk pronunciation: "almond." The dad said, "I grew up farming ammonds"—his first syllable rhymed with "ham"—"but everybody calls them al-monds. But you don't call salmon sal-mon."

As the mother explained that they were just now moving to Boise, her daughter got up onto a water fountain next to me and began climbing the adjacent traffic pole.

"If you go to Central California," said the mom, "you'll hear a lot of ammond versus almond. Everybody that grows them calls them ammonds, but the whole rest of the world calls them almonds." Now all three triplets were climbing things.

"The consumers are buying something a little different!" I said.

"The machine, the shaker, grabs the tree trunk and shakes the ammonds," said the triplets' dad, "so there's a running joke that maybe they're almonds when they're on the tree, but the shaker shakes the *l* off."

¶

In St. Louis, Missouri—about 1,400 miles southeast of Boise—I spoke frankly with a reporter named Ashley about the pronunciation conflicts within my marriage. I confuse Brandt by doing things like pronouncing the names Don and Dawn identically.

That is how it goes with us West Coasters who become entangled with easterners.

"My husband and I have the same argument over these two words," said Ashley, holding up a pad on which she had written "cot" and "caught." "So it's the same sound, right?" she asked.

"For some of us, yeah," I said. "That's called the cot-caught merger." Meaning in some parts of the US, those words sound the same. In other parts, they don't. In my mouth, they do.

"Do you say those two words differently?" Ashley asked Brandt.

"Quite!" exclaimed Brandt. We all laughed. Brandt is unmerged.

"And do you say them the same?" Ashley asked me.

"Yes. We've been together almost twenty-six years," I said, "and early in our relationship, we were arguing over . . . I think it was 'taught' and 'tot'—*t a u g h t* and *t o t*. Brandt was saying they were different, and I said, 'They are not! They're the same.' He said, 'They're different.' And I thought he was out of his mind. I just couldn't believe it."

Ashley laughed. Ashley got me and my vowel sounds. Ashley was westerly like me.

"And I went and looked them up in a dictionary," I said, "and the pronunciation key for the two words was different. I remember that as one of these pivotal moments when you think you know more than you do and you realize that you should always be a little bit careful about that. When I'm teaching grammar, I actually talk a lot about humility, because there are always surprises. You think you have a handle on things, and then you realize there are surprises."

¶

In Iowa City, I found additional vowel kinship. I was planted on a street corner with the Iowa state capitol in view behind me when three smiling young people approached the table.

Dustin, wearing a red sweatshirt, said, "We walked by earlier, and I'm like, oh my god, I'm like a grammar freak."

"Are you really?" I asked. "How did that happen to you?"

"My grandpa was an English teacher," said Dustin. "And so ever since I was really young, he would always correct my English and everything I said, like, it's not 'Joe and me,' it's 'Joe and I.' Like all that."

"Did you like it at the time?" I asked.

"Not at the time," said Dustin.

"But now you appreciate it," I said.

"Now that I'm older and I sound more educated than everyone else, I kind of like it," said Dustin.

We all conferred on possible topics of discussion. "Is

there anything I should know about Iowa, like any Iowa slang or anything?" I asked.

Dustin guffawed.

"We say beg," said Alexis, a smiling young woman with long brown hair.

"We say beg," agreed a second man, Leo, who was also smiling. Iowa sure seemed friendly.

"Beg is a big one," said Dustin. "Beg or beg."

"What are you saying?" I asked, confused.

"Can you grab my beg?" demoed Dustin.

"So you say these the same?" I asked, showing them "bag" and "beg" on my notepad.

"I pronounce them the same," said Dustin.

"Beg," said Alexis. "Yeah."

"Based on the context, I know what someone's talking about," said Dustin.

"That's good, because they are kind of different," I said, laughing.

"Yeah," said Leo. "So like, it's the same for us, but other people, it's like baaaag."

"Like, that's a beg," said Dustin, pointing to a bag on the arm of a passing woman.

Alexis nodded. "It's a beg."

"Oh, okay," I said. "I would say 'I beg for the bag.'"

"Oh!" said Leo, looking shocked.

"I'd say 'I beg for the beg,'" said Alexis.

"I beg for the beg," said Leo. "We beg for the beg. I beg for the beg."

"I beg for the beg," said Alexis.

"For the beg," said Leo.

"Brandt grew up in Connecticut," I said. "And if I look up pronunciations in the dictionary, they pretty much always match what he says. Whereas I have fewer vowel sounds than he does, so as an example, I say these two the same." I held up my notepad, on which I had written "stalk" and "stock."

They looked at the page and said in a chorus, "Stock and stock." No difference. I asked Brandt to model his pronunciation.

"Stalk and stock," said Brandt, just like a walking *Merriam-Webster's*, with clearly different vowels.

"Whaaaa?" said Leo. The three visitors were amazed.

"And these names sound the same for me," I said, writing down Don and Dawn. "Do they for you?"

They erupted in a chorus of Dons. There was no difference.

I looked at Brandt expectantly. Anticipation built. Everyone laughed.

"Don," said Brandt, "and Dawn." A new chorus of Dons exploded from the three.

"This is funny, because I've read that west of the Mississippi River, those vowels are more likely to sound the same," I said. "And we crossed the Mississippi last night when we were driving here. You're the first people I've talked to here about vowel sounds, and I feel as though except for the whole weird bag/beg thing"— they laughed—"I'm among my peers. I feel so affirmed, because Brandt doesn't always know what I'm saying."

"You're with your people!" Brandt told me.

¶

In Spokane, Washington, two friends named Scott and Amanda disambiguated breast coverings and meat pies for me. The word in question was "pasties."

Scott, who wore khaki shorts, said, "We had lunch over at the pub, and we were discussing 'pasties' versus 'pasties.'" Scott pronounced the first "pasties" as pass-teas, and the second "pasties" as pay-stees. I will use these pronunciation spellings to facilitate discussion here.

"Oh, for the thing on your boob?" I asked.

"Yes!" said Scott.

"Yes, thank you," said Amanda, who was carrying an instrument case on her back.

"So pay-stees for that, right?" I asked.

"It is pay-stees," confirmed Scott.

"And a pass-tea in Irish food is like a little pie," said Amanda.

"I did not know that," I said. "Is it really pronounced that way? Because whenever I've read about the little pies, I've always in my head pronounced them as pay-stees."

"Yes," said Amanda. "They're pronounced two different ways."

"Pass-tea for food, pay-stee for the other," said Scott.

"It's really pass-tea for the food?" I exclaimed. "This is going to mess up all the novels I've read over the course of my life. I honestly just said this word yesterday. I'm not kidding."

"I asked the waitress how to pronounce it," said Amanda. "I pointed to the word on the menu, and she said pass-tea. And I was like, Cool." She gave a thumbs-up to illustrate the coolness.

"But then you started talking about the other," I said. She nodded.

"Well, that was more interesting anyway!" said Scott.

As we were talking, I discovered that *Merriam-Webster's Collegiate Dictionary* had no entry for a single pastie/pasty as in breast covering. I could only locate "pasties."

"I guess it's just plural because there are two of them," I said, making a reflexive and unnecessary gesture indicating that I, too, had two.

I read the definition aloud: "Small round coverings for a woman's nipples." I added, "I really feel there should be a singular listed there too."

Then I looked up "pasty," *p a s t y,* and found the pass-tea pronunciation for the food.

"Wow," I said. "You've blown my mind today."

"What does it say for pass-tea?" asked Scott.

"Pass-tea is dough, a meat pie, a turnover," I said.

"Yep," said Amanda.

"Okay," I said, "but what I find most hilarious about this whole thing, aside from the fact that I've been pronouncing the word for the food wrong my entire life,* is that there's no singular listed for the breast version."

"Right," said Amanda. "Because you have two." Then she, too, indicated her chest to help clarify this point.

"Why is that?" asked Scott.

"They must be sold singly," said Amanda.

"What if you just have one?" asked Scott.

"What if you're working in Vegas and you lose one?" asked Amanda.

These were all excellent questions, exactly the kind of thing I hope to explore at the Grammar Table.

"Maybe they figure that you can improvise," I said. "I'm just double-checking that there's no singular listing

---

* Well, I have almost never said this word aloud, but the pronunciation has echoed in my head whenever I've read it.

for pasties, because maybe the singular for that is spelled
p a s t i e."

"Oh, see, now we don't actually know," said Amanda.

"No, we don't," I said. "Because it hasn't told us the
singular."

"I would guess it would be spelled with a *y,*" said
Amanda.

"Okay, what I'm going to have to do on this one is follow up with Merriam-Webster," I said. "That's this dictionary, and I'm going to file a complaint about the lack
of singular for 'pasties.'"

"You could be famous," Scott told Amanda.

"I'm a language geek, actually," said Amanda.

"This is really funny," I said. "We're linking meat pies
with breast coverings!"

"Which is beautiful," said Scott.

"Which I think is beautiful, because it's all positive,"
I said.

Scott had sudden second thoughts. He began worrying that this discussion might come across as misogynistic.

"Misogynistic?" I said. "No! I don't think so."

"Okay, good—as long as you don't think so," said
Scott.

"No, I don't at all," I said. "This was like the best kind
of thing that could possibly come up here."

"I just love this kind of thing," said Amanda. "I get a
kick out of it, but I don't ever get to talk about it."

"I'm so glad that I encountered you," I said. "You taught
me something. Because I had no idea and I might mistakenly have ordered breast coverings in a restaurant!"

Months later, back in New York, I did in fact follow
up with the marvelous Peter Sokolowski, who is editor at

large at Merriam-Webster. He noted that the research for that particular entry is now fifty years old.

"We'd do it differently today, and when the term gets revised, the entry will reflect changes in our ideas," he said. Fifty years ago, the manual collection of paper citations — meaning examples of a word used in print — was laborious and by definition incomplete, but today computers swiftly search enormous language databases for references. Right away Peter found a few instances of a singular "pastie" reference — spelled *p a s t i e*.

"In general," Peter emailed me, "we enter words as plural nouns where the singular form doesn't exist ('undies,' 'glasses,' 'rabbit ears'). Parallel examples more like 'pastie' are 'falsie,' 'spat,' 'galosh.' In this case, I assume the definer could find no evidence for the singular, but even the largest paper citation file in the world has limitations when it comes to very rare forms. This probably should be entered as 'pastie.'"

This is great news. The lost lonely pastie may one day have a home in *Merriam-Webster's*.

¶

In downtown Starkville, Mississippi, a young woman told me, "It took me over a year to finally get 'hearth' right." Her name was Addison, and her hair was bundled into brunette braids.

"To get what right?" I asked.

"Uh, isn't it . . . is it harth?" asked Addison, suddenly uncertain. "Or hurth?"

"*H e a r t h*?" I asked.

"Yes," said Addison.

"No, you're right!" I said. "It is pronounced harth. But

what surprised me about that one is that I don't have any occasion to say it. Do you say it often enough to even think about it?"

"We have a fireplace at our parents' house," said Addison.

"It's funny," I said. "I never thought about it, but hurth would make so much sense because there's 'dearth' and 'earth.'"

"It took me so long to figure out that it was pronounced harth, and that was from Merriam-Webster," said Addison. "You can hear the pronunciation there."

"Yeah, I listen to pronunciations there all day long," I said. "And 'hearth' I used to encounter a lot when I would read novels."

"That's why I started wondering," said Addison.

"I love that example," I said. "It's kind of a romantic word, too. I associate it with novels with these female heroines who are facing adversity and they gather around the hearth and they discuss things. I think there were hearths in *Little Women*."

"I haven't seen that," said Addison. "That's cool though. I don't know where I saw it. Maybe they mentioned it in *Pride and Prejudice*."*

"I think it's entirely possible," I said. "Maybe it appears in just about all nineteenth-century English novels."

"I feel like it's a word that would," said Addison.

¶

---

* Addison was right. There's a hearth. Bingley and Jane stand over it, but there will be no plot spoilers here.

Kelly in Toledo, Ohio, had a beef to share. "Pronounce *v i g i l*," she told me. We were in a corporate park, near the banks of the Maumee River.

"*V i g i l*," I repeated. "Vigil." I was not sure where this was going.

"Vigil!" she said. "Right!" She paused. "My pet peeve is, I keep hearing people on the news saying vid-ju-al."

"No!" I said.

"Yes!" said Kelly.

"Where do you hear that though?" I asked.

"*On the local news!*" said Kelly. "And the thing is, it's always when someone died!"

¶

There were also pronunciation complaints in St. Louis, this one from a visitor named Elisa who had strong opinions about George W. Bush's pronunciation of "nuclear," famously more like "nucular."

"Let's see if his pronunciation is actually documented in the dictionary," I said, opening *Merriam-Webster's*. "I think it's probably in there along with the standard noo-klee-ur."

"Because George Bush says it," said Elisa.

"So many people say it, though," I said.

"Yeah, they're all wrong," she said. "Listen, I can't help myself," she continued, "especially on Facebook, and, like, I get that you make typos and stuff, but there are just some things—like, it's not 'Sorry for your *lost*.'"

Here she made sounds of lingua-despair over the use of the word "lost" for "loss." "Blood curdling over here!" she said.

"Yeah, so they do document Bush's pronunciation:

noo-kyoo-lur," I said, having found it in *Merriam-Web-ster's.*

"Yeah," said Elisa. "They document it as the wrong one! Like, 'Don't say this!' It's kind of like, remember in magazines, they've got those black bars over your eyes? Yeah, don't do this! That's what that was. 'It was pronounced like this, but don't do that!'"

¶

In Chicago, a member of the previously mentioned large group of high school students had a pronunciation concern. "I don't know if this counts," said one student, a girl named Emma, "but you know 'sherbert'?" She pronounced this word with two *r*'s.

"Yes," I said.

"It's 'sherbet,' right?" asked Emma. "Like, there's no extra *r*."

"Yeah, there's no extra *r*," echoed another student.

"But why does our society put in an extra *r*?" asked Emma.

"Maybe it's because once you get going down that *r* path, it just feels like you should keep going," I said. "Let us just see—"

"I'm pretty sure it's sher-bet," said Emma.

"Yes, but *Merriam-Webster's* might list an alternative pronunciation," I said. "Do you all know dictionaries serve a descriptive function? Is that something you've heard about?"

"Yes," chorused the entire group.

"They document language as it is," I continued. "I mean, with limitations, but that's the idea. That's why I'm wondering whether there might be a listing for the second pronunciation. Let's see. Oh! There's a second spelling here."

"With the *r*?" asked Emma.

"Yes," I said.

"Whoa!" said another girl. "So it's both."

"But you know what?" I said. "Sometimes when alternatives are listed, you don't really want to go there. If I'm writing in a professional context, I'd want to see what's conventionally accepted. Similarly, when you're taking the SAT, you probably want to pick the answer that will get you the point."

I wanted to check another source, so I opened *Garner's Modern English Usage* and read aloud: "'Sherbet' is commonly mispronounced with an intrusive *r*: 'sherbert.' Because of this mispronunciation, the word is sometimes wrongly spelled 'sherbert.'"

I'm a checker. My entire life I've checked locks, stoves, and multiple language resources.

Also, I don't eat sherbet. Why eat sherbet when you can have way more fat-filled and delicious ice cream instead? But if I *were* to eat sherbet, I would eat it with just one *r*.

Quizlet

∙∙

The food "pasty" _____ (is, is not) pronounced like "pastry" minus the r.

Answer: *is not*

20

I Saw ___ (a, an) UFO
on Main Street

In Richmond, Virginia, a polite teenager waited patiently in the background while I helped someone with "lie" and "lay." Only when the visitor had left did the teenager walk up and announce, "Hi, I have a confession. Do you know the brand Ukrop's? Like the old grocery store brand?"

I didn't, so she wrote it down for me on my notepad. Her name was Rachel.

"It's a grocery store brand that used to be in town," she said, "and the big debate at school has been, is it '*an* Ukrop's bag' or '*a* Ukrop's bag'?" She pronounced it you-crops.

"Oh my gosh, I love this one so much," I said. "Tell me what you think."

"I think it's 'a Ukrop's bag,'" said Rachel.

"And you are right!" I said.

"Yes!" said Rachel.

"Do you know *why* you're right?" I asked.

"Why?" she asked.

"Because it is not based on spelling," I answered. "It's based on sound. What comes out of your mouth first? Yoo. So you're saying it like you-crops, and the *y* is a consonant sound." I wrote this explanation down next to where she had written "Ukrop's."

"Okay," said Rachel happily. "Thank you!"

¶

People move around these United States a lot. In New Orleans, I met people from all over the country—all over the world, in fact—including a woman from Minnesota.

"What's correct?" she asked. "'*An* occupied table' or '*a* occupied table'?"

"This is so specific that I'm wondering whether this became a subject of discussion with someone," I said.

"Yes," she said. "An editor."

"Okay," I said. "Well, it's definitely 'an.'"

"An occupied table," she said. "So does the article connect to the noun or to the adjective?"

This was interesting. She knew parts of speech. Silently in my head, I diagnosed this as a case of overthinking things.

"It's determined by the first sound after the article," I explained. "So 'an occupied table.'"

"Okay, and is that an issue of controversy at all?" asked the woman. She was clearly disappointed.

"No," I said.

Here are some fun* things to consider, though:

I am _____ (*a, an*) *RN.*

I am _____ (*a, an*) *FBI agent.*

What determines the choice is the first sound, as I told the Ukrop's questioner. If you speak the letters *r n*

---

* Were you taught not to use "fun" as an adjective? I decided some years back that that prohibition was a senseless destroyer of fun.

and *f b i*, the first *sound* in each case is a vowel, even though the first *letter* in the abbreviation is a consonant.

RN = are-en

FBI = eff-bee-eye

So it would be "an RN" and "an FBI agent," even though R and F are consonants. What about this one?

I am _____ (a, an) UFO specialist.

Let's say you are an expert on UFOs and the phrase "UFO specialist" is on your business card. Then you would tell someone you were *a* UFO specialist, not *an* UFO specialist. That's because UFO is pronounced yoo-eff-oh; the first sound, *y*, is a consonant.

Also in New Orleans, a woman named Reagan, with red hair and wearing a blue sweatshirt, arrived at the Grammar Table with a different article-related question.

"For the official final answer," she asked, "is it *a* historic moment or *an* historic moment?"

I waited for a loud truck to go by before answering, then told her, "I say '*a* historic moment,' because I don't say 'istoric'—I pronounce the consonant in 'historic'—so for me there's no reason to go with 'an.' What do you do?"

"I believe it's 'an,'" said Reagan. "We had a debate over it. And I think I actually ended up googling it and looking it up, because I've heard it both ways. And I've heard that there's actually no correct answer, that it's both."

"For me it's very simple," I said. "If I did 'an historic event,' there would be no other word combination with an article like that in all of my English usage, where I had a consonant sound and I put an 'an' before it. So why should that be an exception?"

If you speak a dialect of English in which you do not pronounce the *h*, then "an" makes sense, but I have a clear, conspicuous sound there that no one will fail to hear.

"Don't you feel a little bit funny putting an 'an' in front of your *h*?" I asked Reagan.

"No," said Reagan.

A reporter overhead this discussion and vented after she left.

"It drives me crazy," he said. "I mean, you wouldn't say 'an history book.' I've never understood that. To me that's just wrong!"*

Quizlet

••

I just met _____ (a, an) UN employee while jogging along the East River.

Answer: *"a," because UN is pronounced yoo-en, meaning the first sound after the article is a consonant.*

----

* I try to stay calm and flexible about language topics, so I'm going to hide this confession in a footnote: I don't like "an historic" in American English. I think it sounds weird and anachronistic. Please keep this between us and this footnote.

21

Compound Sentences

"Grammar and I do not work well together," announced a college student named Lee, a blond woman in beige. It was hot in South Bend, Indiana, and I was stationed near a chocolate shop.

"You sound really good, though," I said. "Are you sure?"

"I am," said Lee with confidence.

"Do you have a particular pressing problem that's bugged you that I could resolve for you today?" I asked.

"I don't like commas," said Lee. "Unless it has fanboys afterwards."

"You learned fanboys?" I asked.

"I learned fanboys," she confirmed.

In case it is unfamiliar to you, fanboys is a mnemonic device sometimes used to teach children how to punctuate compound sentences formed using one of the seven coordinating conjunctions: "for," "and," "nor," "but," "or," "yet," and "so." It's how I was taught back in the day.

Here's how the rule works. You start with an independent clause: a group of words, containing a subject and a verb, that can also stand alone as a sentence. If you then use a coordinating conjunction to combine the first independent clause with a second independent clause, you should typically put a comma before the coordinating conjunction. Below is a brief demo consisting of one sample sentence per conjunction.

> *Structure = [independent clause],* <u>*coordinating conjunction*</u> *[independent clause]*

f for   I studied coordinating conjunctions, <u>for</u> today is National Grammar Day.

a and   Marie likes her Japanese classes, <u>and</u> Conrad likes his Russian tutor.

n nor   Benedict doesn't like to write essays, <u>nor</u> does he like to read essays.

b but   They could have cleaned up, <u>but</u> instead they read a linguistics book.

o or   Would you like to read some US history books, <u>or</u> would you prefer to take a history class at the junior college?

y yet   He needed to prepare for his French final, <u>yet</u> the allure of Welsh grammar was too much for him.

s so   I can't envision a life without writing, <u>so</u> I have decided to quit my banking job.

"For everything else, I don't like commas," said Lee.

"So you learned that if you have what could be a complete sentence and then one of those seven words and then another complete sentence, you put a comma before it," I said.

"Yeah," Lee said, then added, somewhat contradictorily, "If I take a breath, I throw in a comma. I'm like, that's where I need to breathe."

"But what if you're just out of breath?" I asked.

"Then that's a period," she said. We laughed.

I encountered a young man with greater grammar confidence in Detroit. "I know a lot about grammar," said the man, who was wearing a blue shirt.

"I had a feeling you might," I said. "You had the air of someone who did. So you're a grammar nerd."

"Yep, in a way," said the man, whose name was Terry. "I wanted to go into linguistics."

"And then what happened?" I asked.

"I'm in HR now," he said, laughing. He told me he and a friend had just been arguing—"because he thinks he's more grammar than I am"—about a comma rule.

"Which comma rule?" I asked.

"I told him the rule is, when you have two independent clauses joined by a conjunction,* you're supposed to add a comma, and he was like, that's optional," said Terry.

"First of all, that was so cool the way you just said that," I told him. "The fact that you just tossed out the whole independent clause thing like it was nothing. You know that most people can't do that, right?"

Terry laughed. "Yeah, I know."

"I'm appreciating you right now," I said. "On very short clauses combined with 'and,' though, like 'Dogs bark and cats meow,' you don't always need a comma."

---

* This idea applies to the seven coordinating conjunctions discussed above, not to all conjunctions.

"Yeah yeah yeah," he said.

"I've actually been affected a little bit by social media," I told him. "So I play with that guideline more than I used to. In formal writing, I still almost always put the comma, though."

As we chatted more, Terry confessed, "I think I have an inner nerd about grammar and I just don't like to admit it." He looked around furtively.

"I can confirm that you do," I said. "And you've just admitted it on camera."

"I know," he replied. "If I say 'independent clauses' to my co-workers they're like, *Whaaat?* When I say you need to put a comma after every introductory phrase,* they're like, What does that mean? I'm like, okay. Or appositives—"

"Did you just say the word 'appositive'?" I asked. This was exciting.

"So that's why I said, what's going on here?" said Terry, eyeing the Grammar Table.

"You have the vocabulary, I'm telling you," I said. "Not many people know what an appositive is."

"I think I just like rules," said Terry. "Obviously—I'm in HR, right?"

¶

Some months later, the Grammar Table was on a pier. It was late on a chilly October afternoon in New Castle, Delaware, and Brandt and I had just blown into town.

---

* I put commas after many introductory phrases, but definitely not all of them. Terry is stricter than I am.

We set up as quickly as we could by the water's edge, trying to get in some grammar time before sunset.

To my delight, young people in formal attire started arriving soon after we got there. There was apparently a dance that night, and the town's parents were out on the water taking pictures of girls freezing in evening dresses.

It was my first Grammar Table formal!

"Hey," said a dad in jeans and dreadlocks who noticed us from about thirty feet away. He was there with his camera and some teenage girls. "How are you?"

"Fine!" I called out. "Are you guys* doing homecoming tonight?" From afar they confirmed that they were.

"You look very stylish," I semi-yelled. "We're making a documentary about grammar. Do you like grammar?" There were some noncommittal "um"s.

"Do you want to come talk to us?" I asked.

"Oh, okay," said the dad. "Like English grammar?" He started walking over.

"All right!" said one of the five girls, and they all headed over, too.

"You're all dressed up," I said. "Usually people come up in sweatpants and jeans. I feel that you're adding—"

"Glamour!" said Brandt.

"Yeah, you're adding glamour to grammar," I said. The dad tossed his hair dramatically. I learned that the girls were all sophomores and juniors in high school.

"Do you have any grammar questions for me tonight?" I asked.

---

* This "you guys" habit is very hard for me to shake. I grew up constantly saying "you guys" in my California all-girls school. There was not a boy in sight.

"Nothing off the top of my head," said a girl in a peach dress.

"I'm going to come up with one!" said her friend, who was wearing a black satin pantsuit. She thought as the other girls shivered, then finally asked, "What is the correct way to use 'but'? Because some people say that you use 'but' and then comma, and then some people are like, you don't need to use the comma."

"Comma, then 'but,'" I said, correcting the order. "If you have a 'but' between what could be two complete sentences, the convention is to put the comma before it. If you don't have a complete sentence after the 'but,' you don't necessarily need one."

The girls continued to shiver as I gave them these two sentences:

I got a new dress, but <u>it ripped in the car door</u>.

I got a new dress but <u>forgot it at home</u>.

"Did you hear the part after the 'but' in the second sentence?" I asked. "Not a complete sentence—'forgot it at home'—so you could leave out the comma there if you wanted to. Now you're all set for any formalwear-related punctuation emergencies."

"Oh my gosh!" said the girl in the black pantsuit. "Thank you!"

"You're going to use that for your next test," her friend told her.

"Yeah!" she said.

"I'm impressed by your bravery in being out in this weather," I said.

"I'm very cold," she admitted.

¶

"If everybody could write like J. K. Rowling," said an un-kempt bearded man on the streets of Asheville, North Carolina, "they'd have like five billion dollars in the bank right now."

"Probably not everyone could do that," I said. "That was a little unusual."

He moved closer. "Do you know that she surpassed Oprah?" he asked.

This is the Grammar Table, not the Billionaire Table, so I replied noncommittally, "She's pretty wealthy." I was in that moment trying to have a Very Important Conversation about Icelandic with a copy editor who had come home from Reykjavik for Thanksgiving, and this money discussion was getting in the way.

"The Harry Potter books and the movies made out of them," said the man. "She's walkin' on money."

Then he surprised me. He told me he loved my dictionary, then added, "I was never good in grammar, but I know you can take two independent clauses, and put a subordinating conjunction in it, comma subordinating conjunction and then the other what do you call it, an independent clause, and the names of the subordinating conjunction are boyfans."

"Fanboys!" I exclaimed.

"Or boyfans," said the man.

"Those are the coordinating conjunctions," I said, but I was impressed.

"'But,' 'or,' 'yet,' 'nor,' 'for,' 'and,' 'so,'" said the man.

"Right on," I said. "You got it. Good work."

"Thank you," he said, then offered me a parting joke:

"Why'd the cheetah not got good luck playing hide-and-seek?"

"I don't know," I said.

"Cuz she's always spotted," he said, and exited stage right.

¶

In Vermont, I met a woman named Andrea, who told me she was a former editor. "It was just an academic journal," she said, "but I'm probably a little bit hard-core and overly picky." She and her husband, Mike, were on the Middlebury College campus for the annual Fall Family Weekend.

Mike told me, "These guys give me a hard time if I have a list of four items, and it's A comma B comma C and D. I want to put a comma in there."

"I always want to put it in, too," said Andrea.

"You're allowed to," I said, assuming we were talking about the Oxford comma.

"I thought you told me to take it out," Mike told his wife.

"No," said Andrea. "Here's what you want to do." She gave this example:

Andrea and I went to Middlebury, and then to Maine.

"And I want a comma there?" asked Mike.

"You want to put a comma before 'and then to Maine,'" said Andrea. "You don't need a comma there, because the second part is not a full sentence. If you said 'We went to Middlebury comma and then we went to Maine,' that would need a comma. But if you just said 'We went to Middlebury and then went to Maine'—"

"You just said the same thing twice," said Mike.

"No, she left out the subject in the second part," I said, providing Grammar Table marital communication facilitation services. These services are included in the standard Grammar Table package.

Here were the two sentences Andrea was comparing:

We went to Middlebury, and then we went to Maine.

We went to Middlebury and then went to Maine.

"Oh, the 'we,'" said Mike.

"Isn't that right?" said Andrea. "Tell us, Grammar Woman!"

"Tell her how picky that is," said Mike.

"And you'd better side with me," said Andrea.

"Are you two married to each other?" I asked.

"Only thirty years," said Mike.

"And I'm right!" said Andrea.

"You know, in my experience the wife *is* usually right," I said.

Mike laughed. "Okay," he said.

"There you go," said Andrea. "She's very smart. I like Grammar Woman."

I do generally follow the punctuation principle Andrea laid out. For example:

Pablo painted a picture, and Agatha wrote a letter.

but

Pablo painted a picture and drilled a hole in the wall.

"But even if there's not a full clause after the conjunction," I said, "there are times where there's something maybe a little twisty or turny about the piece after the conjunction that leads me to make an exception and add a comma. But it's got to have something a little bit jazzy going on."

"My stuff's usually pretty jazzy," said Mike.

"Okay, fair enough," said Andrea. "We've reached a compromise!"

"Thank you," said Mike. "From now on I have an excuse for that comma. That's the Jazzy!"

"This has been very helpful," said Andrea. "You've headed off a lot of fights now."

"I've enjoyed this visit very much," I said.

"I feel vindicated," said Mike.

"We have enjoyed it, too," said Andrea.

"This was our first Grammar Table!" said Mike.

Quizlet

••

In the sentence below, put a comma before any coordinating conjunction you see that is combining independent clauses.

> The Zoom call started out well but then Talia spilled her coffee on her keyboard and disappeared for fifteen minutes to dry it out.

Answer: *The Zoom call started out well, but then Talia spilled her coffee on her keyboard and disappeared for fifteen minutes to dry it out.*

22

Semicolonphobia!

The semicolon inspires an array of emotional and intellectual responses: curiosity, anxiety, indifference, affection, and disdain.

Parents are often important in semicolon dissemination. In Chicago, Annie, a mom who visited the Grammar Table with her husband and three children, told me, "I love the semicolon."

"You do?" I asked excitedly.

"Our kids are nine, ten, and thirteen, so it's interesting to try to start getting them comfortable with it in their own writing," said Annie. "Do you know what I mean?"

"Yeah," I said. "I have no memory of when I started using it. At all."

"I think for me it was probably in college," said Annie. She asked her husband, Thomas, "What about you?"

"What's that?" said Thomas.

"When did you start using the semicolon?" asked Annie.

"Maybe senior year of high school or something," said Thomas.

"Yeah," said Annie, "but I mean, you want your nine-year-old to feel comfortable, certainly your ten-year-old and your thirteen-year-old, you want them to be comfortable with the semicolon."

"And not have semicolonphobia," I said.

"Yeah! You have to own it!" she said. "And not misuse it. Do you know what I mean?"

"You seem like really good parents," I said.

¶

One day when I was stationed in Verdi Square, a little boy and his father came by to visit. The boy, whose name was Arthur, studied the sign.

"Semicolonphobia," he read. "That sounds to me like the fear of semicolons."

I looked at him. "What grade are you in?" I asked.

"Fourth," he told me. "High five!" he said, and held up his hand for a high five. I high-fived him.

He wanted to know how to use a semicolon. I got out my notepad and asked for a sentence — any sentence — to start us off. No problem! He offered, "My teddy bear Wrigley loves to eat," and I wrote that down.

"You use a semicolon in places where you could put a period, but where you want to make the ideas more closely related," I told him. "So we could put a period now, but tell me something related and maybe we can use a semicolon instead. For example, what is Wrigley's favorite food?"

"His favorite food is everything," he told me. I wrote down:

My teddy bear Wrigley loves to eat; his favorite food is everything.

I gave him the paper. "High five!" he said, holding up his hand again for more high-fiving.

"I'm glad you told me how to spell Wrigley," I told him, "because I was thinking it was *w r i g g l y.*" He scrunched up his face and thought that through, then smiled.

"Since you figured out 'semicolonphobia,' does that mean you know a whole bunch of other phobia names?" I asked. "Have you seen the movie *Arachnophobia*?"

"No," he said. "Why would there be a movie about a fear of spiders?"

If you have chronophobia (fear of the future) because you're dwelling on the supposed shortcomings of young people, Arthur and the many other curious, congenial, amusing children I've met at the Grammar Table are evidence you need not be concerned.

¶

"How do I use a semicolon?" asked Jason, the construction worker playing hooky in Decatur, Alabama. "I feel like a semicolon is something that I should use, but I don't."

"There's no minimum daily requirement," I said, "so if you don't use it a lot, it's not a big deal. I'll give you a couple of examples."

"Perfect," said Jason. He seemed giddy.

"This is going to be a depressing one," I said, writing down a sentence I often use in the business writing classes I teach.

"You have beautiful handwriting," said his friend Jack, not for the first time.

"I went to Carlthorp Elementary School, and it was one of the most important things," I said.

"Very nice handwriting," repeated Jack.

"Every year they gave out awards in handwriting and citizenship," I said. "And in second grade I didn't get either, and I'm still bitter about it."

"Look at that *g!*" Jason said. "You didn't win. You didn't even win with *that*?"

"I don't understand how it happened, frankly," I said. I showed them the sentence, which was a run-on.

Revenues were plummeting we decided to close two stores.

"Yes, ma'am," said Jack.

"Plummeting, then semicolon," said Jason.

"Yes," I said. "So you use a semicolon where you technically could put a period but you want to bring it a little closer together so it's not as big a pause." Like this:

Revenues were plummeting; we decided to close two stores.

Next I gave them a new version with a "therefore."

Revenues were plummeting therefore we decided to close two stores.

"Therefore!" exclaimed Jack.

"Revenues were plummeting comma therefore comma," said Jason.

"No. No commas, just the period at the end," said Jack. "That's the way I would do it."

"No, I would put comma 'therefore' comma," said Jason. "See, I overuse commas way too much. Especially when I'm texting, I use commas. All the time — like a disgusting amount."

"It's hard to imagine a disgusting amount of commas," I said. "I'm not sure what that would look like."

"Gross!" said Jack.

"I punctuate like I think I would speak, but I just use commas in place of everything," said Jason. "Just commas instead of everything else."

"I do think maybe you overdid it on the commas here, so I have a question for you," I said. "Could I put a period after the word 'plummeting' if I wanted to?"

"Um, you could," said Jack.

"Absolutely, yeah," said Jason.

"I could," I said, "and if the answer to that is yes, then you need something stronger than a comma there."

"So that's where you use a semicolon," said Jason.

Revenues were plummeting; therefore, we decided to close two stores.

Jason was listening. People surprise me.

¶

Semicolons followed me down a path in Zilker Park in Austin, Texas, the forty-fourth state on the Unofficial National Grammar Table Tour.

"Semicolon," said Nick, a fortyish man wearing a T-shirt that said ANTI in big yellow capital letters. "When do you use it?" He was accompanied by his wife and two children.

"Usually between what are known as two independent clauses, which means what could be two complete sentences,"* I said. "And they have to be closely related, and the combination needs to flow well."

"Why not just make two sentences, though?" asked Nick.

"Because sometimes you want a slightly smaller break," I said. "The semicolon brings the ideas closer together. You create an intimacy between them."

"Okay," said Nick. A shirtless male runner stopped and looked on for a moment, then ran off.

"So it's a slightly different rhythm than with a period," I said, then added, "Or a full stop. Are you from a 'full stop'–saying country?" He and his family members had English accents, and periods are called full stops in England.

Nick confirmed that they were indeed from a "full stop"–saying place—London—so I translated my semicolon explanation into British. "With the full stop, your pitch drops more than with a semicolon, and it's a bigger break, so it's different stylistically," I said.

"Okay," said Nick.

"But I do not use semicolons as an excuse to build never-ending sentences," I said.

"Do you think semicolons are going to survive?" asked Nick. Apparently my semicolon marketing presentation had not enticed him.

"I do think they're going to survive for now," I said. "But I can't speak for what happens after I'm gone."

-----

* "Sentence" and "independent clause" are not synonymous. A sentence can consist of a single independent clause—"The rutabaga is rotten"—but it can also consist of many clauses (preferably not a reckless number) of different types.

Quizlet

Identify any semicolon opportunities in the following sentence.

Lisbeth never works out and claims to have no athletic skills, however, she is more adept with a TV remote than anyone we've ever known.

Answer: *Lisbeth never works out and claims to have no athletic skills; however, she is more adept with a TV remote than anyone we've ever known.*

23

Labyrinthine Lists

Normally when you think lists, you think commas, right? But sometimes commas aren't big and bad enough to do the job.

"I just finished one of my research papers," said a woman named Christa in Detroit, "and I was feeling a lot of distress over the difference between using a comma and using a semicolon. I don't quite get that rule when I have not just a list, but a list of longer things."

"You mean when you have a list of complex items that already have commas within them?" I asked. In such cases, it is sometimes necessary to escalate your punctuation. You may need semicolons rather than commas to divide up those unruly comma-containing items. Like this:

This year we will hold regional client events in Lexington, Kentucky; Red Cloud, Nebraska; Concord, New Hampshire; and Boulder City, Nevada.

"If the individual items don't have noticeable commas within them, I don't really worry about it," I said. "I don't graduate to semicolons quickly. I find that some people do."

For example, if there is even one comma in an item in

a list, some will rush into the arms of the nearest semicolon without fully considering their options. Consider
this example:

> *I opened the front door to find a squealing hamster,*
> *a hungry, angry cat, and a giant pile of spun-out toi-*
> *let paper.*

The only item with a comma in it is "a hungry, angry
cat." That complicates—just slightly—the task of identifying the boundaries between items, but it is probably
fine. Let's try semicolons and see if that's any better:

> *I opened the front door to find a squealing hamster;*
> *a hungry, angry cat; and a giant pile of spun-out toi-*
> *let paper.*

It's okay, I guess, but it takes a fairly simple and fan-
ciful list and clogs up its playfulness with heavy punctuation. If the comma collection in the previous version
bothers you, we might be better off relocating the cat to
the end of the list—something I would accept as a solution only if I felt it didn't negatively affect the content of
the sentence.

> *I opened the front door to find a squealing hamster,*
> *a giant pile of spun-out toilet paper, and a hungry,*
> *angry cat.*

I like it! In fact, I think it is funnier with the cat in
last place; now we have a dramatic pet denouement.
You first cross paths with the two seemingly unrelated
victims, and then you learn that they have a common

feline victimizer. The last item in the series still contains a comma, but it has been distanced from the two commas punctuating the list.

"In general," I told Christa, "unless there are commas within items that then create confusion about where the boundaries are between those items, I don't worry about it." Here is an example that calls out more conspicuously for a semicolon:

> *I invited Jayne Everhart, the director of marketing and PR, Timothy Packard, the senior vice president of sales, and Abelard Ogden, the director of training.*

"When people do use semicolons in lists," I told Christa, "the question arises a lot—and it's frequently mishandled—of what to do with the punctuation before the 'and' just before the last item." I asked what she would put there.

"Oxford comma," said Christa.

"If you've already committed to semicolons in the list," I said, "then you have to put another semicolon before the 'and.'"

"Okay," said Christa. "So it's like an Oxford semicolon."

I laughed. "I never thought of that!" I said. Here is the sentence with the Oxford semicolon.

> *I invited Jayne Everhart, the director of marketing and PR; Timothy Packard, the senior vice president of sales; and Abelard Ogden, the director of training.*

"I don't have a lot of pet peeves," I said, "but if I had to name a few, that might be one: that people abandon the semicolon list punctuation they've committed to and then I can no longer—"

"Determine where the next item is," said Christa.

"I mean, I can," I said, "but it's like someone has the picture tilted on the wall."

She laughed and said, "I like that the Oxford semicolon is my new technical name."

"So do I," I said. "And I'm sure Oxford will appreciate it, too."

I can't remember the last time I constructed a sentence with a list that needed semicolons. There are often creative solutions to avoid them, such as this one:

Invitees

Jayne Everhart
Director of Marketing and PR

Timothy Packard
Senior Vice President of Sales

Abelard Ogden
Director of Training*

However, some people's work involves more listy stuff than mine does (hi, lawyers!), so you may have needs that I don't.

---

* These business titles are capitalized because they are in a formatted list. In a regular old sentence, I would not be capitalizing them. For example: "Timothy Packard, senior vice president of sales, will speak at 4:00 p.m."

¶

You may think semicoloned lists are a specialty topic, but they are not. When you see people relaxing on, say, a beach, they may in fact be considering semicolons in a list.

I know this because when I was at the Grammar Table on the Venice Beach Boardwalk, a man walked up and asked, "When is the proper time to use a semicolon when you're making a list of things? Because I looked it up on Google, and then I did it, and it looked wrong."

"Were you using the semicolon because there were commas within elements in the list?" I asked. "Is that what caused you to do that?"

"Yeah," said the man. "I was making a list of dates and times I was available. And then I wasn't sure—and I used a semicolon anyway."

"That's a good one," I said. I wrote down a sentence with dates for him, like this:

I'm available on June 2, 2021; July 23, 2021___ and January 3, 2022.

"The big challenge, now that you've started on this semicolon jag, is what you do when you get to the place right before the 'and,'" I said. "This is the part that freaks people out, because they think it looks weird to have a semicolon next to an 'and.'"

I added the missing semicolon to my sample sentence:

I'm available on June 2, 2021; July 23, 2021; and January 3, 2022.

"But you've got to be consistent," I said. "I'm very particular about that."

"Okay," said the man.

"As a souvenir of this discussion, I would like to offer you this slip of paper," I told him.

"Thank you," he said. "I appreciate it."

Now if only we in the US could just do as they do elsewhere and write our dates like this: 2 June 2021. That solves so many problems at once. Look:

> *I'm available on 2 June 2021, 23 July 2021, and 3 January 2022.*

How tidy is that? Now the need for semicolons is gone. It's like hiring a personal organizer for our sentence.

Quizlet

....

Does this list need semicolons?

> Karl picked up snickerdoodles from the
> bakery in the morning, cooked three pe-
> can pies at home during the afternoon,
> made eighteen mango ice pops for the
> barbecue this Saturday, and fell asleep
> on the floor with his head on a stuffed
> bunny.

Answer: *No, because there are no commas within individual elements
—only between them.*

24

Colonoscopy

We were in Fargo, North Dakota, and the Grammar Table was parked downtown under the giant marquee of the Fargo Theatre. Brandt had obtained permission from a theater employee inside for me to sit there. That day was one of the hotter days of the year in Fargo, which excels at being cold but on that day was making me sweat, and I was relieved to have the shade.

A social worker named Carter came up to chat. Carter wanted to talk colons. "When is an appropriate time in a sentence to use a colon?" he asked.

"People often use them before a list," I told Carter. "But a list isn't enough. You also have to have a kind of equivalency."

As I began writing a sentence for him, I asked, "Are there any food products around here that would be unique to the state that I could stick in the sentence? What can I order here that I couldn't order somewhere else?"

"A bison burger!" said Carter. I wrote down a sentence that I felt merged the spirit of North Dakota and Manhattan:

I ordered three things: a bison burger, a salad, and a triple cappuccino.

"Sometimes people put a colon as soon as they feel a list coming on," I said.

"Yup," said Carter.

"But you have to have kind of an equivalency thing happening with the list," I explained. "What happens immediately to the left of the colon has to be equivalent to what's on the right. So you have 'several dishes' on the left and then you have the dishes on the right, so that would be fine."

"When would you use a colon without a list?" asked Carter.

It's a similar idea when there's no list. What's on the left of the colon still cues up what's arriving on the right. Here are a couple of list-free colon examples:

Willard had just one life goal: to loiter languidly.

The judges' conclusion was final: Deanna would share the spelling bee prize with Igby.

In each case, the words on the right of the colon amplify what is on the left. "Often colons and dashes occupy the same spaces, but dashes are more flexible," I told Carter. "You see dashes in more random spots."

I consider this last type of colon use an advanced writing skill. There's no need to rush into it if you don't feel you have a handle on it. It's something I feel people get a sense for after seeing its permutations over time in excellent writing. In conclusion: read.

Quizlet

....

How's the colon use in the following sentence?

On our first visit we went to several popular tourist destinations, including: Gilly's Yarn Museum, Serge's Ant & Bee Museum, and Millie's Pepper Palace.

Answer: *Bad, because the word "including" quite specifically does not set up equal values on each side of the colon. Remove the colon! Another way to think about this, if you know about direct objects: the colon is separating "including" from its direct object, and we don't normally do that.*

25

Comma Volume

"I've got one question for you," said a man named Andrew in Minneapolis. He had just ordered at a nearby taco stand. "I work on a small team, and I notice that one of my co-workers uses way too many commas. All the time. What's your best way to influence someone to limit commas?"

"Can you give me a specific type of comma situation where they use it too much?" I asked.

"I think it would be where she naturally pauses when she's talking," he said.

"I sometimes teach grammar to adults," I said, "and people often tell me that they put commas where they feel a pause. And my response to that is, if that were all that determined punctuation, we wouldn't ever have to study rules, because you would just go by feeling. But that's not how modern punctuation works."

"Right," said Andrew.

"Do you have time for an example, or do you need to check on your taco?" I asked.

"I don't see it yet, so we're good," said Andrew.

"Okay," I said, writing. "'I went to St. Paul, Minnesota,

on July 4, 2019, to buy some . . .' What could one buy in St. Paul that would be—"

"Uhhh," said Andrew.

"Cheese!" offered Brandt cheerfully from behind the camera.

"Yeah," agreed Andrew. "Cheese curds."

"Cheese curds!" I said. "Okay, perfect. So technically this is the punctuation that you put, and I'm not reading it with all those pauses."

> *I went to St. Paul, Minnesota, on July 4, 2019, to buy some cheese curds.* *

"There are conventions about where commas go that a lot of people who are involved in publishing and editorial stuff agree on," I said. "They aren't all associated with pauses. Do you want to give her this sentence?"

"I'd better not," said Andrew cautiously. "She's been in her role for twenty years. It's definitely not my place to say. It would be a lot easier if I could put a Grammar Table down in the office."

¶

As night fell in The Villages, Florida, I talked commas with Beth, a retiree who joked in an earlier chapter about her incomplete mastery of "thee" and "thou." Beth told

---

* Again, if I lived outside the US, I could rearrange my date and write this instead: "I went to St. Paul, Minnesota, on 4 July 2019 to buy some cheese curds." But the grammar call is coming from inside the house.

me she had recently edited a book, a task that required her to contemplate grammar more than usual.

"Is that what you do professionally?" I asked her.

"No," she said. "I have a brother who wrote a book, his first novel, which has been published, and he asked me if I would be his editor. I had to keep correcting him on his use of grammar, and he decided he must have been absent that day. Or week."

"Did you manage to stay friendly the whole time?" I asked.

"Oh, yes," she said.

"That's good," I said, "because sometimes even when you get along with someone, that kind of stuff can turn into a thing."

"Yes, exactly," said Beth. "And I kept apologizing, 'Sorry, but I have to tell you this again,' and he said, 'Oh, I don't know what it is with me and commas. I seem to fling them out like a monkey throws poop at his keeper in the zoo!'"

"How wonderful that you were able to do that together and enjoy it and that you both got something out of it," I said.

"And we're still friends," said Beth.

"That, quite frankly, is the most impressive part of it," I said.

"Yes, I'm rather proud of him," she said. "He's my baby brother, and I'm sixteen years older than he is. By the time he was in second grade, I was already out of college and teaching elementary school, so we'd go to my mom's house and I'd go, 'Hey Timmy, let's go do your homework! Let's go read a book!' So I helped him learn to read, and then I edited his first book. Isn't that awesome?"

It was! Family grammar's the best.

¶

Back in Decatur, Alabama, Jason's comma commitment continued unabated. He wanted to put a comma before "you" in this:

Hey, you, I had a great time last night.

"Every time you address someone with the pronoun 'you,' you should put a comma before that, correct?" he asked. He was so serious and intense about it that I started to laugh.

"Right here?" I asked, pointing to the space between the "Hey" and the "you."

"'Hey' comma 'you,'" he said. "Yes."

His friend Jack objected. "No!"

"That is what I was taught to do," I told him. "But now most people don't do it. What about in email? What if you were saying 'Hi Mary'?"

"I don't do email," Jason said. He was now crouched down next to the Grammar Table scrolling through his phone. He was taking this extremely seriously, so I did too.

"Look," he said. "All right, so Snapchat."

"You don't ever email?" I asked.

"Not really, no," he replied. "But I will totally text-message an individual."

"I was raised to put a comma there, but I don't bother anymore," I told him.

"No, that's weak," said Jason. "That's weak."

"Because I wouldn't have friends,"* I said. Jack guffawed.

---

* This was slightly exaggerated. I do have friends who use that

"No, I wouldn't have no friends either," said Jason. "Fuck 'em. I don't need no friends that don't use commas."

"So you still put the comma here?" I asked.

"I do," said Jason, as though he and the comma were exchanging wedding vows.

"I think that's really cute," I laughed. "Seriously." He had his phone out now to show me.

"Like, I even put 'lmao' comma," said Jason, slashing a comma in the air. "I put commas after my 'lmao's or my 'lol's. Like, read that text message." I did. It said:

Lmao, that's hilarious. And no, definitely not. That would be crazy weird.

"Yeah, it's good," I said.

That was not enough enthusiasm for Jason. "Is that good punctuation?" he asked.

"It's excellent punctuation," I said.

"I do try to punctuate everything," he said.

"I feel that is very responsible of you," I said.

"Thank you so much," said Jason. "Yes! Oh my god, give me knucks." I was not familiar with the definition of giving someone knucks, but it turned out to involve fist-bumping.

"Can I get a zoom-in on that text?" asked Brandt, who was still filming.

"Dude, yes, you can!" said Jason. "You absolutely can! Because I'm so happy somebody is finally appreciat-

---

comma, and I like them just as much as I like my friends who don't use that comma.

ing my punctuation!" He enthusiastically reopened his phone, and Brandt pointed the camera at it.

"Will you just say one thing for me?" his friend Jack asked me.

"What?" I asked.

"Roll tide," said Jack.

"Roll tide," I said, for the first time in my life, and Jack was happy.

¶

I do actually use fewer commas today than I did some years ago, and I doubt I am alone in this. I can catalogue my own comma reduction as follows:

1. After years of internal struggles, I finally stopped worrying about the comma that I was taught to put between "hi" and a name, at least in email.

    ~~Hi, June,~~

    Hi June,

2. In email and on social media, I am less likely to put a comma before "too" at the end of a sentence, as in

    I ate one too.

    I have seen elaborate mythologies about this comma and how its absence or presence affects the meaning, and so far I am unmoved. I put it

in when I feel like it, and in this book I often
felt like it, but I estimate that my overall "too"
comma rate has dropped at least twenty-five percent since I was in my twenties.

3. I've already mentioned that I am less likely to
put commas before coordinating conjunctions in
short compound sentences. I could put a comma
before "and" in the following example, but I am
also happy to go without:

She'd prefer ice cream and he'd prefer fruit.

4. I am less likely to put commas after opening
phrases, as in

By half past noon the clock was broken.

Though I still love reading books and articles with long,
romantic, comma-filled sentences, I don't miss the commas that are disappearing from my own writing. I hope
you have so far been finding my approach acceptable.

Quizlet

••

Is there a comma in here that can't be in here?

> A goose, a duck, a sparrow, and a tur-
> tle, appeared to be conducting a lunch
> meeting on a sunny rock.

Answer: *Yes, the post-"turtle" comma has to come out, because it is separating the subject from the verb. In modern English punctuation, that is VERBOTEN.*

26

You Can Read This Chapter in Five Minutes or Fewer*

One of the more popular topics at the Grammar Table is the distinction between "fewer" and "less." Not long ago a friend of mine sent me a link to a *New York Times* story entitled "51 Vegetarian Dishes You Can Cook in 30 Minutes or Fewer." It was illustrated with an appealing picture of a meal featuring feta and colorful, cheerful vegetables, but that could not distract me from the headline, in which I saw linguistic instinct being trampled by overzealous adherence to a poorly understood grammar principle.

Yes, the idea is *generally* that you use "fewer" with countable nouns. Countable nouns are, unsurprisingly, nouns you can count, like this:

one apostrophe, two apostrophes, three apostrophes, . . . one trillion apostrophes

one tufted puffin, two tufted puffins, three tufted puffins, . . . one billion tufted puffins

Uncountable nouns, also often called mass nouns, are nouns you can't count. These are nouns we discuss

---

* I would never actually say or write "fewer" here.

and evaluate in what I like to think of, unscientifically, as blobby form. We use the word "less" rather than "fewer" with these uncountable nouns. For example:

Could you put <u>less chocolate syrup</u> on my son's ice cream sundae than you did on mine?

<u>*Less cilantro*</u> *next time, please!*

I would say "less cowbell"* but "fewer cherries." Some nouns can be both countable and uncountable, depending on how they are used. For example, sugar and salt are usually uncountable, but these words are also used as shorthand for salt and sugar packets, so at a takeout restaurant you might hear someone say, "I'd like four sugars and three salts."

On Martha's Vineyard I was talking to Vicky, a woman with long white hair who told me, "I was introduced to 'less' and 'fewer' by my significant other, who was fifteen years my senior when I met him. He was horrified when I used 'less' for 'fewer.' He said 'fewer' for number, 'less' for amount. What happened is I watched and I got to like 'fewer.' I got to like 'There are fewer people in this room'!"

I laughed. "However," continued Vicky, "then I saw in the dictionary that we are now accepting 'less people.' And so today I'm putting this before you."

I had *Merriam-Webster's* with me, so I opened it and began reading aloud on this topic: "The traditional view

---

* In a classic *Saturday Night Live* skit about a fictional Blue Öyster Cult rehearsal, Christopher Walken's character repeatedly requested "more cowbell." It was a lot of cowbell.

is that 'less' applies to matters of degree, value, or amount and modifies collective nouns, mass nouns, or nouns denoting an abstract whole while 'fewer' applies to matters of number and modifies plural nouns. 'Less' has been used to modify plural nouns since the days of King Alfred* and the usage, though roundly decried, appears to be increasing. 'Less' is more likely than 'fewer' to modify plural nouns when distances, sums of money, and a few fixed phrases are involved." Examples included "less than one hundred miles" and "in twenty-five words or less."

That last bit — about distances, sums of money, etc. — is where people go overboard, in my opinion.

"You say 'less than a hundred miles,' not 'fewer than a hundred miles,' right?" I asked Vicky.

Vicky agreed that she did.

I told her, "I would say, 'I ran less than six miles today,' not 'I ran fewer than six miles.' I also wouldn't say, 'My pet pig weighs fewer than one hundred fifty pounds.' I would say 'less than one hundred fifty pounds.'"

Pet pigs would find "fewer" pretentious and pedantic. Pounds, like miles, are countable, but they are evaluated in blobby form — hence "less."

"It's a good point," said Vicky. "I noticed it in the media, because that's the first place we saw 'less calories.' Which still makes me hit the side of my head" — here she actually hit the side of her head — "because they finally went for it and they said, We're ignoring you. We're not going to use 'fewer calories.'"

"You do see it in advertising," I said, "and people get upset about it."

"What do you think?" asked Vicky.

---

* Alfred the Great, AD 849–899, word-promoting king of Wessex.

"I'm careful about using 'fewer' for countable nouns," I said, "with the exception of the cases that I've mentioned. And there are also some select cases where I'm a bit of a renegade, according to some friends, though I personally don't think I'm a renegade."

"Those who are renegades always think they are non-renegades," said Vicky.

"I'll give you an example," I said, "and you might find this scandalous of me, but I don't like 'fifteen items or fewer' in the express lane at the grocery store. I feel it sounds stupid."

"Fifteen items or less?" asked Vicky.

"Less" sounds natural to me; "fewer" sounds like someone once had an English teacher who made a proclamation. And by the way, "fifteen items or less" is comparable to the "twenty-five words or less" example from *Merriam-Webster's* that I mentioned a few paragraphs ago.

"Interesting," said Vicky. "I like the sound of 'fewer' now that I know it. I see your carve-outs—that's a really good point, but I'm just wondering whether it's official."

"There's no official, is the great thing about English," I said. "It's like the Wild Wild West."

Quizlet

••

How does this sound?

> "I have fewer than thirty dollars in my wallet."

Answer: *Terrible and pedantic. "Less" is sometimes more.*

27

Possessed by Apostrophes

In New Orleans, a reporter doing a segment on the Grammar Table asked Brandt, "If you misplace an apostrophe, do you wind up sleeping on the couch?"

"It hasn't happened yet," said Brandt.

That is true. I married a man with apostrophes in all the right places.

Apostrophes, by the way, were a hot Grammar Table topic all over the United States. Visitors brought up apostrophes in New York, Georgia, New Mexico, California, Tennessee, and quite a few of the other states Brandt and I visited.

In Minneapolis at a downtown art fair, a large man named Patrick came up to the Grammar Table wearing a green T-shirt that said MINNESOTA.

"I'm the son of Nibbles, the hot dog cart," he said, pointing to a cart to the left of me. "They've been down here for thirty-six years. And then I helped run them this year."

The son of Nibbles wanted to discuss apostrophes. He knelt down in front of the Grammar Table for our conversation.

"When I was in elementary school," I told the son

of Nibbles, "I recall learning a more complicated set of apostrophe rules than is typically taught today. But there are a few basic things that are good to know."

I began to draw dogs. "A very basic one, which people get right, is 'the dog's tail,'" I said. "So one dog, one tail. Right? But let's say you had multiple dogs. Then the apostrophe would go after the *s*."

"Okay," said Patrick. "So what's the actual goal on that then?"

"Wait, let me just finish drawing my dogs," I said, "because I feel this is critical to the discussion."

the dog's tail
= the tail of the dog

the dogs' tails
= the tails of the dogs

the dog's tails
= the tails of the dog

"In 'the dogs' tails,' the *s* is already on the end, it's already plural, so you don't add another *s*," I said. "What confuses people is, for example, 'the children's dog,' because 'children' is already plural even without an *s*."

Patrick stood up. He was a sweet guy, but big. I

wondered whether he might have been told he seemed less threatening when he knelt down. If so, it was kind of him to have been careful with the Grammar Table, which is only thirty inches tall.

"So when do you put the apostrophe after the *s*?" asked Patrick.

"When it's a regular plural," I said. "But not all plurals in English are made by adding an *s*. That's why I brought up 'children.'"

"Right," Patrick said. "Kind of like 'goose' and 'geese'?"

"Yes, exactly," I said, and wrote this down:

the goose's tail

the geese's tails

To make "goose" plural, instead of adding an *s,* you change a vowel sound in the middle of the word: *oo* becomes *ee*. "That's why the apostrophe goes before the *s* there," I told Patrick. "On regular plurals, put the apostrophe after the *s*. On irregular plurals, you're going to see the apostrophe before the *s*."

That's why it would be "the children's tricycles"— "children" apostrophe *s* — but "the kids' tricycles," with an apostrophe after the *s* in "kids." I told Patrick I appreciated his apostrophe curiosity.

"Communicating is important," said Patrick. "I'm a photographer," he said. "I do portraiture. I usually communicate with photographs, but to write is another level."

"I am a crappy photographer, so my preferred medium is words," I said. "I take perfectly good photographic opportunities and ruin them."

¶

On Martha's Vineyard, a man with a dog asked, "Say my last name were Roberts. The possessive of that is Roberts apostrophe s: Roberts's. Right? Yes."

What did he need *me* for? He was a self-answering grammar-question asker!

"Then it would be *s* apostrophe, or *s* apostrophe *s*," I said, and wrote down these options:

Martin Roberts'

Martin Roberts's

"The *New York Times* would do *s* apostrophe *s*," I said. "Roberts's."

He and I then said in unison, "Which is what I do."

I add *'s* to almost all possessive singular names, regardless of what they end in. It keeps my life simple and, in my mind, logical.

Abbie's

Russ's

Tex's

"Because I actually say that extra syllable," I said. "I don't need to be stingy about writing it."

"Well, that's true," he agreed.

¶

"Do you have a grammar situation?" I asked a woman and two men standing near the Grammar Table on the Venice Beach Boardwalk.

"Yes!" said the woman, a buoyant brunette in a red shirt. "We do have a grammar situation. If we're talking about multiple witnesses and their testimonies—witnesses' testimonies—how would we write that?"

At first I was thrown by the plural "testimonies," since I usually use "testimony" in singular form. "I have many witnesses' testimonies before me today" was the example Luke, who turned out to be her husband, offered.

"Many witnesses' testimonies," I pondered aloud. "That's idiomatic? All right."

"I don't know if it's ever used that way," said the woman. "But we want to see you shine right now."

"You're asking about the apostrophe, right?" I asked, holding up my notepad to show them this:

witnesses' testimonies

"Yeah!" said the woman. "So you think it's *s s e s* apostrophe at the end."

"No, I don't just think it," I said, looking at her. She laughed.

"You've got an *e s* after double *s*," said Luke.

"Because it's just like any other noun," I said. "You know, like 'dress.' What's the plural of 'dress'? 'Dresses.'"

"Yeah!" said the woman, with enthusiasm.

"So don't get thrown by the syllable count," I cautioned.

"Okay!" said the woman. "Thank you!"

"Do you want this page as a souvenir?" I asked.

"Yes," she said.

"I've got to use it for mock trial," said Luke. He then decided he needed the singular form too, so I took back the paper and wrote this down for him:

witness's testimony

"Really? That's what it would be?" asked Luke.

Multiple consecutive *s*'s trouble many English speakers. But "witness" is a common noun — meaning not a specific name of someone or something — and on singular common nouns ending in *s*, you should always add the *'s*.

The bus's brakes broke.

Ashton Kutcher starred in the movie My Boss's Daughter.

If it's a name, however, you have a choice, I told them, giving them two examples:

Bess' testimony

Bess's testimony

"With names, both versions are considered correct," I said. "The *Wall Street Journal* does the bottom one, the *New York Times* does the bottom one, and the *New York Post* does the top one."

"I was taught the top one," said the woman. "The bottom one I was taught was wrong. Are they both correct?"

"They're both in use, and they have been for ages," I said. "It just depends. People get confused about this because everyone does different things."

"Put a star next to the one you would do," Luke told me.

I starred "Bess's." "I think it's logical because you don't say 'Bess sister,'" I said. "You actually pronounce the syllable. So why not put the apostrophe *s*? That's how I feel about it."

"Okay!" said the woman. "Okay!" She added, "My mom is a grammar freak."

The second man, who turned out to be her brother, confirmed her account. "We grew up with our mother correcting our English our whole lives," he said.

Pointing at Brandt's camera, I told the woman, "You should say hi to Mom!"

"Hey, Mom!" the woman yelled into the camera. She waved enthusiastically at it and moved closer to the Grammar Table microphone. "We're at the Grammar Table. Just where you want us to be! Workin' on our speech and punctuation!"

"And we know how to do 'Tess's sister' as well as 'Bess's sister'!" added Luke.

"My name's Tess!" the woman told me. She then told the camera, "You would not approve of how she's writing 'Tess's,' though."

To me, she said, "She's old school—not with the three *s*'s. I grew up with just the two *s*'s." Like this, she meant:

Tess'

"Are you sure she left off the final *s*?" I asked.

"I'll double-check," said Tess. "I don't want to put you on blast, Mom!" she told the camera.

"Are you sure you know your mother?" I asked, laughing.

"Is this a game show?" asked Tess.

"Look, I have *The Chicago Manual of Style* right here," I said, holding it up. "This is influential in publishing — this is like the publishing bible — and they add the *s*."

"Okay, I'm going to ask her," said Tess.

"If you find out anything surprising, I would love to hear about it," I told her.

I pointed out the up-to-date nature of my reference materials. "This is the current edition!" I said, banging on my *Chicago Manual of Style,* seventeenth edition. "This is not an old and out-of-date version, okay?"

"Well, she would probably prefer an older edition because it would be more purist," said Tess.

"Seventeen!" said her husband excitedly. "Seventeen!" He took a picture of the seventeenth edition of *Chicago*.

"I love you, Mom!" Tess yelled at the camera.

¶

I was discussing pronouns with the St. Louis writer, Ashley, when she brought up possessive constructions such as "Ellen and I's friend."

"Oh!" I said. "I've heard it on *The Bachelor*."*

"Yes!" she said. "All the time on *The Bachelor*. *The Bachelor* is the worst."

"But it's great for hearing new pronoun combinations that I've never heard before," I said. "I had never noticed that one before *The Bachelor*."

"You wouldn't say 'I's friend,'" she said.

"You've got to admit, though, it's a little bit inventive!"

---

* Please don't be horrified; it's a professional must if I'm going to keep up on the latest genitive trends.

I said. "Normally, if you have a joint ownership only the second thing gets the possessive." For example:

Sheila and Ellen's party

But when the second possessor is a pronoun, Sheila normally turns possessive, too. "So then it's 'Sheila's and my party,'" I said.

"Just say 'our party'!" said Ashley.

"Yes," I said. "Or just get rid of Sheila because it's not worth the trouble with the possessive forms."

"But, yeah, they would never write out 'Sheila and I's,' I don't think," said Ashley.

"I wonder if they would," I said. "I'm going to google 'and I's' and see if I can find it. I bet I can."

I did google it later, and I did find it.

The problem with "Sheila's and my party" is that it sounds ugly to many people. People don't have to use it, fortunately. There are almost always ways around it that are even better. Here's a sentence makeover for you:

Before: *I am writing to tell you about Sheila's and my party Saturday! Can you come?*

After: *Sheila and I are having a party Saturday. Can you come?*

Now you are ready to party.

¶

"I'm curious what this is all about," said a man in a blue fleece vest in Memphis. Brandt and I had set up across the street from a mall located in a towering mixed-use complex called Crosstown Concourse.

"This is the Grammar Table. Do you have any grammar questions, comments, or complaints?" I asked.

"What?" exclaimed the man, whose name was Don.

"Seriously," I said. "It began in New York City. This is our thirty-seventh state."

"And it's about any kind of complaint, or only about grammar?" asked Don.

I laughed. "If you have a broader one, I'm happy to listen," I said.

"I've got a lot of bitchin' to do!" said Don. "We're a grammar family in my house. My mother-in-law is an English teacher." Without asking, he put some food and drink down on the Grammar Table so he could take a picture.

I always feel glad when people are comfortable enough to do things like that. Well, unless an open container of a brightly colored or dark fluid is involved. Also excluded is eating my lunch apple.

"I'm extremely fascinated," he told me. "I wish my mother-in-law were here. She's an English teacher. Well, let me just call her. If I don't reach her, I can try any of my family members, because they're all grammar nerds."

"This is cute," I said.

"I'll be so upset if she doesn't answer," said Don.

She didn't answer.

He tried his wife. She didn't have a question. He tried his twelve-year-old son. He didn't have a question either (though he did mention that he knew what relative pronouns were before he hung up). But then Don's phone rang.

"It's my mother-in-law," he said triumphantly. "Wendy!" he answered.

"Hey, did you call me?" asked his mother-in-law.

"I did," said Don. "This is a really out-of-left-field thing I'm calling you about. You have other people on speaker-phone with us. But I'm at Crosstown and I'm picking up some Christmas stuff, and I ran into this lady who's been traveling the country to all fifty states with this thing she's got, called the Grammar Table. And her mission in life is to answer any grammar question or kind of language or punctuation question that anybody might have."

At that moment, a large and unsmiling security guard began walking toward us from across the street. Uh-oh. I don't mind violating faux grammar rules, but I do mind trespassing.

His back to the security guard, unaware of the approach, Don told his mother-in-law, "I thought you of anyone might have a grammar or punctuation question that either number one, you've wondered about all your life, or two, that we could maybe stump her with."

Brandt was now talking quietly with the large security guard. There was a situation. They seemed to be negotiating whether the Grammar Table could stay outside the Memphis Crosstown mall.

Wendy, the mother-in-law on the phone, said, "Okay, why do most books put Chris apostrophe for the possessive of Chris? And now the new grammar books say Chris apostrophe *s*."

In other words, she used to see

Chris'

but now was seeing

Chris's

"My preference is to put the *s,* so I would do Chris apostrophe *s,*" I told her telephonically. "But I have two style guides on my table right now. *The Chicago Manual of Style* encourages the addition of the *s. The Chicago Manual of Style* is huge. Your son-in-law is looking at it. You can confirm that it's huge, right?"

"It's large," confirmed Don. "A very large book."

"Yes, and it governs a lot of what people do in publishing," I said. "*The Associated Press Stylebook* governs what people do in newspapers and magazines to a significant degree, and AP doesn't add the *s.* However, they are currently contemplating a change that would add the *s.*"

In other words, although in AP style you might see someone discussing *Chris'* cauliflower, the discussion could in the future concern *Chris's* cauliflower.

"Right," said Wendy. "Okay. So we're starting to see the *s* apostrophe *s.*"

"Yes, and I like it," I said, "because I don't pronounce it like 'Chris book.' I say 'Chrissez book,' so I like putting the *s.*"

"All right!" said Wendy. "Well, great! Thank you. You sound like you know what you're talking about." And* that was the last thing that happened before we were expelled from mall property in Memphis, Tennessee.

¶

---

* I regularly begin sentences with "and" and "but." If you read good literature and journalism, you will see that there is no prohibition against it, no matter what you may once have been told back when your shoe size was still changing annually.

One day back in New York, when I was stationed next to the staircase leading to the northbound 1, 2, and 3 trains in the Seventy-Second Street subway station, a fortyish man in a suit and tie approached me and said, "I have a question for you I've been wondering about for a while now. How do you write the possessive forms of Jesus and Moses?"

"That's a good one," I said.

I learned at one point to omit the *s* after the apostrophe in biblical and classical names already ending in *s*, even if you tend to include it on other names ending in *s*. So even though I would have written "Charles's desk," I told him, at one point I would have written "Jesus' teachings" or "Moses' wife."

I no longer do that. *The Chicago Manual of Style* supports homogeneous treatment, which strikes me as sensible:

Charles's desk

Jesus's desk

Moses's desk

The man had been edging around the Grammar Table as I talked, and now he was on my side of it, next to me. That was strange.

I glanced up and noticed that in just the past few minutes, a tiny group of Jehovah's Witnesses across the subway station from me had turned into a big group. They were standing there quietly with their rolling literature carts, clearly waiting for me to vacate my prime New York City real estate, begrimed and begummed though it was, at the top of the Seventy-Second Street subway stairs.

"Wait a second," I said to the man. "Are you over here because you care about grammar, or because you're wondering when you can get my spot?"

"Well, I didn't want to be pushy, but we *were* kind of wondering how long you were going to be here," he said.

"You can have it," I said. "I was about to leave anyway." Which was true. Otherwise there would have been not the slightest chance of my moving. First come, first served, all's fair in grammar, et cetera. I rose and packed up my table, stool, Grammar Table sign, and grammar books.

As I exited the station, awkwardly carrying the stacked furniture and heavy books, the man extravagantly held open the gate for me while shoving some Jehovah's Witnesses literature into my tote bag.

"So you can check our writing!" he said.

To this day, the Jehovah's Witnesses remain the Grammar Table's chief competition for table real estate.

Quizlet

· ·

Add or fix apostrophes as needed in the sentence below. Assume monogamy.

My cousins husbands are taking their childrens classmates to the water park.

Answer: *My cousins' husbands are taking their children's classmates to the water park.*

28

Plural Possessive Holiday Extravaganza

One of the things I love most about the holiday season is that you get to spend so much time talking about plurals and plural possessives of proper nouns. I absolutely love talking about the plurals and plural possessives of proper nouns.

Normally you form the plurals of names the same way you form the plurals of common nouns, by adding *s* or *es,* as shown in the names below.

Wilhelmina and Egbert Arnold = the Arnolds

Tim, Marco, and Suzanne Batts = the Battses

Ethel and Robin Felix = the Felixes

Abel and Renata Matthias = the Matthiases

Please keep in mind, however, that you should not introduce your neighbors Sydney, Rachel, Marly, and Bobby Fish as the Fish. They are the Fishes. Similarly, your colleague Joan Foot and her husband, Tim Foot, are not the Feet; they are the Foots. Even if the name is identical to a common noun with an irregular plural, you treat it as though it is regular and add the usual *s* or *es* ending. The plural of the last name Cary is Carys, not Caries. Don't call your friends tooth decay.

¶

On Venice Beach, a man named Michael asked, "When you have a name ending in an *s* — for example, Jones — how do you form the plural of Jones?"

"That's our last name!" said a stunned young woman in red, who had just arrived at the Grammar Table carrying a baby. She was accompanied by a man and a sleepy toddler. "That's our last name right here!"

"Oh, it is?" said Michael mildly, as if it were totally natural that the possessor of a surname, albeit a common surname, would pass by at the very moment we were discussing how to make it plural.

Multiple Jones family members are "the Joneses."

Since we already had the actual Joneses with us, I decided we should take it up a notch.

"Let's do 'the Joneses' house,'" I said. (Unlike you, they couldn't see how it was written; they could only hear it. You have the inside scoop.)

"This is so crazy," said the woman. She waved her hand to indicate the craziness of this. "We just got married on Valentine's Day!" she added excitedly.

"Do you want to guess where the apostrophe goes in 'Joneses'?" I asked. But there was a lot going on on that boardwalk, what with babies and coincidences and new marriages, so I decided to go ahead and show her:

the Joneses' house

"But if you really hate that," I said, writing, "you could do this and avoid the whole thing."

the Jones family's house

"This is so crazy," said the woman in red, newly a Jones, still holding the baby.

"What's your first name?" I asked.

"Jessie," she replied.

"Okay," I said. "You have a choice in this one." I wrote:

Jessie Jones'

or

Jessie Jones's

I handed the sheet to Jessie and said, "I feel you should take this."

"I do too!" She was so smiley. "This is so awesome right here! Who would have ever thought you'd be talking about Jones? That was awesome, though!"

"Thank you," I said. "Congratulations on getting married!"

¶

In Bozeman, Montana, a woman approached and said, "I have a question for you. So last names that end with a *z* or an *s*—"

"That's just going to cause your children lifelong grief," I interrupted her. I laughed; she did not. Her name was Brandy, and she was accompanied by two elementary school–age children.

"We have friends by the name of Phipps," said Brandy. "When we do our Christmas cards, how do we do their name? The Phipps family? The Phippses?"

"First of all, this is one of my favorite topics," I said. "I could talk about this for three hours. The plural is Phippses. For example, 'The Phippses like to fish.'"

"Okay," said Brandy. "That's what I thought."

"But then the plural possessive throws people off," I continued, showing her this:

The Phippses' fish spoiled in the car.

"Okay," said Brandy. "So it is with the *es*. With names ending in *s* and *z*, it's the same?"

"Yes, right," I said. It's also true of names ending in *sh, sch,* and sometimes *ch*.

The Fishes' granddaughter enjoyed the aquarium.

Someone stole the Riches' fossil collection.

With *ch*, the choice depends on how it is pronounced: Do you have to add another syllable in speech to get an *s* on the end? With the name Rich above, the answer is yes, but if Bach is pronounced like the composer's name, you can just add an *s*, as in

The Bachs' house is at the end of the lane.

How do you know how to make a name ending in *ch* plural if you don't know how to pronounce it? Well, you don't! Fortunately, there is the internet, and that makes name-pronunciation research much easier than it used to be.

Quizlet

. . . .

What is the last name of the people in each of these phrases?
1. Curt Bert's shirts
2. Curt Berts' shirts
3. Curt Berts's shirts
4. the Berts' shirts
5. the Bertses' shirts

Answers: *1. Bert 2. Berts 3. Berts 4. Bert 5. Berts*

29

Peculiar Pasts

Lisette, a business professor, was in a fast-moving ticketholders line snaking past the Grammar Table toward the entrance of Fifth Third Field, where the Toledo Mud Hens minor league baseball game was about to begin. She wore a floppy red sunhat and big sunglasses, and there was a purple cast on her left arm.

"I might have a grammar question," she said as she was drifting by. "You know the past tense of 'lead'? When you say 'I was led astray'?"

"Yes, right!" I said.

"Most of the time, I thought the past tense was *l e d,* like 'I have been led,'" she said. "But my autocorrect and everything else always says *l e a d.*"

"No, you are right," I said. "It's *l e d.* Maybe autocorrect isn't reading the context correctly." (Lisette's example contained a past participle rather than the past tense, but they are the same form: "led.")

Then Lisette was swept away with the ticket line. I yelled after her, "You just keep on doing what you're doing. I have faith in you!"

Here are some "lead" and "led" examples for you:

present	Every game he <u>leads</u> Mrs. Grimball to her seat.
past tense	Last year he <u>led</u> the team to five straight wins.
past participle	Oops, I have <u>led</u> you to the wrong hot dog vendor.

¶

It was dusk in Verdi Square when a woman and two men rolled up with a baby in a stroller.

One of the men asked, "What is the infinitive of 'wrought'?"

People often think this form is from "wreak" or "wring." It's not. I pulled out *Garner's Modern English Usage* and showed them the entry for "wreak," which lists regular verb forms: I wreaked, I have wreaked.

"The past tense is not 'wrought,'" writes Garner, "which is the archaic past tense and past participle of 'to work.'"

That doesn't mean you should start saying, "I wrought until almost midnight last night." These days I mostly see this word in references to wrought-iron fences, wrought-iron shelves, wrought-iron bed frames, and other wrought-iron items. I've also seen it in more than one headline over the years—for example, "What the War in Iraq Wrought" in *The New Yorker* in 2014.

As the two men studied the entry, the woman said to them, "Let the baby look at it. She wants to look at it, too."

So they took *Garner's,* a hardcover book 1,120 pages long, and placed it gently in the baby's lap. The baby looked at the entry, studying and caressing it with wee baby fingers.

New York City preschools are really competitive.

¶

One sunny March Saturday in New York, a smiling woman of about forty in a wheelchair arrived at the Grammar Table accompanied by her smiling look-alike teenage daughter.

"What is this?" asked the woman. I gave her the abridged history of the Grammar Table.

The daughter was fourteen. It had just been International Women's Day, and the mom told me they had decided to turn it into an International Women's Weekend so they could extend the celebration they were having in the city.

"Grammar Table is honored to be a part of International Women's Weekend!" I told them.

At first, they couldn't think of a grammar question. "Oh, I know!" said the mom finally. "What is the past tense of 'to hang'?"

You can hang both people and pictures in the present tense, but once you move into the past tense, the forms part ways.

"It depends on how you're using it," I said. "If you're hanging laundry, it's 'hung.' If you are using it to mean someone puts a noose around someone else's neck and then—" Oops. Here I hesitated as I glanced at the daughter, but the mom waved me on.

"Okay, if you mean 'hang' in the sense of hanging by your neck, then the past tense and past participle are both 'hanged,'" I finished.

I switched to a less macabre subject. "What else have you done for International Women's Weekend?" I asked.

"We went to the museum, we went to Sephora, we got hot dogs, we came to the Grammar Table—" said the mom.

"Wait a second, what do hot dogs have to do with International Women's Weekend?" I interrupted.

"Because it's International Women's Weekend, so we can do whatever we want," the mom said. "And now we're going to get a mani-pedi!"

Quizlet

∙∙∙

Yvette _____ (lead, led) him to the office where Zev had just _____ (hung, hanged) the painting of Tootsie and Scooter.

Answer: *led, hung*

30

Peripatetic Past Participles

In Chicago, a little girl who was in town to visit her grandparents wanted to know what a past participle was. I am charmed by any child who wants to know what past participles are.

"Do you know what a verb is?" I asked. She said she did.

"If you have a verb and you want to know what the past participle is for that verb, then you figure out the form that goes in this blank," I told her, writing this down and showing her:

I have _____.

"Let's say I wanted to know the past participle of the verb 'to cry,'" I said. "What would the past participle be? Fill in that blank with the correct form: I have <u>cried</u>."

When a verb in English is regular, the past participle looks just like the past tense — for instance, "I <u>cried</u>" (past tense) and "I have <u>cried</u>" (past participle). Not a problem! Sometimes even irregular verbs have the same past tense and past participle form. "Read" is an example: "I <u>read</u>" (past tense) and "I have <u>read</u>" (past participle).

"What's the past participle of 'to bake'?" I asked the girl.

"Baked," she said.

"Good!" I asked. "Now what's the past participle of 'to write'?"

"Wrote," said the girl.

"Would you say 'I have wrote' or would you say 'I have . . .'?" I paused to give her an opportunity to guess again.

"Written," she said.

"Exactly!" I said. "That's what you have to do. You have to just make sure you slow down enough—'cried,' 'baked,' 'written.'"

It's when the past tense and the past participle diverge that people often run into trouble. Participlemaker, beware!

¶

Participles diverged in Montana, but my visitor was ready for them.

"I heard about you coming here today," said Barbara, an elderly woman at the Bozeman Public Library.

"You did?" I asked. "How did you hear about it?"

"Friends were talking at knitting this morning," Barbara replied. "We have a group that's met for quite a while, and then I have a quilting group in the morning, and they've met for forty-four years on every Thursday."

She was delicate, gracious, and attractive. In my casual grammar attire—I was wearing a T-shirt that read I ❤ GRAMMAR—I felt like an awkward Dorothy to her Glinda the Good.

"Let's do 'swim,'" she said.

"I'm ready!" I said. "What should we do with it?"

Barbara wanted the different tenses. In English, there aren't many forms to talk about with verbs, even with ir-/regular verbs, because our total verb forms per verb are minimal.

I began writing: "I swam." That was past tense. Done. One form.

I then wrote:

I have _____.

I paused and looked at her.

"Swum," said Barbara.

"Yep," I said. "I think we've run out of things to do now. That's about it. Sometimes people will use 'swam' as the past participle."

In other words, they might say "I have swam" instead of "I have swum." That means they are using the standard past tense form ("swam") as the past participle (conventionally, "swum").

"Yes," said Barbara. "Okay, what's the other one? I miss it all the time."

"Is it another tense thing?" I asked.

"Yes," she said.

"Ones that come up are 'run,' 'drink,' 'sink,'" I said. "Do any of those ring a bell?"

"Let's do 'drink,'" said Barbara. "I'll think of my wine."

"Okay," I said. "I drank and —"

"What made you think of doing this?" she interrupted. Barbara was apparently already done thinking of her wine.

"I don't know," I said. "It just happened. I thought it'd be funny and fun. And I got sick of being on a computer, and I like talking to people."

"I would have went!" she remembered.

"That's the one!" I said. "Right."

"That gives me chills," she said.

"I'm so sorry," I said. In her new example, the past tense "went" was being used in place of the past participle "gone."

"You know where I think the mistakes come up a lot?" I continued. "When there are intervening helping verbs. Like 'I should have went,' 'I should have drank less,' and so on."*

"It would be 'drunk less,'" said Barbara.

"I should have gone, I should have drunk, I should have swum," I said. I ripped off the page on which I had written those and gave her her Grammar Table receipt.

"I love words," said Barbara.

Poetry of the Participle

In modern edited prose, the standard accepted participle forms are often not the same forms that people use in daily speech. Here is a short poem/memory aid to help people avoid common participle missteps, should they wish to do so, in formal and/or workplace settings.

---

* Helping verbs precede the main verb, and you can have multiple helping verbs in a row. The helping verbs in "I should have gone" are "should have." The main verb is "gone."

I run, I ran, I should have run.
I drink, I drank, I would have drunk.
I sink, I sank, I could have sunk.
With rhymes like this, I will not flunk.

•••

¶

Past-participle questions were unusually plentiful on the Venice Beach Boardwalk.

A man named Eduardo, fluent in both English and Spanish, told me, "Instead of saying 'I have eaten,' people say—"

"I have ate," I said.

"I have ate!" Eduardo confirmed. "And I'm like, 'Oh, I have eaten too!'"

Fernanda, looking cool in a white T-shirt, arrived at the Grammar Table a little later. She told me, "The first thing I thought of when I was walking toward you was, If someone says 'I should've went,' it's a deal-breaker. There's no reason someone should say 'should've went.'"

Fernanda was from Brazil. "I'm self-conscious about the fact that I have an accent," she told me.

"You must have come here very young," I said. "I didn't know you weren't a native speaker."

"No, not very young," she said. "Like seventeen. If people spend enough time with me, they can tell that I have an accent. I can fake it for a while, but then there's gonna be words there."

She added cheerfully, "Doesn't it get annoying when you're talking to people who aren't even American but then they have their opinions of how they really hate when people say 'I should've went'? Isn't it like"—here she acted out a scene of grammar conflict—"'How dare you, I'm an American!'" Then she repeated "I should've went!" and giggled.

"No!" I exclaimed. It is fact that plenty of my most linguistically knowledgeable students and friends are non-native speakers of English. In fact, if you ever find yourself confused about whether to use "I" or "me," or "who" or "whom," you will often be better off asking a non-native speaker of English than a native.

Alternatively, you can read the rest of this book!

¶

"She's always getting on me about my grammar," said a young woman in Verdi Square, indicating the middle-aged woman with her.

"Are you related?" I asked.

"I'm her mom," said her mom, who wore an orange cap over her dark hair. "My mom's an English professor, my father was an English teacher, I was an English major, and my daughter is studying communications. 'Josh and I' or 'Josh and me' is a really, really big thing. That's what got us started this morning, and I said people's grammar, even college-educated, has gotten so bad that if you can keep your grammar good, it gives you an edge. I was using an example in my business—I work in tech—and people are always saying 'I haven't ran the data yet,' and it makes my skin crawl. Even my boss."

Her right hand attacked her face like a space alien, demonstrating the gravity of the situation.

"And yes, there's definitely a difference," said the mom. She turned to her daughter and said, "Because it's understanding the past tense. Like 'I haven't run the data' versus 'ran,' which is past tense!"

"I know," said her daughter, Trish, laughing calmly. I was impressed by her equanimity. Trish told me, "We always talk about this."

"Are you her only child?" I asked.

"No," said Trish. "I have a younger brother."

"Okay, so this is distributed over multiple siblings?" I asked. "You seem to have a good sense of humor about it."

"And my nephew, and my cousins," said Trish.

"They all get it!" said her mom. "Because our parents were English teachers."

In case you have a parent who annoys you by getting on you about your grammar: In the early nineteenth century, an Englishman named William Cobbett wrote an epistolary grammar book addressed to his fourteen-year-old son. That means a whole grammar book in the form of letters, written to that son. If you ever feel annoyed by a parent hassling you about your pronouns or participles, just keep in mind that you (probably) do not have a parent who writes you epistolary grammar books.

¶

In Boulder City, Nevada, a woman came up with her husband and asked, "Can I ask you a grammar question?"

"I'm ready," I said. "Hit me with it."

"Okay," said the woman, whose name was Marilyn. "If somebody finishes like three bottles of wine in an evening—"

"Are you sure this is a grammar question?" I interrupted, smiling.

"Yes." She didn't laugh. "Do you say the wine was all drunk, or drunken, or drank, or . . . I know you could say 'consumed,' but if you want to use the word 'drink,' 'the wine was all drunk'?"

Her husband, in a blue cap, had sidled away from the Grammar Table and the cameras. "Drank," he said, from a secure location.

"The wine was all drank, the wine was all drunken . . . Tough one, huh?" said Marilyn.

"Typically 'drunk' is used as the standard past participle, which is what you need in that sentence," I said. "Did this come up in a conversation recently? Is this a holiday topic?"

"No, we don't drink at all," said Marilyn. "We're both teetotalers. It's kind of a tough one, because most people would just say the wine was all consumed or the wine was all gone. Hardly anybody would say the wine was all drunk."

I complicated our discussion unnecessarily by reading aloud to her at length from a usage guide and blathering on irrelevantly about "drunken," which is in use too, adjectivally, often to describe excessive or habitual drinking.

I was off the rails; I focused. "It would definitely be 'The wine has all been drunk,'" I proclaimed.

"Well done," said Marilyn.

"Thank you," I said.

"I'm not going to quibble with you, because who knows?" said Marilyn. "But yeah, you're probably right."

I was right.

"Oh! The wine has all been drunk by the drunken sailor'!" I said triumphantly. "Now we've got both 'drunk' and 'drunken' in one sentence, and I feel good about that."

"Can't be wrong," said Marilyn, without conviction.

Quizlet

• •

On vacation in Thailand, Omar has
_____ (swam, swum) daily, Coral has
_____ (ran, run) daily, and Theodore
has _____ (drank, drunk) daily.

Answer: *swum, run, drunk*

31

What's Passed Is Past

"Can you! help! me! figure out! when! to use! 'pass,' 'past,' and 'passed'?" asked Alicia as she and her companion Tara stood before the Grammar Table on the Venice Beach Boardwalk.

This "pass"/"past"/"passed" thing appeared to be an emergency.

"I feel like I knew this at one point," said Alicia, "and then I didn't remember, so now I just avoid those three words altogether." You met Alicia in an earlier chapter. She was the diminutive woman who gleefully pronounced the effect of the "affect"/"effect" discussion to be victory.

"I'm going to give you a sentence for each of these, and then you can tell me if that helps," I said. "'Pass' can be used in different ways."

Alicia said, "Like present tense: 'I pass the ball.'"

"Yeah, or 'I want to pass this test.' 'Passed,' *p a s s e d,* is the past tense of 'pass,'" I said, offering these examples:

I passed the ball.

He passed the test.

"Passed" and "past" are homophones. They are different words but sound the same. Homophones are rascals.

I explained, "'Past,' *p a s t*, is normally used to refer to time that happened already. Like 'in the past.' Oh! I'm going to put two in one sentence for you!"

"Do it, do it!" said Alicia.

I did it. "It's a twofer," I said, writing this:

In the past, I passed that test.

"What about 'passed by'?" asked Alicia. "I'm trying to think of when I would try to use it."

I wrote down a sentence with a blank and showed it to her. "You can fill in the blank," I said.

Yesterday I _____ (passed, past) by the Grammar Table.

Alicia was unsure, but her companion was confident. "That's *e d*," said Tara.

"So, 'In the past, I passed by the table'—is that the same word?" asked Alicia.

"No," I said.

"'In the past' would be with the *t*," said Alicia.

"Yes!" I said.

"'Past' with a *t* is time," said Tara.

"Yes," I said. "I'm going to give you a little list of phrases with *p a s t* in them. I think that will help." I wrote down:

in the past

the past tense

a past girlfriend

"Okay, what about someone dying?" Alicia asked.

"He passed away, *p a s s e d*," I said. "Again, it's acting as an action verb. Can you hear that?"

"Yeah," said Alicia. "So if it's a verb, I use *p a s s e'd*."

"Yeah," I said. "*P a s t* is normally going to be used for noun and adjective."*

"Noun and adjective, okay," she said, nodding eagerly, her chin in her hand. The ocean behind me was now swallowing the sun. We had been there all afternoon.

"Are you trying to get out of here?" asked Tara.

"Tara has a question," Alicia told me. She asked Tara, "Has your question *passed*?"

"Nice!" said Tara.

"Wait!" I said. "How do you spell it?"

"*P a s s e d*," said Alicia.

"Yes," I said.

"Yes?" said Alicia.

"Yes," I confirmed, giving her the page.

"Boom!" said Alicia, high-fiving me.

But then I took back the paper from her, saying, "I feel I need to add this one form, because we didn't cover it."

I *have* *passed* the test.

"That's like a past participle?" said Alicia.

"Oh my gosh," I said. "What are you, a closet gram-marian?" They both laughed. "Do you know how rare it is for people to come up with that term?"

---

* "Past" can also be a preposition: "Victor walked past the school."

"What? Is that right?" Alicia asked. "That's right?" She made a triumphant gesture with her fist.

"Yes!" I exclaimed. "And you know what? This is coming full circle because 'past participle' has *p a s t* in it!" I gave her the piece of paper—and included here is a chart I made for your records, too.

PAST
(noun)   Tell me about your past.   SPEED DATING

PAST
(adjective)   I think I was a cat in my past life.

PASS
(verb)   Please pass the kale.   Gladly.

PASS
(noun)   I lost my backstage pass to the library panel.

PASSED
(past-tense verb)   After we passed the Greek test, we passed out.

"Oh my god!" Alicia threw up her arms and did a triumphant circular grammar victory walk.

"This is really exciting," I said.

"Chills," said Alicia, pulling up her sleeve to show us. "Are you here every Saturday?"

Quizlet

••

More than once in the smoothie-making course she is taking, her _____ (past, passed) experiences with kale have _____ (past, passed) through her mind.

Answer: *past, passed*

32

Gerund v. Present-Participle Smackdown

In Falls Park in Sioux Falls, South Dakota, water was cascading over rocks behind me when two men stopped to talk. Greg, a scientist who had seen a segment about the Grammar Table on CBS a while back, seemed completely unsurprised to encounter me on a random bit of winding path at the falls. He was accompanied by his cheerful twenty-year-old son.

"I never understood what gerunds are," Greg told me.

"This is one of the best questions," I said excitedly. "I love when someone can come up with the word 'gerund,' because it doesn't happen to me on a regular basis." I wrote down two sentences and showed them the page.

I am running.

Running is fun.

I explained, "In general, when you see these *-ing* forms, they're referred to as either a gerund or a present participle. In the sentence 'I am running,' 'running' is acting as a verb. It combines with 'am' to tell you that you're in the middle of doing this thing. In that context, 'running' is called the present participle. And then, in 'Running is fun'—"

"It's the subject," said the son.

"—it's the subject, and it's a noun," I said. "So it's an -*ing* form, too, but you use it as a noun." I wrote down another pair of examples:

I was eating spaghetti.

Eating spaghetti is great.

"These aren't very literary sentences," I said. "This isn't the Literature Table. In 'I was eating spaghetti,' 'eating' is a verb, right? But in 'Eating spaghetti is great,' 'eating' is a thing. It's the subject of the sentence. It's acting as a noun, so that one would be called a gerund."

"Oh," said the son. "So a gerund is a present participle acting as a noun."

"That was excellent," I said.

"Yes!" said the son triumphantly.

When you combine present participles with a present-tense form of the verb "to be," you are using what is known as present continuous. In school you may have learned this as present progressive, as I did; they're the same thing. In the following sentence, the present continuous tells you that the speaker is in the middle of eating the spaghetti.

I am eating spaghetti.

Why do you need to know this terminology? Well, technically you don't. You can live a long and happy life without knowing it. I love knowing it, though. I think it's

· ·

For your ongoing spaghetti-eating needs

I am eating spaghetti. = present continuous
I was eating spaghetti. = past continuous
I will be eating spaghetti. = future continuous
I have been eating spaghetti. = present perfect
  continuous
I had been eating spaghetti. = past perfect
  continuous
I will have been eating spaghetti. = future
  perfect continuous

· ·

fun. And if you're reading this book, either you care a little bit or someone has assigned it to you for class against your will, in which case I'm very sorry, but I do hope you are enjoying yourself at least a little bit anyway.

¶

On a warm and sunny day in New York City, a pair of little boys, one about five and the other maybe four, walked up to the Grammar Table in Verdi Square. The bigger boy asked, "What's a gerund?"

I looked around. No adult in sight. This was peculiar, but my first duty as Grammar Table proprietress is to answer questions, not ask them.

"It is an *-ing* verb form that you use as a noun," I told my tiny grammar students. "Like in the sentence 'Reading is fun,' the word 'reading' is a gerund."

They looked at me. "Do you know what a noun is?" I asked.

"I'm not sure," said the big one.

Doubtful that I could break down nouns and verbs for the pre-elementary crowd, I changed the subject. "Are you two related to each other?"

The bigger one said, "Yes, we're brothers!" as the littler one said, "No."

"Oh, so you two aren't in agreement on this," I said.

"That's because he doesn't understand what that means," said the older one. Then he wrapped his hands around his little brother's neck and started choking him.

The littler boy made a *glugluglugluglug* sound as his brother shook him back and forth.

A violent incident would definitely damage the reputation of this public grammar enterprise, so I took action. "No choking of your brother at Grammar Table!" I yelled.

A man, probably the dad and also, presumably, the origin of the gerund question, popped off a nearby bench. As he flew toward us to forestall fratricide, I yelled at the boys, "Hey! That was a gerund!"

¶

Some weeks later in nearly the same location, I talked to a man named Nathan, perhaps in his thirties, who told me his boss had a thing for gerunds. Nathan asked if he could film our conversation to show his colleagues, and when I agreed, he pulled out his phone and began recording.

"So I'm out here with Ellen in front of the—are you the grammar queen?"

"I don't really have a name yet," I said. "Maybe Grammar Table lady. We're sorting that out. Or Ellen. Ellen works."

On his phone, Nathan showed me a slide from his company's recent town hall. In the business world, a town hall is a large meeting run by upper management for all employees. Ideally it is also a bonding experience.

"Our CEO always includes a grammar lesson," said Nathan. "In this one, he actually did the grammar lesson first. Often he does it at the end, but for this one, he actually led with it. So this was our company update, and the very first thing that we got to was a lesson on gerunds."

"That's hilarious," I said, reading the slide on his phone, which looked like this:

GRAMMAR

- GERUNDS
- What are they?
- I appreciate you/your living the values
- Promotions are contingent upon one/one's living the values

"This is a very precise, focused kind of topic," I said. "I'm interested in this. People have come by and complained that people don't use possessives with gerunds when they're needed, so your boss is tapping right into that current of dissatisfaction."

"I see," said Nathan. "Well, that's good to know. Also good to know is that right after the gerund lesson came reporting on our record sales and profits. But the important things first."

Now, I would use the possessive forms—"your" and

"one's"—in the sample sentences Nathan showed me if someone made me use that exact wording. But it is more likely that I would rewrite them, because the possessive-plus-gerund syntax can sometimes sound a bit stiff.

Nonetheless, I have spontaneously uttered countless possessive-plus-gerund structures many times in my life. For example:

> *I appreciate your helping me peel the potatoes.*

I would not use "you" in this potato sentence—it would feel weird to me—even though it is common enough in the US and acceptable in the UK to many educated speakers.

Still, if anyone ever tells you you should always have a possessive in front of an *-ing* form, you can use this counterexample:

> *I saw him walking down the street.*

People don't tend to argue that that should instead be this:

> *I saw his walking down the street.*

Some months later, I saw Nathan walking through Verdi Square. It was Christmas Day, and he was with his wife and two small children. We were all bundled up in coats.

"Wow, you're really toughin' it out here in the chilly weather," said Nathan. "On Christmas?"

"That's right," I said. "I take this very seriously."

"Remember I was the guy whose boss is the grammar nut?" asked Nathan.

"Yes," I said. "Did you show him the video?"

"I did," said Nathan. "We have a grammar interest channel, and I uploaded the video of me talking to you. Everybody got a kick out of it."

"The video of me talking to you" is a perfect example of the issue Nathan's boss discussed in his slide about gerunds. Don't overdo this possessive-before-a-gerund thing. Which do you prefer?

I *uploaded the video of me talking to you.*

I *uploaded the video of my talking to you.*

I prefer "me talking" here, just as Nathan delivered it. If you pick "my talking," that makes "talking" a gerund and "my" a possessive for that noun. What is the sentence meant to convey? Is it primarily a video of talking, or is it primarily a video of Nathan undertaking a particular action (talking)? I think the latter. If you pick "me talking," that makes "me" the object of the preposition, and then "talking to you" a participial phrase modifying "me." That, in my opinion, is the sense that is intended.

If you disagree with me on that one, what about this? "She uploaded the video of *me* doing a triple cartwheel." I definitely wouldn't say "She uploaded the video of *my* doing a triple cartwheel." Would you?

If I am able to do a triple cartwheel, I the cartwheeler want full credit!

Quizlet

···

Is the underlined word a gerund?

Babies like <u>eating</u> items that they encounter on the floor.

Answer: *Yes, it is acting as a noun.*

33

Horizontal-Line Lessons—Hyphens and Dashes, A–Z

"I'm an editor, my mom's an editor, and we saw an article about you," said Ava, a young woman with her hair in braids. "I'm going to tell my mom I saw you!"

At that moment I was sitting at the Grammar Table inside the West Seventy-Second Street subway station, next to a staircase leading to the uptown tracks. "So editing is like a genetic thing in your family," I said.

"Well, it's funny," said Ava. "My dad's an economist. My mom and I are editors. My sister's an English teacher. So he's the odd one out."

"Wow, he's surrounded!" I said.

"Yeah," said Ava. "He complains that there are arguments about em dashes around the dinner table!"

As someone genetically predisposed to em-dash overuse, I enjoyed this home-life description. The various horizontal lines used in text are a popular topic, and not just at Ava's family's dinner table.

Now, before we go even one paragraph further,* this is important: When people talk about em dashes, they are usually referring to what most of us call dashes. The

---

* I *tried* using "farther" here, for the sake of punctilious readers, but I hated it and changed it back. Sorry.

opposite holds true as well. When people refer to dashes, at least in the US, they usually mean em dashes. Em dashes are the longest of the horizontal lines you will see populating professional publications.

I'll explain the other main type of dash (the en dash) shortly, but in the meantime, here is an example of em-dash (a.k.a. dash) use:

> *Being a chocolate taster is hard work—but someone's got to do it!*

There's an unexpected reversal at the dash. It's kind of like an explosive comma.

That was a single em dash, but often em dashes travel in pairs. Pairs may set aside an idea in a dramatic way, as in this example:

> *My friend just got a raise—her first in many years—and promptly moved to Provo.*

When I recite examples such as this one at the Grammar Table, or in my grammar classes, I often do "dash hands" at the places where the dashes appear. Dash hands look a lot like jazz hands, but they are not as well known.

There are also more mundane dramatic applications for em-dash pairs. As one woman told me in Detroit, "Sometimes I use em dashes when there are already a lot of commas." You might see this in a sentence where there is a lot of information bunching up around someone's name. I see examples like this one in my corporate work:

> *Marla Givens, the chief operating officer — and the first woman to hold that position at our firm — was the keynote speaker at the conference last week.*

¶

In Charleston, South Carolina, a family of four talked dashes and hyphens with me. The conversation began slyly, with the dad walking up to me and asking, "What do you use the locative for in Slovak?" I laughed.

Locative is what is known as a grammatical case, and it appears in some languages, but not in English. I had encountered locative before while studying Slavic languages, but I do not know Slovak, nor did my visitor actually expect me to know Slovak.

"I saw the Polish book on your table," said the man, whose name was Frank. "Otherwise I wouldn't have asked." He told me that his grandmother was Slovak and he was taking Slovak Saturday classes with his sister.

"I love that you're doing that," I said. "I love language learning. It's like oil for the mind; it keeps it flexible."

"Yeah, it's supposed to be good for you," said Frank.

"Oh, yeah," I said. "You'll live at least twenty years longer now."

"Wow," said Frank. "I've really got to do my homework then!"

Frank was there that day with his wife and two young adult sons. They had just completed the Turkey Day Run & Gobble Wobble mentioned in an earlier chapter.

"Are you collecting opinions on *any* grammar things?" asked Frank's younger son, whose name was Benjamin.

"Is there something you wanted to offer an opinion on?" I asked.

"I don't know," said Benjamin.

"It says 'Vent,'" noted Frank's other son, Daniel. He was four years older than his brother, but they looked almost like twins.

"Yes, it does," I said. "That has been extremely important in New York, where people like to complain. It comes up a lot there."

"We just read a news article about some grammar things," said Benjamin.

"Oh yeah," said their father. "We read an article about everybody suddenly using the em dash for everything."

"Oh, really?" I said. "Do you do that? Do you em dash—"

"I use it in, like, formal writing," said Benjamin, the younger brother. "Like in English class essays, I use it frequently. Not in texting."

"I just verbed* 'em dash,'" I pointed out. "I don't know

---

* Verbing a noun means taking a noun that does not already double as a verb (as many English nouns do, "cook" being just one example)

if you noticed that, but I said, 'Do you em dash?'" They were subdued in their enthusiasm for my verbal feat.

Daniel, the older brother, said, "I always knew that the computer automatically changed the size of some of the dashes or hyphens or whichever word you use for them, but I always thought it was just because the computer wanted it to look nice. I didn't think there was any actual reason for it. If you showed me a document, I still don't think I would notice how long the dash was."

"Dash length does vary according to fonts," I said, "so sometimes it's a little hard to tell. An em dash in one font will be longer than in another."

"Wait, so is an en dash different than a hyphen?" Daniel asked.

"Yes," I said. "You have three lengths." I drew three lines of different lengths and showed them.

"The hyphen, the shortest one, is for fusing words, or if you break a word at the end of a line," I said. For example:

my first-aid kit

a smooth-talking sales agent

an eight-year-old hacker

You could make a whole industry out of hyphenation in English. Hyphenation is not totally consistent from one dictionary or style guide to the next, and practices

---

and using it as a verb. "I verbed that noun" is an example of verbing the noun "verb."

evolve over time, so whatever you do, don't rely on antique reference materials for your hyphenation advice.

"And then the medium-length line is an en dash," I continued, "but it isn't really used that much. You don't see it in newspapers, for example. When I was working as a freelance journalist, I never used it, but you'll see it in ranges—for instance, time ranges on invitations. Like if you invite someone to a formal event from nine a.m. to five p.m., that could be an en dash."

"Oh," chorused the brothers. They were low-key but seemed supportive of my efforts.

Here's an invitation with an en dash:

> *Please help us celebrate our 98% congenial breakup!*
> **What:** *Breakup bacchanalia, consisting of adult spelling bee followed by drinks and dancing*
> **Where:** *Christy's Urban Bar & Grill*
> **When:** *November 23, 9 p.m.–2 a.m.*

You can also use an en dash in travel routes and scores, if you want to bother, which I usually don't in normal daily life. These examples both contain en dashes.

My Denver–Bozeman flight is late.

The Amityville Alley Cats beat the Carson Crocs 21–7.

There is a complicating factor to be aware of with en dashes: in the UK, en dashes are often used where Americans would use em dashes, so don't be surprised if the dashes in a UK publication look a bit underfed.

"I actually once wrote a poem about the difference between a hyphen and a dash," I told the family. By dash, I meant the em dash. "Do you want to hear it?" I asked. "It's really short."

Benjamin, the younger brother, nodded politely, and I recited my poem:

> *A dash*
> *Is for panache,*
> *A hyphen*
> *Is more triflin'.*

"That's it," I said. No one laughed until I started laughing, and then they laughed too.

"Was it written with any hyphens or dashes in there?" asked Benjamin.

"No," I said. "And now that you've asked, that seems like an oversight." I wrote a note to myself: "Add dash to hyphen/dash poem."

I told him, "Thank you for that. This is going to greatly enhance my literary future."

"In the newspaper article we were reading yesterday, someone said that all the em dashes were turning people's writing into Morse code," said Daniel, the older brother.

"I sometimes work with adults who use an em dash because they don't know what else goes there," I said. "They're like, I don't know if this is a period or a semicolon or a colon, so I'm just going to put a dash."

"Maybe they'll take over," suggested the dad.

I replied, "I feel they won't."

"If there are all these different dashes, then how come there's only one on the keyboard?" asked Daniel. "I feel like in the future people are only going to use one length of dash, because there's just one on the keyboard and they're just going to want to use the easiest thing."

"I'll tell you what," I said. "Let's meet back here in ten years and we can see if that happened." I could hear their mom laughing in the background.

¶

One thing that makes it difficult to discuss dashes and hyphens is that people regularly call hyphens dashes and dashes hyphens. You can tell people they are actually talking about the other thing, and they will correct themselves for about fifteen seconds before reverting to calling them the wrong thing and you're back where you started.*

In Boulder City, Nevada, I discussed dashes with a nice couple. At least I *think* we were talking about dashes.

"Hyphens? They've sort of become like a new punctuation, right?" asked the woman, whose name was Sally. "I don't know. You sort of use it when you don't know what to do."

"It's like a more expressive comma," said her husband, Bill.

"You don't know whether to put a comma or a period, you sort of want to expand the thought, so you put a hyphen there!" finished Sally.

----

* As someone who sometimes absentmindedly calls ellipses colons (come on, they both have dots in them!), I am not throwing stones here.

"That's where I throw it," said Bill. "But I don't really have a rule."

"I don't have any rules in grammar here," said Sally.

"There's a pause here. Does this feel like a comma pause or a hyphen pause?" asked Bill, reenacting his internal punctuation monologue. "It feels like a hyphen pause."

I'm 99.9 percent sure those hyphens were all dashes.

Whatever they were, we then got deep. "I mean, if you really want to get us talking about this, the truth is that grammar terrifies me," said Sally. "I'm so afraid of making a grammatical error in writing that I hate writing. I'm probably not as bad as I think I am, but I'm just afraid of it. I don't want to make mistakes."

"What you're saying is meaningful to me," I said. "I teach business writing to adults, and I often think that it's not so much the writing part that people are hung up on but rather, the concern that they're going to make an error. They don't feel they got a systematic introduction, or maybe they don't remember."

"And I'm judgey when I read something," said Sally.

"You are?" I asked, smiling. She seemed less judgey than self-judgey.

"I am!" she exclaimed. "I'm like, Dude, use a period, or capitalize that, or you misspelled that. I think there's something to be said, at least in business, for taking your time. Make it error-free!"

"I have a feeling you might be extra hard on yourself," I said.

"See?" she said to her husband. "This is turning into a therapy session. This is awesome." She turned back to me and said, "I'm actually a therapist."

"Wait, what?" I asked. "Really?"

"I am," she replied. "But I don't think I've ever had a patient who complained about being traumatized by grammar."

"I would guess that is not the top topic," I said.

"No, not the top one," she said.

¶

I've so far been a little neglectful of the hyphen, the runt of the litter, so let's pay it a little more attention before departing this chapter.

On Venice Beach, a man told me, "Something that's always gotten me, when I'm transitioning from Spanish to English, is the ambiguity of the English language. For example, one time I was driving, and I saw a sign, and it said BIG MATTRESS SALE. And I thought to myself, Well, is this a sale of big mattresses or a big sale of mattresses?"

That ambiguity doesn't happen in Spanish, where word order helps make the meaning clear. In Spanish, you'd see the following:

gran venta de colchones = big sale of mattresses

venta de colchones grandes = sale of big mattresses

The latter meaning—a sale of big mattresses—is highly unlikely, but not long after writing down these examples, I had a nightmare about a scarily huge octuple-size mattress, so be careful about the grammar thoughts you think before bed.

The man told me, "It becomes difficult at work when

you're trying to follow instructions from your boss and you're like, 'Do you mean this, or do you mean that?' It's like, they're both equally valid."

People often use hyphenation to solve clarity problems in English. If it were a sale of big mattresses—which it wouldn't be, but let's just say it was—then you could do this:

a big-mattress sale

That tells you that "big" refers to the mattresses and not to the sale. However, because that is so unlikely a meaning, people would most likely conclude that you didn't know how to hyphenate and assume that it was a big sale of normal-size mattresses anyway!

Quizlet

Identify each of the three horizontal lines in the title of this chapter: "Horizontal-Line Lessons— Hyphens and Dashes, A–Z."

Answer: *The first is a hyphen, the second is an em dash, and the third is an en dash.*

34

Good Fun with Bad Words

In Maryland, our twenty-ninth state, I set up the Grammar Table in downtown Annapolis. I had been talking to a man in a blue vest for a while before he finally convinced his reluctant friend, a man in a black jacket, to come over and talk to me.

"She wants to find out if you have any questions about grammar," the man in the vest told his friend. "Or complaints."

"Well, my only complaint is that people have taken today's English and thrown it to the ground, personally," said his friend in the black jacket. "The words that I hear used today are not the ones that I heard used in grade school."

He elaborated. "The main word begins with an *f* and ends with a *k*. That seems to be part of the vernacular. Which I don't really appreciate. Then again, I was raised in Catholic schools."

"I keep it clean here," I said.

That was a reflexive response, and I'm afraid it does not hold up under scrutiny.

On a street two hundred thirty miles away in Morgantown, West Virginia, a young man in a knit cap was not philosophically aligned with the man in Annapolis.

"Curse words should just be accepted in society," he told me.

"They *are* pretty accepted, don't you think?" I asked.

"I don't know," said the young man, whose name was Philip. He lived in Wheeling, about seventy-five miles from Morgantown.

"Where do you get restricted from using them?" I asked.

"Obviously like around younger people, to make it seem like we don't say these words, but as a matter of fact, we do say these words," said Philip.

"So you feel there's misrepresentation of what's actually happening," I said.

"Yeah," he said.

"I have been known to use a few words," I said, "but I don't use them around children, and I try not to impose them on people I don't know, because people have different relationships with them."

"True," said Philip. "Definitely."

"Oh, you might find this interesting," I said. "There's something called an infix. Have you heard of a suffix before?* An infix is when you stick something in the middle of a word, and so you can use a curse word as an infix—like 'absofuckinglutely.' That's an infix. You stick it right in the middle of the word."

"Give it some emphasis!" said Philip with enthusiasm.

"That's right," I said. "So that's an infix for you. That's my grammar offering for the day."

"Heck, yeah!" said Philip. He fist-bumped me. "You learn something every day!"

---

* If you know prefixes, infixes, and suffixes, you are pretty well fixed for anything. (C'mon, don't groan at me; that was funny.)

I thanked him for visiting the Grammar Table.

"No problem," said Philip. "You guys are doing something cool. I learned something. I'm going to use that!"

Quizlet

....

A fascinating aspect of the f-word is its grammatical versatility: it can be used as quite a few parts of speech. What part of speech is each instance in the sentence below?

> "Can you please stop being so f***ing annoying about the f***ing tires?"

Answer: *"F***ing" #1 is an adverb modifying the adjective "annoying," and "f***ing" #2 is an adjective modifying the noun "tires." (In case you are wondering why I'm suddenly using asterisks instead of writing out the actual word, it's just that this was a lot of f-bombs for one tiny quizlet.)*

. . .

My main experience with the ellipsis (. . .) is as a way to mark material deleted from a quotation. I mostly used it when I was student in the 1980s, in research papers. I have little need for it now, except maybe occasionally to indicate suspense in text messages to friends. Plenty of people like it and use it, but they don't always know what it means when *other* people use it.

The versatility of the ellipsis in casual use means that it remains mysterious, sometimes even ominous, for some ellipsis recipients.

"I have a question about the way people end sentences with the dot dot dot," said a singer and bandleader in New Orleans.

She told me, "In my opinion, I mean I don't want to embarrass myself, and it's been a while, but communications was my major in college, and my debate is always dot dot dot. To me, it means a pause. And I'm always wondering, what was the pause for? No one can ever give a definitive answer to what it means if I text you 'Hey! I'm on my way to lunch,' and your response is, 'okay dot dot dot.'"

Let's see what that looks like:

Hey! I'm on my way to lunch

ok...

"Well, the context is everything with this," I said. "Do you know the name for this?"

"Period period period," replied the singer.

"I'm going to give you the formal name," I said, "because it sounds kind of fancy: ellipsis." I wrote it down and showed her.

"Ellipsis!" she exclaimed.

"The meaning depends partly on the context," I said. "Are we talking about workplace contexts, or just for texting?"

"Work and then in general, because I've received those dots in both contexts, from business email to friends responding socially," said the singer.

"Right," I said. "With friends, I'd say anything is fair game, but for work, I don't really use it unless I'm quoting something and leaving words out in the middle of a quotation."

I pondered her example. "If I saw 'okay dot dot dot' from someone about meeting me for lunch, I would think that sounded a little bit like the person didn't want to meet me. How do you read it?"

"Well, I'm a likable person," she said, "so I would hope that that's not what it means."

"So do you use it, or someone uses it with you?" I asked.

"I use it, and when I use it, I know where I'm coming from," said the singer. "It means that I don't understand everything, or it's a pause for me. Like someone says, 'Oh, let's go have pizza,' but actually I think I might want to have some Indian food. In my mind, it's an 'okay dot dot dot.'" She bobbled her head and rolled her eyes as she said that last bit, and I laughed.

"Right," I said. "So that's not so enthusiastic, right?"

"No," she said.

"Yeah," I said. "That's how I would read it."

"That's how I receive it," she said. "So ellipsis."

¶

A week later, the ellipsis had once again been demoted to a state of anonymity.

"What's the little triple dot called?" asked Jason in Decatur, Alabama.

How delightful to be asked again! I never run out of zest for this question. "It's good to know the names of these things," I told him, "because then at a party, if you run out of things to talk about, you can say, 'So what are your feelings about the . . . ?'"

"Dot dot dot," said Jason.

"The dot dot dot," I said. "But you can use the fancy name and the person will be like, I don't know, because I don't know what that is. This is called an ellipsis."

"Ah-lipsis," said Jason.

"Yeah," I said, holding up the page where I had written it.

"Wait," he said. "I thought an ellipsis was the little . . ." He drew an ellipse in the air with his finger.

"That's the ellipse in math," I said. "Ellipsis does sound kind of mathematical. It sounds scary. So anyway, as I was saying, at a party if you run out of things to say, you can ask, 'So what are your feelings about the use of ellipses?'"

"Ellipses," said Jason.

"That's the plural," I said. "I'll write that down, too."

"I feel like I don't normally talk to girls that are smart enough to know what that is," said Jason.

"You know what?" I said. "Maybe it's because you haven't brought it up before, and you'll find something out."

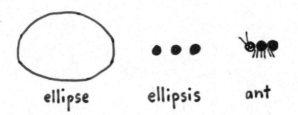

ellipse   ellipsis   ant

"You're probably right," said Jason. "I need to find some girls that know what an ellipses is—" Here he paused and self-corrected: "—sorry, know what ellipses are."

"That was good!" I said. "So do you want to keep this as a souvenir of your visit?"

"Absolutely," said Jason. "Also because you have fantastic handwriting."

"She does," said his friend, Jack.

"Wait, you haven't seen my signature," I said. "I'm going to sign it, because I want you to appreciate my cursive."

"Oh my lord, please do," said Jason. "Yes." They both bent over the table.

"Oh my god," said Jack. "You should sign baseballs."

Quizlet

• •

What is the number of letters in the plural of "ellipsis" minus the number of letters in the plural of "ellipse"?

Answer: *Zero, because the plural is "ellipses" for both. They are pronounced differently, however: ellip-sez for the math concept and ellipseez for the three dots.*

36

Where's That Preposition At?

In Florida, a woman told me, "My uncle, who always corrects people, really hates when people say, 'Where's the party at?' or something ending in 'at.' He'll actually stop a conversation and say something like, 'Oh, I hate when people do that,' and you're like, 'Uh.'"

Prepositions arouse strong emotions in many Americans. There is far too much preposition agitation nationally, I feel. I do not share that agitation. Agitation is not good for blood pressure.

In Verdi Square one day, a woman carrying a big white shopping bag stopped about twenty feet away from me and stared.

She started laughing. "I've never seen a Grammar Table," she said, adding, "The people who need it most aren't going to visit."

She came closer. "Well, you might be surprised," I said. "A lot of people who are confused about something will come up to me."

"Oh, will they?" said the woman. "Okay."

"There's a healthy percentage of that, and then there are also people who complain about other people's grammar," I said.

The woman nodded vigorously. "Uh-huh," she said.

"And I'm sure I make many errors of my own, but my pet peeve is sentences ending in prepositions." She did a sort of body wave to demonstrate her distaste.

"Mm-hmm," I said.

"You don't end a sentence in a preposition," she said. "And I see it all the time, among people who should know better. They've been to college, they've even been to graduate school, and they don't know how to use a preposition. So, good luck!"

And she was gone.

¶

Were you told in school not to end with prepositions? I seem to have picked that idea up in junior high or high school, though I don't recall all the details of those lessons. For a while as a young adult, I made an effort to avoid writing sentences with concluding prepositions and consequently ended up with some awkward and convoluted sentences.

While concluding prepositions can sometimes be a style issue, they are not a grammatical error, as so many Americans were taught in school. They are instead a natural feature of English as it is constructed and used.

Sometimes ending in a preposition sounds lousy in writing. Here is an example:

That's the book I just finished reading the first half of.

Such a sentence could surely erupt spontaneously in speech, and it would be well understood if it did. In writing, if the surrounding context permitted, I would want to rewrite the sentence, possibly like this:

I just finished reading the first half of that book.

Or I might do any number of other things to make the idea fit my paragraph, my intended meaning, and my desire for elegant sentence construction.

Here are several sentences ending with prepositions (left) and attempted revisions without ending prepositions (right):

She wouldn't tell me where she's <u>from</u>.	She wouldn't tell me <u>from where</u> she is.
What was his mother <u>like</u>?	<u>Like what</u> was his mother?
I don't have anyone I can talk <u>to</u>.	I don't have anyone <u>to whom</u> I can talk.
That's what friends are <u>for</u>.	That's <u>for what</u> friends are.
Nathaniel isn't sure where they're <u>from</u>.	Nathaniel isn't sure <u>from where</u> they are.
What are you <u>up to</u>?	<u>Up to</u> what are you?

Every sentence on the left is fine as is. The column on the right is what can happen to you if you don't accept this basic fact of English. English was built for the left column. That you can't end with a preposition is a grammar myth that had some stature for a time, but it has been torn to pieces a bazillion times, for generations now, in reputable usage books, in articles, and all over the internet. Prohibitions from childhood, unfortunately, are like grass stains on white pants: they resist efforts to scrub them away.

¶

"I love it," said Lara, a petite brunette in Detroit, as she surveyed the Grammar Table. "My kids all went to public school, so— Aaagh! What was that, like whole-language learning?" I gathered she was not keen on whatever grammar-lite approach they had had in school.

"You definitely need a Grammar Table postcard," I said, handing her one.

"So what are you?" asked Lara. "What is going on here?"

I explained myself. She tried to think of a grammar question. "I seriously never end a sentence with a preposition," she told me.

"That is a superstition about English," I told her. "Let me give you an example."

"That was an imperative sentence, right?" asked Lara.

"It was!" I exclaimed.

"Ha-*haaaaa,* ha-ha, ha-ha!" Lara raised her arms triumphantly in the air. "Let me tell you one more thing," she continued. "I was a French major in college, so I know what subjunctive is all about."

"I have a whole book on French subjunctive on my bookshelf!" I told her.

"Loved it!" Lara said. "You know, when you start it, you're just like, What the hell is this?" She did a robot imitation to demonstrate the absurd and alien nature of subjunctive. "'This is not real.' It's like, yeah, it is; it's just that nobody's using it in English."*

"Okay, I have a sentence for you that ends in a preposition," I told her. "What if you were writing an email to someone and you typed, 'That's the book I was telling you about'? Would you say to yourself, I can't end in a preposition and change it to 'That is the book about which I was telling you'? Would you notice?"

"If it were a friend, I would end in 'about,'" said Lara. "If it were not a friend, I would rewrite the sentence. I would say something like 'Here's that book we discussed last week.'" She leaped sideways and made a triumphant beeping sound upon landing.

"I'm just going to show you," I said, "if you don't mind spending another moment with me."

"I'm actually working," said Lara. She pointed off into the distance. "That's my office over there, so I'm on the clock!"

I pulled out a reference book to show her what it said about prepositions. "This is one of a bunch of things people were taught in school that aren't actually true," I said.

"Okay, yes," said Lara. "Which makes sense."

---

* I was not going to be tempted away from prepositions by seductive subjunctive references, but here is an example of subjunctive in English, in case you would like one: "It is essential that she <u>attend</u> this meeting." In this sentence, the phrase "it is essential that" triggers subjunctive in the verb that follows. The regular present tense would be "she attends," so the difference is a dropped *s* in the subjunctive. Not all English speakers use subjunctive in this spot, but it is automatic for me.

"I was taught some of them," I said, "and actually many people in our age range were taught that stuff."

"So young!" said Lara.

"Exactly," I said, and we laughed with the wisdom and maturity of our youthful years.

I had the reference book open to the preposition section. "Do you want to take a picture of this?" I asked.

"Well, Sister Mary Anne's probably dead now, but . . ." she said, and snapped a picture anyway.

¶

"Grammar is one of my favorite things," said a woman in a yellow vest in Morgantown, West Virginia.

"It is?" I asked.

"Oh yeah," she said. "Since my sixth-grade English teacher."

"She hates it when I end with a preposition," said her companion, who was wearing a yellow cap. He seemed quite cheerful about it.

"But he doesn't do it in writing," she said. "He only does it verbally, but it drives me crazy."

"You never do it yourself in speech?" I asked her.

"Oh, I do, but—" she said.

"It's pretty rare," said the man. "I'll give her credit. It's pretty rare."

"Because it grates on me," she said.

I asked, "So were you taught that back in the day?"

"Yeah," she said. She told me about her elementary school teacher in southern West Virginia. "He was an excellent teacher," she said. "He passed a couple of years ago but is very well remembered at the local high school."

He made them memorize prepositions, she said.

"About, above, across, after, against," she recited. "It's still up there."

"When I was teaching," said her companion, "I used to be pretty good at grading papers, but I enjoyed running them through her, because what she learned from her teacher helped her pick out some things I missed."

"And I'm by no means perfect," she said. "Because I've gone into computers as a profession, so it's not something that I am professional at, but— See? 'At'!"

"It doesn't bother me," I said.*

"At which I am professional!" she said, laughing.

¶

Needless grammar guilt crossed state lines into Charleston, South Carolina, where a woman stopped at the Grammar Table and told me, "I'm a retired English teacher and newspaper editor."

In fact, she and her husband, who was there with her, had both been English teachers in Alaska.

"That's where we retired from," explained the woman, who then promptly added, "I'm sorry. I just ended in a preposition."

"Oh, that's actually a myth anyway," I said.

"Yeah, it is," said her husband.

"It is?" asked the woman.

"It is," I said. "It's well documented. I have ammunition here." I gestured at the books on the Grammar Table.

---

* Try saying "It's something at which I'm not professional" to people you know and see to how many parties you are invited.

"Yeah," her husband agreed.

"I think it needs an object,"* said the woman.

"But then why did you want to do it?" I asked. "Because it's natural."

"Because I was raised wrong," she said, and we all laughed.

Prepositions came up again about forty minutes later in the same location.

"What is this about?"† asked Shannon, who had red hair and was accompanied by two women. They had all just finished the Thanksgiving Day five-kilometer race.

"I answer grammar questions," I said. "Do you have any?"

Shannon and her companions laughed. "I don't off-hand, but—" started Shannon.

"Is it proper to ask a question with the last word being 'at'?" interrupted a woman with long brown hair. Her name was Amelia.

"Where's Mom at?" offered Shannon as an example.

"Do you argue about this or something?" I asked.

"Yes!" said Amelia. "I'll say, for example, 'Where's my husband at?'"

"Behind the 'at'!" replied Shannon.

"Every time," said Amelia. "I could be across the room. Across the street. If she hears me sayin' 'at' at the

---

* Her sentence does actually have an object: "where." And you could spend a lot of fruitless time trying to rearrange perfectly natural English sentences for no reason—or you could use that time to go for a walk, or eat a banana, or read a page of a book, or pick up a dirty sock lying on the floor.

† Shannon's question ended, felicitously, in a preposition: "about."

end of the sentence, it's always"—here she feigned long-distance bellowing—"*Behind the 'at'!*"

"Okay, so—" I began.

"So is it proper?" interrupted Amelia.

"'Proper' is a loaded word," I said, which caused everyone to laugh. "I find it charming, but I do encounter a ton of people who say, 'Don't stick that unnecessary "at" on the end.'"

In other words, the complaint is that this does the job:

Where's my husband?

"So it can be said, and you think it's charming, but should it be said?" said Amelia.

"I think about language pragmatically," I said, "so if I feel that something I do is going to bug people, I consider adjusting it."

"You lost me at 'pragmatically,'" said Amelia. Shannon guffawed.

"Practically," I explained. "Sorry about that."

"I'm not going to be an English major anytime soon," said Amelia.

We chatted a bit longer, and when we parted ways, Shannon shook my hand and said, "Good luck on your travels."

"Come on, dear!" Amelia yelled to her husband cheerfully. "Where you at?"

Quizlet

···

How many prepositions are there in the following sentence?

> Marge told me about the puppy she got for Ricky at the farm near the intersection of Route 2 and Ebbet Lane.

Answer: *Five. Marge told me <u>about</u> the puppy she got <u>for</u> Ricky <u>at</u> the farm <u>near</u> the intersection <u>of</u> Route 2 and Ebbet Lane.*

37

Faces and Facets of "They"

"I have a lot of beefs about grammar," said an elegantly dressed older man in a seersucker suit in Salt Lake City. "My biggest one is the use of a plural pronoun to achieve gender neutrality."

"So, no singular 'they' for you," I said.

"No," he said.

"Do you have another solution?" I asked.

"Oh no," he said. "There's no word in English for it. My solution is 'he' and 'him.'"

"They" and "their" have a long history of singular use in English writing and speech, in contexts ranging from mundane daily speech to the most celebrated literature, and a long history of being needed and desired for singular use, regardless of arguments that emerged in the eighteenth century against this usage—arguments that influenced my own schooling a couple of centuries later. Pronouns such as "somebody," "everyone," and "nobody" —all of them singular—caused us poor kids to produce pretzel-like writing in their wake as we struggled to stay singular. For example:

Everyone should bring his or her eclipse glasses or he or she might get retinal burns.

Today you see "they" in print to refer to a person whose gender identity is nonbinary or whose gender is unknown. Top news publications use a person's requested pronouns, and so do I. "He or she" and "his or her" are no longer broadly acceptable, as they are not inclusive, so I have dropped that practice completely. But the "everyone"/"their" struggle continues for many.

Two days and 333 miles after my Salt Lake City exchange, I encountered another pronoun philosopher, this time on the streets of Steamboat Springs, Colorado, where I set up on the main drag downtown. This location is memorable to me as the only stop in the country where the Grammar Table was passed at regular intervals by trucks carrying long loads of long logs.

"I was a copywriter," said a loquacious blond artist who approached me. "We break every rule, and we're always trying not to say 'he.' So you do weird tricks to try not to make it always masculine."

I had a similar experience as a freelance writer. In the late 1990s, I sometimes wrote case studies for banking and technology companies, and I would want to talk about a singular customer experience, but then what? You refer to the person as "the customer" the first time, but what happens when you switch to a pronoun? I couldn't keep using "he or she," "him or her," "his or hers," and so on. And no way would anyone doing my job, even long ago in the 1990s, have wanted to use just "he" as a generic stand-in for all possible versions of humanity. Whatever your pronoun philosophy, it's simply bad business.

But "they" and "their" were not broadly accepted in this role in print at that point, so I acquired tricks: making the subject plural where possible, or replacing the possessive adjectives "his or her" with an article if I could.

Ugh: *The customer should bring his or her receipt to the bank teller.*

Alternative #1: *Customers should bring their receipts to the bank teller.*

Alternative #2: *The customer should bring the receipt to the bank teller.*

It was a nightmare.

Those tricks solve a lot of challenges, but not all, because often I didn't want to, or couldn't, make my singulars plural, and there were also many cases where I couldn't replace a possessive such as "his or her" with an article. The sentence "The customer touched *a* nose" does not convey the same idea as "The customer touched *his* nose." The latter might result in the offer of a tissue; the former might result in expulsion from the bank branch.

What I wanted was this:

The customer should bring their receipt to the bank teller.

It's what I would probably have *said,* after all. But in professional writing it was not generally accepted, on the principle that "customer" was singular and "their" was plural. Even today, it remains unacceptable to many, and whatever you decide as a writer, the reader may or may not be with you.

Increasingly, though, respected publications such as the *Washington Post* and *The Associated Press Stylebook* accept "they" and its associated forms in this singular gender-neutral role. Here is The Associated Press's current position: "'They'/'them'/'their' is acceptable in limited cases as a singular and/or gender-neutral pronoun, when alternative wording is overly awkward or clumsy. However, rewording usually is possible and always is preferable. Clarity is a top priority; gender-neutral use of a singular 'they' is unfamiliar to many readers." The message isn't that you should do it often. It's more like "It can be done."

¶

Let's visit a few "they" conversations from the Grammar Table. In downtown South Bend, Indiana, amid loud construction, a sixtyish woman in a white T-shirt said, "Tell me what you think about the matter of third-person singular pronouns."

The drilling got louder. It was so loud we had to shout.

"Are you talking about, for example, if I say 'Everyone should bring their whatever,' versus 'his,' 'her,' or 'his or her whatever'?" I yelled.

"Yes," yelled the woman, whose name was Hannah.

"That's *my* question," yelled an orange-capped man standing nearby. He was of a similar age.

"In speech," I yelled, "it's just fact that for a long time people have said 'their' in this case, and then for writing they often put 'his or her,' or 'his.'"

"Yeah," yelled Hannah.

"It's very awkward to do 'his or her,' and I usually refused to do 'his,'" I yelled. "If I'm writing a blog entry, I would use 'their' without worrying about it. But for formal writing, I still have concerns, because it's about audience, and not everyone's accustomed to it. What is your position on it?"

"I am not enthusiastic about using 'they' or 'their,'

singular, in normal writing," yelled Hannah. "However, I think there is a need for a gender-neutral singular pronoun. And in fact, if you google it, you know that there have been a lot of possibilities proposed down through the years. And I think people are just sliding in a lazy and unimaginative way to using 'they' and 'their.'"

"But it already exists," I yelled. "We don't have to make up a new word. It's been in use for a long time, so why not have that be the word? Because, for example, in Spanish you would use the word *su* to mean 'his,' 'her,' 'their,' so it could be like our equivalent of *su*."

su familia	her family
su familia	his family
su familia	their family
su familia	your family (formal)

"Well, the option that I like best is simply using the letter *e*," yelled Hannah.

"Oh, so you want a new one," I yelled.

"Well, it's not new," yelled Hannah. "And various options have been proposed since the 1800s."

"So you're open to the idea of a word that's not in common use being introduced into the language," I yelled.

"Yeah," yelled Hannah. "Actually, in Sweden they have done that. They use the word *hen*!"

"Right!" I yelled.

The man with the orange cap yelled, "I like your point. You must not like the *s* slash 'he.'" He made a face about the awfulness of "s/he."

"It is just awkward," yelled Hannah. "It's an effort to deal with the issue, because I think everyone recognizes that there is a need for a singular pronoun. I realize I'm fighting a lonely battle."

It's not lonely, though. Many people are interested, and they want to get it right.

¶

The topic was important to the ponytailed girl in the group of high school students in Chicago with whom I previously discussed octopuses, octopi, and octopodes.

"They have a bunch of errors on the SATs," she said, "and it's really annoying. I found errors on practice SATs I've taken."

"Do you have any examples?" I asked.

"I have an example from an SAT, but I don't know if this is, like, technical," she said. "So like on a lot of the writing and English sections, they say that using 'they' and 'them' as, like, a singular pronoun is, like, incorrect."

"Right," I said.

"Which I understand conventionally—like, it is," said the girl with the ponytail. "But I think in this day and age they should change it so that 'they' and 'them' can be used as, like, a correct singular pronoun for certain situations in literature and, like, to make it more normal in, like, our society."

"Awesome," said another student.

"Well, there's also historical precedent," said a cute boy in stripes, who then proceeded to tell us about early grammar books.

"Is this a summer program for smart kids?" I asked.

¶

In Richmond, Virginia, a woman named Brooke came by with a cute baby in a blue hoodie, a dog, and her husband, Stan.

"What are you doing?" she asked.

"Answering grammar questions," I said.

"Awesome," said Brooke.

"Taking complaints," I added.

"Taking complaints?" said Brooke. "I love it."

"You should share your joke from earlier today," said Stan.

"Okay," said Brooke. "What did the thesaurus eat for breakfast?" she asked me.

"I don't know," I said. "What?"

"Synonym rolls," said Brooke. I put my head in my hands, and the couple laughed.

I learned that Brooke used to teach English as a foreign language and now worked placing teachers in high-need urban schools. Brooke and Stan had met in China, where they were Peace Corps volunteers teaching English to Chinese students.

Brooke asked, "What is your feeling on the APA's recent endorsement of 'their' instead of 'his or her'?" APA stands for American Psychological Association, and their style guide, *Publication Manual of the American Psychological Association,* is used heavily in the social sciences.

"To use 'their' as a gender-neutral singular?" I asked. "My philosophy is that if you can write around it elegantly, go for it, but if you can't, it's fine."

"Right," said Brooke.

"I write around it a lot," I said as their dog wiggled. "Your dog is so enthusiastic," I observed.

"He loves people," said Brooke. "He loves to be out. He's very friendly."

"Do you have a feeling about it?" I asked.

"I have very mixed feelings about it," said Brooke. "Prescriptively, it kind of hurts me to use it. But I understand the need for inclusivity. There are some people who use 'them,' 'their,' 'theirs' as their pronouns. So to honor that inclusivity and get with the times, I see that as not a bad thing, but it is hard for me to transition to using that when I know prescriptively that's not the right thing."

One thing to be aware of grammatically is that singular "they" can create antecedent complications that are the writer's responsibility to resolve. Not long ago, I read a news story about the engagement of a nonbinary person who used the pronoun "they." The story contained a pronoun-reference problem that I have replicated in this example, in which a nonbinary person with the surname Carter is about to be proposed to:

> *Carter and Jones spent the morning roaming Central Park and appearing smitten with each other. Carter did not know what awaited <u>them</u> later that day.*

In this example, "them" is intended to refer to Carter rather than to Carter and Jones, but that isn't clear. The example can easily be rewritten to avoid antecedent confusion. One option is this:

Carter and Jones spent the morning roaming Central Park and appearing smitten with each other. Carter did not know what would transpire later that day.

Throughout our pronoun discussion, Brooke and Stan's dog had been enthusiastically supervising the goings-on at the Grammar Table.

"Do the dog and the baby get along?" I asked.

"They do," said Brooke, without conviction. "The baby loves the dog more than the dog loves the baby. The baby loves to be around the dog, but the dog likes the baby in his own time and space."

"The dog used to be the baby," said Stan. "Now the dog is not the baby. The baby is the baby."

Quizlet

. . . .

What are the antecedents for the underlined pronouns in the following sentence?

> Does anyone have <u>their</u> employee badge with <u>them</u>?

Answer: *"Anyone," which is singular, is the antecedent for both. This is an example of effective — and incredibly common — singular "their" and "them" use. What would sound absurd while simultaneously being noninclusive is this: "Does anyone have his or her employee badge with him or her?"*

38

The Precarious Case of
the Pronoun Case

To he or not to he: that is the question.

On Venice Beach, I met a middle-aged writer who told me, "For a while, I was dating a woman who kept saying things like 'him and I.' I corrected her a couple of times, and she was really defensive. She didn't want to be corrected. She was a teacher, so I kept thinking, she's exposing a whole new generation to bad grammar."

"Is it that she didn't want to be corrected, or she just didn't want to be wrong?" I asked.

"Both," he said. "For the sake of the relationship, it was smart to shut up."

Pronouns inspire passion and can even lead to break-ups.

In Verdi Square, a Grammar Table visitor told me that once at a therapy session, her therapist said "between you and I."

"Oh, that's hard," I said. "Did you manage to get past it?"

"No!" she said. "At my next appointment, I told her, 'I don't think I can see you anymore.'"

¶

In snowy Santa Fe on Christmas Day, I encountered similar pronoun passion in another visitor, a gray-haired man in a black leather jacket.

"I'm an English teacher," he said, "and I have a grammar question."

"I'm listening," I said.

"I see professional people on television say 'me and my wife,' 'me and my family,'" he said.

"You mean at the beginning of a sentence," I said.

"Yes," he said. "Why is this happening? It's becoming a habit."

"It's to torture you," I said.

"It does!" he said. "I wince every time it happens!"

"What about this one?" I asked. "'He gave the book to Marshall and I.'"

"Right," he said. "That's also wrong. The objective instead of the nominative."

Oh, he was good.

I replied, "But that colloquial 'me and someone,' that's very common. I don't do it personally."

"Well, it's gotten out of hand," he said.

"I can file an official complaint for you," I told him.

"Yes, please," he said. "The name's Robert Parker. Professional people are doing it."

¶

At Middlebury College in Vermont, I talked pronouns with Andrea, the former academic editor, and her husband, Mike. You may recall Mike from Chapter 21 as the husband whose stuff was usually pretty jazzy.

"The thing that confuses me," said Andrea, "is when I

answer the phone and someone says, 'Is Andrea there?' I think it's correct to say 'This is she.'"

I've said "This is she" plenty of times in my life. The reason for "she" rather than "her" is the verb "is": I was taught, after a verb of being, to preserve the subject form. It's a convention many of us were taught, but the intersection between that taught prescription and our linguistic instincts does not strike me as high in English—especially not when you are talking about the first-person singular.

"If I rang someone's doorbell and they were expecting me," I told Andrea and Mike, "and they called down and asked 'Who is it?' there's no way on earth that I'm going to say 'It is I.'"

"Not unless you were wearing a Shakespearean outfit or something," said Mike.

"I would say 'It's me,'" I said. "But I still use 'This is she' on the phone."

Those are basically the same construction, but in one I use a subject pronoun—"she"—whereas in the other I use "me," an object pronoun. The first-person singular "It is I" sounds extra terrible to many people even as they bemoan the incorrectness of "It is me" or "It's me."

"Saying 'This is she' doesn't feel unnatural to me," I said.

"It doesn't feel as pompous as 'It is I,'" said Andrea.

"No," I said. "But often I just say 'This is Ellen' and skip the whole pronoun thing."

"Yeah!" Mike was enthusiastic. "That's what I try to do: avoid it."

I added, "I definitely won't say 'This is her.' But I will say 'It's me.' Like when I call my husband and he picks up the phone, I don't say 'It is I, your wife!'"

"Because then he'd have to say 'Huzzah!'" said Mike.

Here's a thought. The French for "It is I/me" is not *C'est je* (*je* is "I") but rather *C'est moi*. The word *moi* is part of a special class of pronouns in French called "stressed pronouns." Depending on context, *moi* can be translated into English as "I" or "me." Therefore, for people who are bothered by "It's me," my proposal is that we simply view using "me" in that position as a classy French affectation.

¶

In Iowa City, Leo—one of the three young people who in an earlier chapter begged for the beg—said, "My biggest pet peeve is when people are telling a story and they say, like, 'Me and this person.' It's 'This person and I.'"

"Do you hear that a lot?" I asked.

"All the time," said Leo.

"Okay, but 'Joe sent Jack and . . .'" I stopped.

"I," said Leo.

"Are you sure?" I asked.

"Yes," said Leo. "'Joe sent Jack and I the book.'"

"What do you think?" I asked the others.

"'Joe sent Jack and I,'" agreed Alexis, the sole woman in the trio.

"No, 'and me,'" said Dustin. He was the one with the grammarian grandpa.

"'Jack and I' sounds normal, though," said Alexis.

"No, it's 'me,'" said Dustin. "It's 'me' because you wouldn't say 'Joe sent I a book.' You say—"

"'Joe sent me the book,'" said Alexis.

"Because Jack's there, it's 'Jack and I,'" said Leo.

"If there were no Jack there, what would you say?" I asked.

"It'd be 'me'!" said Leo.

"And it's the same thing with Jack there," I said. That caused an instant hubbub.

Dustin said, "I know when to use it because my grandpa went psycho on me."

"Is your grandpa still around?" I asked.

"Yes, he is," said Dustin.

"Can you thank him for me?" I asked.

"Yes, I will," said Dustin, to laughter from his friends.

"You can thank him yourself right here," said Brandt.

"Thanks, Grandpa!" Dustin yelled into the camera.

"It depends whether it's an object or a subject," I said. "Every night before you go to bed for a week, I want you to say 'Joe sent Jack and me the book.'"

"It sounds wrong," said Leo.

"But it's right!" said Dustin.

"It sounds wrong partly because so many people say it wrong," I said. "It's 'The store fell on Jack and—'"

"I," said Leo.

"No," I said. "Me. 'The store fell on me.'"

"Pretend Jack isn't there," said Dustin. "You wouldn't say 'The store fell on I.'"

"Jack doesn't change it," I said. "Jack's also crushed by the store."

"Jack is now dead," Leo said. "They're both just dead."

"Yeah, you and Jack both get it," I said. "It's over for both of you."

❡

Pronoun tribulations come up frequently in Verdi Square in New York City.

"The worst problem is when someone uses 'I' instead of 'me,'" said a musician named Cara, who stopped by on her way to a sound check for a performance at the nearby Beacon Theatre. "My Grandma Hall always said, 'People think "me" is a dirty word.' No! Use 'me'!"

"They do," I said. "That's true."

"I'd rather have them say 'Me and him went to the store' any day than saying 'Please give that to Linda or I,'" she said.

"I agree with you on that," I said.

"I mean, it's so stuck up," she said. "It's like, 'Oh, I'm speaking correctly. I'm going to say "I." Please hand that to I.'" She walked off.

On another day there, I spoke to a woman named Helen. "I would love to bring my granddaughter and her mother, my daughter-in-law, to you about 'Me and him went,'" she told me. "I die when I hear that from my daughter-in-law."

"Does she say 'John and I' at the end of a sentence?" I asked.

"Yes, the 'I' at the end of the sentence," Helen replied. "And I say 'No, it's "me."' And she ignores me and goes ahead, and I say to myself, 'Shut up.'"

I laughed.

"You know?" she continued. "There's nothing to be gained here. I'll just end up with a bad relationship with my daughter-in-law. So I stopped."

"So much language education comes from the parents," I said.

"Yeah, exactly," said Helen. "But I think to myself, Don't do this to my granddaughter, you know? And my son—my daughter-in-law's husband—he loves to speak down. He'll say 'Me and her went,' and I say 'Stop it!' He knows how to speak correctly. He does that because he wants to sound like a Brooklynite—you know, where he was born."

¶

On Venice Beach, I talked for quite a while to that nice family of five from Connecticut: the one with the mom, the two boys, a smaller girl, and the dad, Peter, who in an earlier chapter was seen angling to sit on *my* side of the Grammar Table. I will refer to him from now on as Intense Grammar Dad—or Grammar Dad for short.

Grammar Dad told me they had been working on this sentence:

Dave and I went to the park.

"Right?" he said to the children. "Not 'me and Dave.'"

Grammar Dad wasn't done with them, though; he had a second sentence at the ready for kid quizzing:

Does anyone want to go to the park with Dave and _____?

"What would you say?" he asked them.

"Dave and I?" asked the middle child, who had red hair.

"You would say, 'Does anyone want to go to the park with Dave and I?'" asked Grammar Dad. "Is that what you all would say?" He began polling the children individually.

"I'd say 'Dave and me,'" said the youngest child, a little girl in a bathing suit.

"Does anyone else want to go to the park with Dave and me?" Grammar Dad asked the boys. "Or do you want to go to the park with Dave and I?"

"Dave and I," said the middle child, semi-confidently.

"'Dave and I' is right," agreed the oldest son. It was the boys against the girl.

"Well, kids," said Grammar Dad. He looked at me. "Judge?"

"Your sister's right," I said to the boys.

"That's where you use 'me,'" said their mother.

"So how many times have I told you, you take out . . . So what's the trick?" said Intense Grammar Dad. "You take out 'Dave and.'"

"And that leaves 'Do you want to go to the park with I?'" said their mom.

"Right," I said.

"Got that?" asked Grammar Dad.

"Even if you put three hundred names in there, it would still be 'me' at the end," I said. "But it would also be a really bad sentence." Here's an example with somewhat less* than three hundred names, just so you can have the flavor of the experience.

Does anyone want to go to the park with Dave, Sue, Hans, Charlotte, Tonya, Roberta, Mark, Phineas, Suzanne, Sandy, Albert, Jonas, Trixie, Janet, Sophie, and me?

---

* This "less" was a conscious choice. See Chapter 26.

"So cool," said the mom.

"This is great," said Grammar Dad. "I'm going to set up an I AGREE WITH YOU table right next to you."

¶

In Salt Lake City, a woman in a turquoise sweater told me, "Last night at Back to School night, my kid's language arts teacher said, 'You can give it to myself.' And I'm like, Ohhhh."

She made a face of grammar horror and said, "I feel like you only use 'myself' if you have just used 'I' or 'me.'"

"Right," I said.

"I wouldn't say 'Thank you for giving that to myself.' I would say 'Thank you for giving that to me,'" she said.

"Right," I said again.

"But I feel like it's this epidemic that people are saying 'You can give that to myself or Joe.'"

"Myself" and other reflexive pronouns—which are the ones that end in -*self* or -*selves*—are mostly for cases where the action doer is the same as the action recipient. For instance:

I cut <u>myself</u> while peeling grapes.

You also occasionally see these pronouns used for emphasis:

I <u>myself</u> do not believe that!

I told the woman, "A lot of what you're talking about has to do with 'me' evasion. People have this instinctive revulsion to the word 'me,' and I think part of it is because you weren't supposed to say 'Me and Joe want to go to the movies.'"

"Joe and I," she said, reflexively.

"It's called hypercorrection when you fix something that wasn't wrong to begin with, thereby creating a mistake," I said. "So you're overdoing it: you're overeliminating the 'me's."

"Right," she said. "What do we do about this?" This was a woman of action.

"It's going to continue in spite of our wishes," I said, "so it's important to achieve a state of inner peace about it."

¶

In New Orleans, a woman in yellow came up to the Grammar Table and asked, "What first-person singular pronoun would you use for the object of a preposition?"

I burst out laughing.

"Come on, it's not so tough!" she said, glaring at me.

"'Me'!" I said. She looked at me sternly, as though she was waiting for me to change my answer.

I shrugged. "First-person singular pronoun, object of a preposition: 'me'!"

"For you and me," said the woman, whose name was Beth. She was visiting from Colorado.

"Yeah!" I said. "You were looking at me like I had it wrong, and I knew I didn't. Are you an English teacher? Are you a plant?" She laughed.

"No, but I was an English major," said Beth. "So many people use 'I' when they should use 'me,' because they think 'I' sounds more correct."

"That's right," I said.

"And it's wrong," said Beth.

A blaring speaker, probably from a nearby restaurant or nightspot, informed us, "You can't boogie no more."

¶

In Morgantown, West Virginia, I encountered a student with curly hair and a grammar philosophy problem. He told me, "I know it's right when you say 'Will you go to the bar with Emily and me?' Like, that's correct."

"Yes," I agreed.

"But I don't want to sound stupid," said the student, "so I just say 'Emily and I,' because people don't know that. When you say 'Emily and me,' people correct you. And you don't want to get into arguments, so you're just like . . ." He shrugged to indicate the hopelessness of the situation.

"If you do something right grammatically but most people think you're wrong, then that's a bummer," I summarized.

"Yeah!" exclaimed the student.

"But I'll know you're right," I said. He and his two friends laughed. "I mean, there are still lots of people who'll know you're right. I'm actually very happy that you know that."

"Okay, cool," said the student.

"It's impressive," I said. "I teach adults, and I teach them to use 'me' in that case. Sometimes people who know it's right get really bugged by the error. They might think, Well, this person doesn't know the difference between the subject and object pronoun. And you do, so you should get credit for it."

"Okay, cool," said the student happily. "I will start my journey as a 'me' guy."

Quizlet

••

1. Zelda handed the skateboards to Ariana and
   ____ (I, me).
2. Zelda wanted Ariana and ____ (I, me) to stay for
   chocolate lava cake.

39

Whom Ya Gonna Call?

I was sitting on a Detroit street corner when a brunette woman arrived in a state of agitation.

"Can you sit up straight so I can see your shirt?" she said.

Ahem, I was not slouching. Women's T-shirt fronts are often hard to read because of certain biological realities. I straightened out my shirt so that she could see that it said I ❤ GRAMMAR.

"I don't know what's going on," she continued. "My niece just posted something about grammar, and it was a nightmare."

"Do you want a postcard?" I asked her.

"No," she said. "I don't understand. I mean, like, is this going on around the country, like promotional grammar this week?" She seemed irked that it was confusing.

"Only because I'm moving around the country," I said. "I'm on a Grammar Table tour. This is my pop-up Grammar Table stand from New York City."

"Come on, are you serious?" said the woman.

"This is my husband, and we're driving around the country." I pointed to Brandt.

"But why?" she asked.

I gave her a brief history of the Grammar Table, and she said, "Just as I was walking here, it popped into my head that I still don't know how to use 'whom.' I'm a lawyer. I will rewrite entire paragraphs so that issue does not come up."

"Have you ever seen this book?" I asked, holding up *Garner's Modern English Usage*. "He's a legal lexicographer and I really recommend—"

"Are you taking my picture?" asked the lawyer, noticing Brandt's camera. "Don't take my picture."

"It won't appear anywhere unless you sign a release," I said. "Garner's a lawyer and legal lexicographer and—"

"You know what?" said the lawyer. "I've got to get going, okay? I just realized I'm late for meditation."

"—you can look up 'who' and 'whom' in there," I finished. She was already walking away, but perhaps unable to resist the allure of lawyer-sourced "whom" advice, she came back and snapped a picture of *Garner's*.

"Good luck," I said sunnily as she left.

A reporter standing next to me said, "I assume that's a fairly common question."

"'Who' and 'whom'?" I said. "Yes, but usually when people ask about it, they stick around for the answer."

¶

In New Orleans, a woman named Trina was visiting the Grammar Table with her sister. Trina wanted to know, "When is it proper to use 'whom' versus 'who'?"

"The best way to get those right all the time is to know

grammar inside out and upside down, because you have to see the word relationships," I said. She smiled at this. "But I can give you two key examples!"

I wrote this down for her:

Evan, who/whom I admired, just robbed a bank.

"Mmmm," said Trina disapprovingly.

"I know; it's not good," I said. "It's the end of my admiration. But in this case, see how the commas are there? Ignore everything around the commas, and you just look at the words in between them."

"Right," said Trina.

"I admire . . ." I began, and paused.

"It's 'whom,'" said Trina.

"Whom," I said. "It's an object form. Now I have one more for you."

Evan, who/whom I thought was an honest person, plagiarized two paragraphs of mine.

"'Whom' again," said Trina.

I explained that everything outside the commas was irrelevant. "I thought *he* was an honest person," I said. "It's the subject form, so you go with 'who.'"

"Oh," said Trina. "All right."

"All right," I said. "This is your slightly messy souvenir."

"Thank you," said Trina.

"For whom are y'all doing this for?" asked her sister, and we all laughed.

"Now see, you are just a troublemaker," I said.

"She is," confirmed Trina.

"Yes," I said. "You have time-out over there."

"Yes, ma'am," said her sister.

¶

Newlyweds are extra fun at the Grammar Table. In Austin, Texas, a pair of them came up to me as I sat under my tree along a Zilker Park trail. I greeted them and asked if they had any grammar questions.

They looked at each other in excitement. "Oh, man!" said the man.

"Can you think of any?" the woman asked him.

The man, whose name was Jacob, wanted to know when to use "whomever." A pronoun scene from the comedy series *The Office* had triggered this interest, which just goes to show you, watching TV can be educational.

"I can give you a 'whomever' example that I did wrong in my past," I said. "I'm going to confess."

"Okay, yeah, I want to hear," said Jacob.

"Back in the early nineties," I began, "someone was stealing my newspaper from my front door every day before I got up." They both looked horrified, which I found gratifying.

"Oh, so savage!" said Jacob.

"I know, right?" I said. "This was in the days before there was any internet."*

"Okay, this is important," said Jacob.

"Yeah!" said his wife, Emily. "Yeah!"

What an enchanting, insightful, discerning audience!

---

* Well, the internet existed, but it wasn't yet being used by all the regular folks.

"It was my link to the world," I continued, "so I wrote a nasty note. This was in New York City, and—well, it wasn't that nasty, but I very pretentiously wrote, 'To whomever is stealing my *New York Times,* cut it out!'"

They both laughed. "That's awesome," said Jacob.

"Anyway, that one I would definitely regard as wrong now," I said. "Do you remember prepositions, or should I give you a quick refresher?"

"I definitely need one," said Jacob. "She probably doesn't. She's so much smarter."

I provided a quick preposition refresher that included "over," "under," "near," "toward," and "to." I told them, "Generally, if you put a word after a preposition, it's going to have the object form."

subject	object
I	me
he	him
she	her
we	us
who	whom
whoever	whomever

"But in the case of my missing newspaper," I continued, "the object of 'to' is not 'whomever' but rather the whole idea." It's not "to whomever," but rather, "to *x*," where *x* equals this:

_____ *(whoever, whomever) is stealing my* New York Times

A clause — in this case, "whoever is stealing my *New York Times*" — can be the object of a preposition. I don't remember learning such a thing in school, but if I didn't, I definitely learned it later, when I was more fully formed — and I say this for the benefit of anyone still taking memories of seventh-grade English as grammar gospel. The choice between "who" and "whom" is based on the internal grammar of that clause, not the preposition.

"It's not 'whomever,'" I said. "You wouldn't say 'Him is stealing my *New York Times*.' You would say 'He is stealing.' So I would say now, if I wrote this very strict note —"

"Years later," said Jacob.

"Yes," I said. "I'd say, 'To whoever is stealing my *New York Times,* cut it out!' But I get it electronically now."

They burst out laughing.

"Problem solved!" said Emily.

"I learned something," said Jacob. "I'm so happy that I got some peace and clarity."

"This is incredible," said Emily. Those two were sunbeams. It was a happy new marriage of two sparkly sunbeams.

¶

I was sitting in view of St. Louis Cathedral in New Orleans when a man in a turquoise plaid shirt approached with a problem.

"I have a master's degree," complained the man, whose name was Adam, "and I don't get the difference between 'who' and 'whom.' Isn't that terrible?"

"No," I said. "'Who' and 'whom' are genuinely tricky, because they're a rarity in English. There aren't that many English words that change form based on how they're used, so English-speaking brains aren't really trained to deal with that. And actually, if someone would put me in charge of pronouns, I might like it if there just weren't a 'whom,' because we don't need it to understand one another."

"Oh, we don't need it," said Adam. "It's kind of like the penny in the financial world. It's useful at times, but not necessary." But he wanted to know how to use them anyway, so I began explaining.

"'Who' and 'whom' are pronouns," I said, "and in places where you would use 'he' and 'she' and 'I,' you would also use 'who.' Those are all what are known as subject pronouns."

"Okay," said Adam.

"And then 'whom' matches up with places where you might use 'him,' 'her,' and 'me,'" I said, "so those are all objects."

"'Him,' 'her,' and 'me' are objects?" Adam asked.

"Object pronouns," I said. "Let me give you—"

"Hang on," said Adam. "Let me get a little deeper on that piece of it. Is the language changing just a little bit just to get away from objectifying 'him' or 'her'? Can we use something different than 'object'? Can we, you know, get with the times in terms of not objectifying people?"

"Oh!" I said, taken aback. "When I say 'object pronoun,' it's really just a grammatical function, so I'm not talking about doing anything bad. It's just the difference between saying 'He wrote a book' and 'The book was about him.' That's all it is."

"I know, but you're in the language business," said Adam.

"Yes. Well—" I began.

"So can we somehow change the object terminology for 'him' and 'her'?" he persisted.

"You think it should be called something else?" I asked.

"Maybe something different," said Adam.

"It's very kind of you to be concerned about the objectification of people," I said. "I guess I'm so used to thinking about it as a grammatical function that it's not even in the same bucket in my head."

"Yeah," said Adam, unimpressed. He didn't want to hear any of my lousy grammar excuses.

"But I hear what you're saying," I said. "I could file a complaint on your behalf and see if it goes anywhere."

"Okay," he said. "Not on my behalf, but just on the behalf of people."

¶

On Venice Beach, the sun was gone, but Alicia and Tara were still eager to talk grammar. Alicia asked, "Is it 'by whom' or 'by who'?"

"Yeah!" exclaimed Tara.

"I say 'by whom,'" I said. "But I sometimes don't say 'whom' when it's technically called for. Like, would you say 'Who did you call?' or 'Whom did you call?'"

"I don't know," said Alicia.

"I would say 'who,' always," said Tara. "I've never used 'whom.' I just don't know when to use it."

The pronoun is an object there, so I have often said

"whom" in sentences like this, but I have also occasionally had misgivings that it's a bit too much for the twenty-first century.

"Yeah," I said. "It can sound pompous, I think, to say, 'Whom did you call?'"

"Right?" said Alicia.

"Unless you're talking about *Ghostbusters,*" said Brandt from behind the camera. "Whom ya gonna call?"

We all laughed hard in the dark on the beach with the waves and the sand and the gulls sleeping silently somewhere.

Quizlet

••

_____ (Who, Whom) is your first choice for mayor?

Answer: *Who*

40

Bewitching Whiches

It was the second day of the Detroit presidential debates in the summer of 2019, and I was on location talking to a man with a NO GRAND PRIX BELLE ISLE sign.

By on location, what I really mean is not on location, since I was stuck behind the street barricades about a third of a mile from the actual debates. But around me were protestors for every cause, and this particular man's cause was that he did not want the annual Grand Prix to be held on a local island called Belle Isle. He was in the middle of telling me about it when a family of five— mom, dad, and three children—showed up.

"Teach these guys!" said the protestor, graciously stepping aside.

"We have a question for you," said the father. "We were just chatting about 'that' and 'which,' and we were hoping you could help us out. What's the rule for that?"

"It depends a little bit on where you live," I said. "No matter what I say here right in this moment, you're going to go out and find different things depending on where the thing that you're reading was published."

"Do you say that before every question you answer?" asked the dad. "Sort of hedging bets?" His wife laughed.

"No, I don't," I said. "That would create some very

long conversations. I say that because 'that' and 'which' are used interchangeably a lot more in the UK than they are here. I'm going to make a special page for you with two examples."

"Wow!" said the man with the sign. He was a good Grammar Table booster.

I wrote:

I threw away the books that were water-damaged.

I threw away the books, which were water-damaged.

"What's the difference in meaning?" I asked, showing them the pad. "Do the children want to participate? Are you all related?"

"Yep!" said Mom. "Kids."

"I'm not," said the protestor, raising his hand, and everyone laughed.

"Do you know what the difference in meaning is between those two sentences?" I repeated.

There were some fumbled guesses from a couple of family members, and then the youngest child, a girl of about ten, pointed at the comma in the second sentence.

"Yes!" I said. "In American usage, you usually have a comma before 'which.' And that indicates that the information after it is fundamentally removable without totally destroying the meaning of the sentence."*

"Uh-huh," said the dad, in the same tone of voice par-

---

* In the UK, you will often see "which" used in places where Americans would be more likely to use "that." For example: "I threw away the books which were water-damaged." In that case, the comma-free "which" is acting like an American "that."

ents use with a child presenting the case for a later bed-time.

"'That' is used for critical information," I said. "No comma. It limits the books to what category of books? Only the books that were water-damaged."

"So you just throw away the water-damaged books, and you keep the clean books," I continued. "With the comma plus 'which,' the idea is you threw away all the books. You could cross off the whole 'which' clause."

I threw away the books, ~~which were water-damaged~~.

"Like 'by the way,'" said the mom.
"Yes!" I exclaimed. "That's actually how I explain it.

It doesn't mean it's not important or interesting; it just means it's not critical to the sense of the sentence."

"Got it," said the mom. "So when you use 'which,' you should be using a comma, and when you use 'that,' you don't need to."

Mom was mostly right. That is a pretty good guideline that will usually hold true. But if you are expecting uniformity across national borders or even within the confines of these United States, you are sure to be disappointed.

While I try not to douse people with grammar terms, there are a few terms that might come in handy for you here, especially if you want to explore this area in more detail on your own.

"That" and "which" are relative pronouns. You find relative pronouns at the beginning of what are known as relative clauses, and a relative clause modifies a preceding noun or pronoun. In the previous examples, "which were water-damaged" and "that were water-damaged" are both relative clauses that modify the word "books." However, "which were water-damaged" is a nonrestrictive relative clause, and "that were water-damaged" is a restrictive one.

You've seen the terms "restrictive" and "nonrestrictive" before, in Chapter 12 on appositives. It's the same idea. Restrictive appositives and restrictive relative clauses are not optional or removable; nonrestrictive appositives and nonrestrictive relative clauses are. Restrictive appositives and restrictive relative clauses do not take commas; their nonrestrictive counterparts do.

On the Middlebury College campus in Vermont, a man with glasses resting on top of his shaved head asked, "Do you ever use 'which' without a comma?"

"I don't use it as a restrictive relative pronoun," I said. "I don't personally. But it doesn't bother me. It's common in British usage."

"My British colleague says that it's totally fine to use it that way," said the man.

"Yes," I said. "You see it in English novels."

In *The Return of Sherlock Holmes,* which I read in its entirety in a bathtub in 1994, though not all at once, Arthur Conan Doyle had both a restrictive and a nonrestrictive "which" in this sentence: "From a rise of the road on the shoulder of Crooksbury Hill we could see the grim Hall bristling out from amidst the ancient <u>oaks, which</u>, old as they were, were still younger than the <u>building which</u> they surrounded."

The comma makes the difference, not the word choice. In American publishing today, the first underlined instance — a nonrestrictive example with a comma plus "which" — would have been preserved, but a copy editor might have inquired about replacing the second "which," which is restrictive, with a "that."

In *Walden,* written in the nineteenth century, Henry David Thoreau did the same, with two restrictive instances of "which" in this one tiny sentence: "That <u>time which</u> we really improve, or <u>which</u> is improvable, is neither past, present, nor future." Thoreau was American, so don't blame this on British people.*

"And I disagree that it's fine," said the man. "But at least you see what I mean."

"Yes, I do know exactly what you're talking about," I

---

* Perhaps you can blame it on American lawyers, though. In the US, my (untested) impression is that lawyers have an above-average tendency to use "which" as a restrictive relative pronoun.

said. "I don't use 'which' like 'that,' because I think it adds clarity to distinguish."

"I agree," said the man. "I appreciate it."

Quizlet

···

In which sentence below did some portion of the brownies fail to entice?

1. The brownies that didn't have nuts in them were a hit at Lois's party.
2. The brownies, which didn't have nuts in them, were a hit at Lois's party.

Answer: *Sentence 1*

41

Punctuation Location
Contemplation

"What's your position on the period inside the quotation marks or outside the quotation marks?" asked Warren. Brandt and I had just arrived in Red Cloud, Nebraska, population 1,095 human beings. Warren was married to a man who had grown up there, and they were visiting from their home in New York City.

"In American usage, I just go with the flow," I said.

"Period inside the quotation marks," said Warren. He meant like this:

My mother refers to my second cousin as "the apostrophe assassin."

"Inside," said his husband. "It drives me crazy when it's out."

"It does?" I said. "That's because you're so used to having it tidily tucked in. I would prefer for it to be logical. I would be in favor of a reform of that. But since that's not how American English works, I'm just going to go with the flow."

When Barack Obama was president, I heard a rumor that he was an advocate of what is sometimes called "logical punctuation," as shown in this example:

My mother refers to my second cousin as "the apostrophe assassin".

Logical or not, that's not how things are normally done in the US, so like any punctilious punctuator, I promptly emailed the White House to inquire further. Unfortunately, no one answered me, and for now, that's the end of my story. Maybe one day I'll find out whether it was just a rumor.

¶

"Welcome to the Grammar Table," I said to a lean young man with brown hair and reflective sunglasses. This time I was sitting along a canal in Bricktown, a hip part of downtown Oklahoma City, as the Grammar Table is nothing if not hip. "Do you have any grammar questions?"

"Oh geez," said the man, whose name was Tim. "I do. How do you use punctuation in a quotation? Does it go inside, or does it go outside?"

"It depends on punctuation type," I said. I wrote down this example, leaving the ending blank:

He called his boss "an interminable bore__

"What goes first now, the period or the quotation marks?" I asked.

"I would put the period inside," said Tim, who described himself as "a Nebraska product and then a Navy product."

"Yes," I said. "That's the rule in American English. The period is always inside." Like this:

He called his boss "an interminable bore."

The same is true of the comma:

Because he called his boss "an interminable bore," he was fired.

This practice frustrates many Americans who find it illogical, but that's life. Right now is the only time in this book that I will tell you this: *Turn off your brain!* Just turn it off, stop seeking logic in all things, shove that comma and period inside the quotation marks, and move on.

Next Tim wanted to know what to do when you quote a whole sentence that ends at the end of your sentence.

In class today, my teacher said, "Kids need to study more at home."

"Does that period at the end count twice, so to speak?" he asked.

Yes, it does — so don't double up. It's like double coupon days at the grocery store: you get double credit for the period.

I gave Tim two more examples to illustrate what to do with question marks and exclamation points. For this portion, please turn your brain back on.

She asked, "Where are my persimmons?"

Did you really call your yoga instructor a "torpid turtle"?

In the first example, the quoted material is itself a question, so the question mark goes inside the quotation marks. In the second example, the writer is asking a question and embedding a brief quoted phrase inside of it, so the question mark goes outside. Exclamation points work the same way. In other words: logically!

Let us now proceed to Richmond, Virginia, where a mom and dad with two little boys, about five and nine, stopped by the Grammar Table. They had just bought a board game at a local store.

"Hi, do you have any grammar questions?" I asked them.

"I do, actually," said the man, whose name was Nolan. "We were having a—"

"—grammar discussion as we walked past your table," continued the woman, Erin, "and we thought we'd come back and ask you."

"Let's say you have a sentence and you're quoting something in the sentence," said Nolan. "Is there ever a time when the period goes outside of the quotation marks? I was thinking like if just part of the sentence at the end has a quote in it."

"No," I said. I wrote this sentence:

He called his colleague "a dictatorial miscreant."

"Okay, I have just a tiny little quote at the end of my sentence," I said. "In American English, it still goes inside. But I would say about half of Americans don't know that."

"Your half," said Erin, pointing at her husband, and we all laughed.

"If you were in the UK," I said, "it would be reversed in that sentence."

"Oh!" said Nolan.

"You would put the quotes and then the period," I said, "because the quotation is embedded in the writer's sentence, and the punctuation for that is handled more logically there than here." Both single and double quotation marks are in use in the UK, so you might see either of these options:

He called his boss 'a dictatorial miscreant'.

or

He called his boss "a dictatorial miscreant".

"If you can't deal with US style," I said, "which I sometimes have trouble doing myself, you may need to move to London."

Nolan looked at his wife. "So having this period on the inside," he said, "is kind of like not being on the metric system."

"It is!" I said. "Yes! Would you like this sentence as a souvenir of your visit?"

"Yes, thanks a lot," said Nolan.

"We're going to frame it, because I was correct," said Erin.

I said to her in a conspiratorially low voice, "You know what? The wives usually are."

The older son objected. "Wait, no, Mom, you said that there wasn't *ever* a time. But there *is* a time."

"Oh yeah, there's a time," Nolan told his son, with expert spousal insouciance. "Like in a different country!"

¶

Connor had been living in Asheville, North Carolina, for several years the day I met him downtown in his adopted city. He had long brown hair and wanted to talk about the single quotation marks he was encountering in some of the novels he was reading.

"Why do they do that?" he asked.

"You might be reading things published outside the US," I said.

"Yeah," said Connor.

"It's observant of you to notice," I said. "There are different practices. In the UK, for example, they often use single quotes where we use double. Also, are you familiar with how here, when we have a quote within a quote, single quotes are used for the inner quote?"

"Yeah," said Connor.

"There you might see it reversed," I said. "Single quotes on the outside quote, double on the inside." For example:

US   Ariel said, "My neighbor called me an 'anti-punctuation activist.'"

UK   Ariel said, 'My neighbor called me an "anti-punctuation activist".'

"Gotcha," said Connor. "Cool."

In case you are wondering, if the neighbor actually said the word "an," you could also begin quoting before "an" if you wanted, like this:

US   Ariel said, "My neighbor called me 'an anti-punctuation activist.'"

I sometimes prefer the momentum of placing the quotation marks after the article rather than before. It's not a meaningful part of the quotation here, and if we leave it out, we will hardly be accused of plagiarizing the indefinite article the neighbor used to insult Ariel.

¶

In Charleston, South Carolina, a young man walked up to the Grammar Table and said, "If I'm writing a quote that somebody said, and the end of the quote is an exclamation point, but that's not the end of the sentence—"

"Then you're just trying to make trouble," I said. He laughed and gave me this example:

"Oh my!" said So-and-so.

"Do you put an exclamation point and then comma?" asked the man, whose name was David. He was accompanied by his stylish wife, Sharon, who was wearing a fedora and sunglasses and who made me feel uncool by comparison in my T-shirt with three commas and a chameleon on it.*

"You just skip it," I said.

"No comma?" asked Sharon.

"You skip the comma?" said David.

"Yeah," I said. "Does it look weird to you?" I held up the page for their review.

"No," said Sharon.

---

* This shirt was inspired by Culture Club's 1983 song "Karma Chameleon." Yes, I know there are five karmas in "Karma Karma Karma Karma Karma Chameleon," but T-shirts have limited punctuation real estate.

"It doesn't," said David.

"If it were a period instead of an exclamation point," I said, "you would replace it with a comma." For example:

So-and-so said, "Oh my."

becomes

"Oh my," said So-and-so.

David seemed glad to have this information. He told me he was writing a daily blog. "We have a year-and-a-half-old daughter at home, so we put up daily Instagram posts that I write in her voice," he said.

"He's really good," said his wife.

"She's clearly very sophisticated, since you're checking on this advanced quotation punctuation thing," I said.

"She'll read it one day," said David, "so I want to make sure that she's well represented."

• •

Quotation Mark Cheat Sheet, American Style

quoted word or phrase before a period
They described their new neighbor as a "chronic participle dangler."

quoted word or phrase before a comma
They described their new neighbor as a "chronic

participle dangler," but they remained polite to him
in the hallway.

quoted sentence
  He said, "Our new neighbor is a chronic participle
  dangler."

quoted word or phrase within a question
  Did they describe their new neighbor as a "chronic
  participle dangler"?

quoted question
  She asked, "Have we told you our new neighbor is a
  chronic participle dangler?"

quoted word or phrase within an exclamation
  They called you a "chronic participle dangler"!

quoted exclamation
  He said, "You, sir, are a chronic participle dangler!"

• •

¶

"What's going on?" asked Kevin, a shirtless young runner
in Austin, Texas. I had seen him jog by shirtlessly in the
other direction a little earlier when I was in the midst of
a serious semicolon discussion.

  "It's the Grammar Table," I said. "Do you have any
grammar questions?"

  "I actually wanted to tell you something I learned today," said Kevin.

  "What did you learn?" I asked.

"I had no idea about this," said Kevin. "I was trying to figure out the punctuation inside parentheses and outside, and I learned that when the sentence is completely parenthesized—or is it parentheseized? Is that the right word?"

"Well, you're inventing it, so you can do it however you like," I said.

"Okay, cool," said Kevin ebulliently. "So whenever the sentence is parentheseized entirely, the period goes inside."

"Right," I said. He meant like this:

At the time, Henrietta was the CEO of the firm. (Her sister-in-law had just been ousted as CFO.)

"And when it's partial, it goes outside," said Kevin.

"Yes," I agreed. Like this:

At the time, Henrietta was the CEO of the firm (though her tenure there would soon end in scandal).

"That's crazy," said Kevin. "I didn't know that. It was always like, whatever felt good in my gut at the moment. But I never really knew."

"Will it be as satisfying now?" I asked.

"Absolutely, yeah," Kevin said. "I appreciate the work you're doing, by the way!"

Quizlet

••

How many punctuation placement errors are there in the sentence below?

> "Where do you think you are going"? asked Fritz, who was the meanest kid in the entire fifth-grade class (but who by the end of sixth would be my dearest friend.)

Answer: *Two errors, one after "going" and one after "friend." The sentence should look like this instead:*

"Where do you think you are going?" asked Fritz, who was the meanest kid in the entire fifth-grade class (but who by the end of sixth would be my dearest friend).

42

Subject-Verb Synchronicity

In front of Caffe Aroma in Buffalo, I met a man named Rick who wanted to discuss wording he had encountered in a book: "a handful of supporters were." For example:

> A *handful of supporters* _____ *(was, were) protest-ing outside the company's headquarters.*

Rick told me, "I was thinking 'handful' was singular, but it was using it as a plural, and then I couldn't decide whether—"

"If you were not thinking about grammar at all, is there a direction you would head by instinct?" I inter-rupted. Sometimes instinct differs from what we were taught to do, or think we were taught to do, and when that happens, the choice may merit fresh consideration.

"Well, I would have thought it was singular," said Rick.

"So it's not just that it's something you remember from school?" I asked. "I was possibly taught to use a singular there, but I don't think that corresponds to common us-age or common sense. You could put 'handful' into the bucket of collective nouns, like 'group' or 'council.' And I often use those with plurals."

"Oh!" said Rick.

Collective nouns are singular in form but plural in concept. Here are some more for your files: "trio," "staff," "team," "board," and "panel." I told Rick, "British people use them with plurals more than Americans do, so I feel this might be my one slight British affectation."

He laughed. What an agreeable and discerning man he was to laugh at my grammar jokes!

"Here's another example," I said. "Would you say 'the couple is arguing' or 'the couple are arguing'?"

"Is," said Rick. (I would have picked "are," but reader, please do not give up on me now when we've already come so far together. This is a carefully considered position.)

I added more conspicuous conflict to the next example I gave Rick, who seemed content to keep conjugating on demand:

The couple _____ (is, are) throwing stuffed elephants at each other.

He picked a singular verb again: "is."

"Doesn't it bother you that you then have 'each other' at the end and there's antagonistic action, so they're acting as individuals?" I asked. "Because it bothers me."

"Each other," said Rick. "Well, that's interesting, but I would say 'is,' because 'each other' sounds singular to me."

"That's not the subject, though," I said. "'Each other' is stressing that they're acting as independent elements. A usage distinction that's often made with collective nouns is that if the individual members are acting in concert, you use a singular verb. If they're not, then it's more likely to tilt into plural, but not so much in the US as in the UK. So I feel I may have to move."

"That's great," said Rick, laughing. "That's helpful. Thank you."

In England, you might see something like "United are in town today," referring to the soccer team Manchester United. Recently online, I saw an American woman who went to junior high school with me in California conjugating the company name Google with "have." That is understandable, because she moved to Europe ages ago, but companies are normally singular in the US.

Here's a basketball-themed example I like:

The New York Knicks ____ *(is, are) on a winning streak, but the Miami Heat* ____ *(is, are) not.*

What would you do? Plural for both? Plural for the Knicks, singular for the Heat? I am definitely an "are"/"are" kind of gal on this one.

The New York Knicks are on a winning streak, but the Miami Heat are not.

For me this sounds weird:

The New York Knicks are on a winning streak, but the Miami Heat is not.

I can't do that. Once again, if this bothers you, please consider it my one British affectation. I think we Americans should all be allowed one.

❡

One day early in Grammar Table history in New York, a girl about nine years old arrived at the table with her mother and asked, "Why do people use 'there's' when the noun after it is plural?"

"That's a really great question!" I said, impressed. She was talking about this kind of thing:

There's some orangutans in that tree.

"Orangutans" is the subject and it's plural, so her point was that the verb should be plural, too. In other words, "are."

There are some orangutans in that tree.

I explained to my young visitor that many people just default to the singular verb after "there," no matter what follows, in part because they don't realize that in a sentence beginning "there is" or "there are," the subject follows the verb rather than preceding it. People also sometimes just think "there" sounds singular. Here's another example.

There's a lot of books here.

I would say and write "are" in the sentence above ("There are a lot of books here"), but it is fact that I have in my life begun sentences beginning with "there," then picked a singular verb, then found myself crashing unexpectedly into a plural subject. When you start a sentence with "there," you don't always know exactly what's going to come next. Things can multiply.

At a local café a few days later, I ran into the conjugating girl's mother. She recognized me.

"You're the Grammar Table lady!" she said. "My daughter was really excited about the Grammar Table, and she's already decided she's going to be a grammar queen for Halloween next year!"

¶

I got a similar question some months later, on Martha's Vineyard. As I sat under a nice big tree in the shade, a woman with shoulder-length gray hair said, "I think it's supposed to be an easy one, but nobody seems to know the answer. When you say to somebody, 'Attached is this and that,' is it supposed to be 'Attached are'?"

"I do 'attached are,'" I said.

"Is that not a grammar issue?" asked the woman, whose name was Melanie. "Is there not a right answer?"

"Well, the subject is technically the two things if you're using an 'and' to combine them," I said. "You're not talking about 'as well as,' right?"

"No," said Melanie.

What I meant was this:

Attached are my time sheet __and__ my status report.

as opposed to this:

Attached is my time sheet __as well as__ my status report.

The subject of the first sentence above is both the time sheet and the status report, so the verb is plural: "are."

In the second sentence, you match the verb with the part before "as well as," meaning "time sheet" alone, so the verb is singular. The status report, while not exactly an aside, is tossed aside when you are picking your verb, so you end up with "is."

Sometimes a grammatical concept or editorial convention comes into conflict with the goal of sounding good or natural. It is rare that such a thing befalls me, but if it does, do I want to choose a verb that sticks out like an oversize rusty bent nail—a *talking* rusty nail— and announces, "I know the grammar and I'm going to demo that, even if it's a style nightmare"?

I do not. And there are many ways to write most ideas.

I told Melanie, "Sometimes even if I have a compound subject after 'there is' or 'there are,' it sounds a little odd to use a plural verb, maybe because the first element is singular and on the longish side and you can't really feel the plural nature of the subject."

I gave her an example:

Attached are an invitation for the Acheson party and an architectural drawing for the new site.

"In that case I might use 'as well as,'" I said, "because then I'm off the hook and I can use a singular verb."

Attached is an invitation for the Acheson party as well as an architectural drawing for the new site.

"I go through all sorts of permutations and contortions for this," I added.

"So you would use 'are' if the two things were simpler, like 'an invitation and a drawing'?" asked Melanie.

"Yes, but I do often prefer to write 'I have attached' in that case," I said. Melanie made a small grammar moan.

"It all depends on how I feel it sounds," I said. "But I have done it. I will do it."

"Okay," said Melanie, resignedly. "I like the 'as well as' trick. I like that, or 'I have attached.' I mean, I could have always done that."

"I usually do 'I have attached,' or 'I've attached,' because it feels more like how I would communicate in speech," I said.

"But this is email," said Melanie.

"I know," I said. "But I email in a style that is pretty close to my speech rhythms. I do 'attached is' or 'attached are' when I already have other sentences beginning with 'I' and I don't want to sound like a complete narcissist."

Melanie laughed. "This is way beyond grammar," she said.

¶

Now, you may have thought we were done with Rick in Buffalo from the beginning of this chapter, but we are not. There is more to report from in front of Caffe Aroma, where Rick demonstrated excellent conjugation-discussion endurance.

After we discussed "handful," I told Rick, "You were taught the same thing I was: that the subject can't be part of a prepositional phrase. You look at the noun before it, and if it is singular, then the idea was, it doesn't matter what's happening after."

"Right, exactly," said Rick.

What are the subjects of these, for example?

Three of the girls were late for trapeze class.

One of my best friends is giving a presentation on fossils.

The manager of the grocery store helped me find the liverwurst.

Did you pick "three," "one," and "manager"? If you did, you are right!

What comes after the "of" is normally not relevant in determining whether a subject is singular or plural. This idea works in many independent clauses, as in the three examples above, but there are complications. Collective nouns as subjects are one of those complications, since they are sometimes treated as singular and sometimes treated as plural.

In addition, math grammar can be messy: what is inside the prepositional phrase does sometimes affect verb choice. I gave my new friend from Buffalo another scenario and asked him which verb he would pick.

One percent of our employees _____ (is, are) using the treadmills at lunch.

"One percent is," said Rick.

"But what if you had five thousand employees?" I asked.

"Ah!" he said, looking amused. "I would use 'are.'"

I definitely recommend "are" in this case. "One percent of" is not comparable to one apple, or one tiger, or one ukulele. It is telling you what portion of a group of people use the treadmills. One percent of the employees could mean a lot of people.

If the one percent were of something uncountable, however, the verb would be singular:

*One percent of the pie is missing.**

"Majority" works the same way:

A majority of our employees are now using the treadmills at lunch.

but

The majority of the pie is missing.

"What I like about these questions is that there's an intersection between grammar and math," I told my new friend Rick. "To me that's fascinating. I sometimes write word problems that combine grammar and math and post them on social media, and so far they've been surprisingly unpopular."

He laughed and told me, "You make people's heads hurt."

¶

A last, possibly head-hurting topic involves subject-verb agreement in relative clauses. This doesn't come

---

* I know, I know—no one ever eats one percent of a pie. Please forgive the appallingly unrealistic example.

up much at the Grammar Table, but I have seen so many people grammarsplaining this topic to strangers online (incorrectly, I mean) that I wish to address it here.

This is one of the trickier topics in this book, so you might want to fortify yourself with snacks before reading further. Let's start with these two sentences.

One of the children <u>has</u> been stealing licorice.

Bo is one of the three children who <u>have</u> been stealing licorice.

In the first one, which is a single simple independent clause, the notion that the subject cannot be part of the prepositional phrase ("of the children") applies. The subject is "one," and the verb is singular to match it: "has."

The structure of the second sentence is different and more complicated. Here the subject is "Bo," and the verb is "is." The pronoun "one" is acting as what is known as a subject complement: it follows a linking verb and points back to the subject.

"One" is modified by the prepositional phrase "of the three children." The word "who" in the relative clause "who have been stealing licorice" has as its antecedent "children." That is why the verb is the plural "have," not the singular "has." Don't get distracted by "one," or "Bo," or "is." Multiple children have been stealing licorice, and Bo is one of the culprits.*

Here is a new sentence with a comparable structure:

Marlene brought me a pile of dolls that <u>were</u> missing their eyes.

Some people will argue reflexively that because "of dolls" is a prepositional phrase, the underlined verb should instead be a singular—"was"—in order to match "pile." I must put my foot down here. First of all, we are talking about "their" eyes, not "its eyes," and that is an important clue. Good grammar requires common sense.

In my sentence with Marlene and the eyeless dolls, "Marlene" is the subject, "brought" is the verb, "me" is the indirect object, and "pile" is the direct object, modified by the prepositional phrase "of dolls."

Next you have the relative clause "that _____ (was,

---

* If you would like me to write more about advanced grammar topics, please write a persuasive letter to my publisher. Thank you in advance.

were) missing their eyes." The way you figure out the verb here is to decide what "that" refers to. A pile wasn't missing "their" eyes; the dolls were missing their eyes. The sensible choice here is the plural verb "were."

I'm sorry for this creepy image, but I hope it will teach relative clause grammarsplainers—I'm not pointing fingers, but you know who you are—an important lesson: Grammar is varied and complicated, and we need to stay humble before it.

As Hamlet told Horatio, "There are more things in heaven and earth . . . than are dreamt of in your philosophy."

¶

Before we depart this chapter, I'd like to take one final look at a couple of poor misunderstood pronouns, whose versatility is underestimated and whose verb-conjugation opportunities are, as a result, unjustly limited.

One winter day, when I was stationed inside the Seventy-Second Street subway station at Broadway, a woman with energetic curly gray hair came over.

"There are so many mistakes now," she said. "It's terrible. People even use a plural verb with 'none.' That's wrong! 'None' means 'not one.' It goes with a singular verb!"

"Well," I said, "'none' is broadly accepted with both plural and singular verbs, and in my own habits, it's actually much more common with a plural verb."

She gave me Grammarian Side-Eye.

"None can mean 'not one' or 'not any,'" I said, undeterred. "When I mean 'not any,' I often treat it as a plural."

For example, in the question "Are any of you going to

the party later?" the subject is "any" and the verb is plural: "are."

My explanation earned me more Grammarian Side-Eye.

"See, this is why I bring all these reference books with me," I said, waving my hand at the books in front of me. "This way you don't have to rely on the word of a random stranger sitting at a table on the street."

I opened one of the books and turned it so she could read the "none" entry more easily. It said the same thing I had just said. She read it. Her eyes were unhappy.

"If you look that up in other reliable usage guides," I told her, "you will find that same point of view confirmed."

There was nothing more to say; she walked off into the gray Sunday rain. I and/or civilization had let her down.

Quizlet

• •

She was one of the students who _____ (was, were) awarded a scholarship to study entomology in Argentina.

Answer: *"Were," because the antecedent of "who" is "students." Another way to think about it: Multiple students received the scholarship, and she was one of that group.*

43

More Than Then

When I was sitting at the Grammar Table on Broadway—in Fargo, North Dakota—a young man approached to chat.

"I'm bad at grammar," he said. His name was Dylan.

"You are?" I asked. "Are you sure? Because people are often bad at self-assessment. The people who say they're really good at it often aren't, and people who say they're bad at it are often just humble."

"Well, I know the difference between 'then' and 'than,'" he said.

"Okay, that's good!" I said.

"Because people on social media rip into you if you do it wrong," said Dylan. "They like to correct you."

"But you've got that straight," I said.

"Yeah, it's 'better *than*,'" he said, emphasizing the *a*. He was right. As in:

This font is better <u>than</u> that font.

He told me he was a cab driver and website developer. As we were talking, a loud, fancy motorcycle went by on Broadway. I told him we lived on Broadway in New York.

"How's Broadway in Fargo versus Broadway in New York?" he wanted to know.

"Cool!" I said. "I really like it." I meant it. I was happily amped up from a magnificent quadruple-shot cappuccino I had drunk a couple of hours earlier at a stylish, spacious café downtown. "I've been wanting to come here for years," I added.

"I'm a Fargo boy, and I take pride in Fargo," said Dylan. "North Dakotans, they're kind of underrated, kind of quiet."

"Not underrated by me!" I said. "There are cool people everywhere."

"Yeah," said Dylan. "People are simple around here. All they want is nice shoes, nice clothes, maybe a gold chain, you know? They're very simple."

¶

One hundred twenty-eight days later, and 1,180 miles away by car,* it was Christmas in Santa Fe and a group

---

* See how I wrote out the first number and then didn't write out the second? According to the style guide I'm using—*The Chicago Manual of Style*—I'm not supposed to write out either large number, but there's also a guideline that says I shouldn't begin a sentence with a numeral (e.g., 128). The format of "one hundred twenty-eight" is now in conflict with the format of 1,180, but that's life. If you are reading this footnote, it means my number-formatting decision survived copyediting. Hi there! By the way, writers will often move a big number from the opening position to avoid problems like this, but that's a drag, because big numbers can be dramatic! And I refuse to be intimidated by a style rule! Except for the one that says I can't begin with a numeral like 128!

of children would not leave the Grammar Table. And to be clear, I didn't *want* them to leave.

There were six of them, and they were accompanied by two women, each of them clearly a mother of some portion of the children, though I had trouble keeping track of whose children were whose. Both the moms were native Russian speakers who spoke English as a foreign language; all the children were natively bilingual in both Russian and English.

"When do you use 'then,' and when do you use 'than'?" asked Clara, who wore a cute winter hat with two pompoms.

"You use 'than' for comparison," I said. "For example—"

"'This one is better *than* that,'" offered one of the women, in blue. "Right?"

"Yes!" I said, then asked Clara, "Is that one where you might get confused?"

"I honestly don't pay attention," she said.

"They sound sort of the same, right?" I asked.

"Yeah," said Clara.

The woman had more examples: "'I went to the store, and *then* I went to the coffee shop.' This is *e,* right?"

"Yes," I said. "So—"

"See, I know that one," said the woman happily.

"Yeah," I said. "So 'then' is time or sequence, so it'd be like 'I ate chocolate. Then I ate cookies.'"

"Do you do SAT tutoring?" the woman asked me.

"Oh my god, Mom," said another teenage girl, in a blue jacket. "I literally just got my scores!"

Quizlet

••

In the following sentences, which instances of "then" are wrong?

1. I like coffee more then Toby does.
2. Kobe is taller then Sarah.
3. Milly's favorite song in high school was "More Then This" by Roxy Music.

Answer: *All of them are wrong. They should all be "than." And Roxy Music spelled it right, by the way, but fans sometimes don't.*

44

It's Time for "Its"!

Because I have always found that quizzing people on their grammar is a fast track to popularity, here's a question for you to try on friends and family at your next social gathering: How many things can "it's" with an apostrophe mean? The answer will arrive later in this chapter.

An "it's"/"its" question came up with the same children I was talking to at the end of the previous chapter in Santa Fe. As revealed there, the girl in the blue jacket, whose name was Nadia, had just taken the SATs.

First Nadia wanted to know the difference between these two words:

it's

its'

The second one does not exist, so we quickly dispensed with that and compared "it's" and "its" instead.

"What you need is some sample sentences," I told Nadia. I wrote "it's" on my notepad.

"Like 'it is,'" Nadia said.

"What else?" I asked. "It can mean one other thing. This is the sticky one that people forget. Does anyone know?" I looked around at the other children.

"Like, belonging to?" asked Nadia.

The girl in the double-pompommed hat, Clara, raised her hand. "It belongs to," she agreed.

"Nope," I said. "Not with an apostrophe."

"Oh," said Nadia.

"The possessive form has no apostrophe. It's just *i t s,*" I said. "Do you know that term?"

"Yeah," she said.

"Like 'its shoes,'" said Nadia's mom. "Or 'It's sunset.'"

"No. That's not —" began Nadia.

"Its apples!" interrupted her mother, hastening to redeem herself.

"I'm going to give you a sentence, and you tell me what the 'it's' in it means," I said. Here it is:

It's been a long time since we last saw each other.

"Has," said Nadia and Clara simultaneously.

"Yes!" I replied. "Very good."

I gave Nadia another sentence, trying to keep myself from adding apostrophes automatically — which is hard since I am an autopilot apostrophe inserter. Here it is:

Its tail was wagging, but its not clear why.

"Does this sentence need any more apostrophes?" I asked.

"No," said Nadia.

"I haven't put any in yet," I hinted.

"Oh," said Nadia. "The first 'its' needs an apostrophe."

"No, it doesn't," interrupted Nadia's mother.

"The second 'its,'" said Clara of the pom-pom hat.

Nadia's mom started, "Because it means the—"

I cut Mom off before she spilled the grammar beans. "The second 'its'?" I asked. "Why do you say that?"

Clara said, "Because it means 'it is not clear.'" Clara was accompanied by several small backup "it is" singers.

"Very good," I said. "Do you want to do one more?" There was a chorus of yeses from the children.

"Can I do one?" asked a small boy, Alex.

"Of course," I said.

"What are you even supposed to *do* at the Grammar Table?" asked a third girl in a blue hoodie.

"It can be anything about words," I said.

"Why does my brother always ask 'Why?'" asked the girl in the blue hoodie.

"Why?" asked Alex, the small boy who had just asked to do a question and who also appeared to be her brother.

"That's a sign of intellectual curiosity," I said. "It's a wonderful foundation for an excellent life."

"Why?" asked Alex. Amid holiday hubbub, I wrote:

The car was clean, but its headlight was broken.

"Do I need an apostrophe in this one or not?" I asked.

"No!" said the children in unison.

"Correct!" I said. "You guys are all over this! Do you feel like you need another one? Oh, I know! Let's say you see your friend and you say, 'It's been too long.'"

Nadia and Clara replied together, "Apostrophe!"

"Because that means . . ." I began.

"'It has'!" said Nadia and Clara simultaneously.

"Do you know what apostrophe is?" the woman in green asked Alex. I concluded that she must be his mother.

"Why?" asked Alex.

"Do you know what it is?" she repeated.

"Why?" said Alex. His mom smiled, shook her head, and gave up.

Quizlet

....

What is the sum of (a) the number of things "it's" can mean and (b) the number of things "who's" can mean?

Answer: 2 + 2 = 4

it's = it has: "It's been ages since I lent you that bicycle pump."
     it is: "It's a downward dog."

who's = who has: "Who's been stealing the pizzas?"
       who is: "Who's a good girl?"

45

More Homophonous Happenings: "Your" and "Their"

In Fargo, an elderly man in suspenders and a black Dakota Heritage Bank cap approached the table.

"One mistake I make all the time is the word 'your,'" said the man, whose name was Paul.

"'Your' versus 'you're,' right?" I asked, writing them down and showing him.

"That's right, and I miss out on this one," he said, pointing to "you're." "I should be putting that down instead of *y o u r*. Is *y o u r* only for possession?"

"Yes, only possession," I said. "And *y o u* apostrophe *r e* is only 'you are.' People sometimes write 'Your welcome' with *y o u r* by mistake."

"That's wrong?" he asked.

"Yes," I said, "because 'You are welcome' is the idea."

"Oh, I put *y o u r* all the time," said Paul. "So it should be like this all the time, huh?"

"Yes," I said, and gave him a Grammar Table postcard.

"This is where it originated in New York City," I explained. "That's right outside our apartment building. And then we took it on the road."

"Oh, for crying out loud," said Paul in amazement.

"My grandmother used to say that," I said. "I miss it!"

"Yeah, we say funny things here," he replied cheerfully. "I often say 'Holy catfish.'"

¶

On Martha's Vineyard, a health coach named Louisa was surveying the Grammar Table.

"My pet peeves about grammar?" she asked, exhaling. "'Your,' 'you're,' and 'yore.' Those are my pet peeves."

Because they are homophones, I couldn't tell which "your" was which in her sentence, or whether "yore" was even really intended to be one of them. But those are the three yores! Or yours. Or you'res. So that's what yore going to here about hear.

Just kidding in that last bit! Totally kidding!

"Have you ever gotten* an email where the whole email was this?" I asked Louisa, showing her this:

Your welcome.

"Yes," said Louisa. "That's what it is."

"If there are two words and one is wrong, it's a fifty percent error rate," I said.

"Yes," said Louisa. "I love it."

I feel sure that the antecedent for "it"† was the Grammar Table rather than the error rate.

---

* If you are from across the Atlantic and are bothered by "gotten" (i.e., rather than "got" or some other verb): "gotten" has existed in English since the fourteenth century, so while it may be conspicuous today in American English, it is older than the US, which means we are not the ones who started it, ahem.

† As a reminder, the antecedent is the noun or pronoun "it" refers back to.

"I tell people that if they're going to write an email that short, they should at least get the spelling right," I said.

"You see 'Your invited'—*y o u r*—on invitations, too," said Louisa.

"And then what do you do?" I asked. "Do you say no?" I cracked myself up.

In exchange for the grammar chat, Louisa handed me a small bottle. "It's mineral sunscreen," she said. "You need that in your life." She was right. I really did. It is sunburning to be a summertime Grammar Table!

¶

From an earlier chapter, you may remember Maddie, the college athlete in Wichita whose grandmother texted "lol" when Maddie's cat died.

Maddie had questions about three commonly confused words. "I don't know how to use 'there,' 'they're,' and 'their' properly," she said. "I've gotten really, really, really yelled at for using the wrong one."

"You're yelled at?" I asked. "That sounds like a harsh reaction."

This was clearly a grammergency. I invited Maddie to guess which of the three homophones would work in these blanks.

_____ *friends are over* _____.

She guessed wrong. "I don't know," said Maddie. "See why I'm asking?"

"I'm glad you're asking!" I said. We filled in the blanks together.

Their friends are over there.

"This first one, 'their,' is usually described as a possessive," I explained. "Since you're talking about whose friends they are, it needs to be *t h e i r*. And then the second one is often a location."

"All right," said Maddie. I wrote some sentences down on a piece of paper for her to use as a reference sheet.

"So you use *t h e r e* for location and also just when you're saying 'there is' or 'there are,'" I said.

Here are some more sentences for you, esteemed grammar book reader, to consider while you are here:

There is an old waffle in my bed.

There are too many hyperactive puppies in this room.

I don't think there's enough ice cream in this ice cream sundae.

"And then, I don't know if you get this one mixed up," I said, pointing at "they're" on the page, "but that's just a contraction for 'they are.'"

"All of them!" said Maddie. "It's not one; it's all of them. I just now learned a semicolon, so I'm getting there."

"Okay, good," I said. "Semicolons are hard for a lot of people. A lot of people never use them."

I decided to give my grammar guest additional examples for her cheat sheet, so I added two more sentences, each of them containing all three words.

They're over there with their friends.

<u>They're</u> not going to bring <u>their</u> bikes <u>there</u>.

As I handed her the paper, Maddie told me, "I'm probably going to keep it and put it in my wallet, not gonna lie. Because I'm probably going to use it for a lot of text messages. I kid you not. It's been a problem!"

¶

This next incident took place at the Grammar Table in front of the Geiser Grand Hotel in Baker City, Oregon.

"I have a philosophical question," said a Grammar Table visitor, a writer doing research for her book. "Say that you knew a guy who was brilliant, compassionate, talented, extremely hardworking, ridiculously handsome, and highly ethical, but who did not know how to distinguish between 'your' and 'you're'? Would you date him?"

"Could we perhaps just attribute it to one instance of carelessness, or are you talking about something serial?" I asked.

"There's a pattern," she said. "And to be clear, I'm not actually thinking about dating him, but it occurred to me that he's extremely eligible. And then I always go, Oh, but he uses 'your' instead of 'you're.'"

"I haven't been tested on this because I've been with this man for more than twenty-five years and he's really meticulous," I said, pointing to Brandt, who smiled. "I think yes, but I might try to teach him the difference." She and I laughed.

"You chose wisely," said the writer. "You're on the side of 'Love will find a way.'"

Quizlet

• •

1. _____ (They're, Their, There) are _____ (they're, their, there) zucchini chocolate chip muffins.

2. _____ (They're, Their, There) not sure that _____ (you're, your) ready to rumble.

Answers: *1. There, their 2. They're, you're*

46

Had Had, That That,
Do Do, Do Be Do!

Remember Kevin, the shirtless runner who coined "parentheseized" in Austin's Zilker Park? "One thing that always got me," he told me, "and that still doesn't make sense to me, is Ayn Rand used 'that that' a lot in *Atlas Shrugged*. I hate that. I hate when there's two 'that's together."

"That that?" I asked.

"I know it's correct," said Kevin, "but it's just so frustrating to read. She used it like a hundred times in that book."

"Occasionally, though, if you take out a 'that,' it's harder to read," I said.

"It is," said Kevin. "Which is weird."

"Because you don't know which kind of 'that' you have left," I said.

For example, let's start with a sentence containing two consecutive "that"s.

It is unsurprising <u>that that</u> new employee showed up half an hour late.

The first "that" is a conjunction, and the second "that" is what is known as a demonstrative adjective. Although

I don't run around seeking out "that"-doubling opportunities, the double "that" doesn't bother me here. In case it does bother you, however, let's see what happens if we remove one of them.

• •

"That" Is a Hard Worker

There's a reason people often end up with lots of "that"s in a sentence: "that" can be multiple parts of speech with multiple functions.

Demonstrative pronoun[*]	<u>That</u> is not my name.
Conjunction	Gaston said <u>that</u> they wouldn't be here by five.
Relative pronoun	I want to hear more about the boat <u>that</u> you saw today.
Demonstrative adjective	I want to hear more about <u>that</u> boat.

• •

---

[*] Other demonstrative pronouns include "this," "these," and "those."

*It is unsurprising <u>that</u> new employee showed up half
an hour late.*

I like this version fine too, but be aware of a small
consequence of cutting the first "that" in sentences like
this one. For a split second now, when the reader reads
the words "It is unsurprising that new," it is possible —
maybe even likely — that that "that" (yeah, I went there!)
will be misread as the conjunction. As soon as the reader
reaches "employee" and realizes that that "that" is actually just a modifier for "employee," then all becomes
clear, but it is a potential minor brain blip, and this sentence is slightly more work than the original version with
the double "that." While I do sometimes delete a "that"
in twin-"that" cases like this, I don't do it with impunity.

"'That' is like that, like, step-cousin you just, like, don't
need but, like, he's there," said Kevin. "It's just like, Why?
Why is it there? But it works for some reason."

"You have a well-developed grammar philosophy," I
said.

"Thank you very much. Well, reach out if you want to
talk about it more," he said, after filling in his contact information on the Grammar Table documentary release
form. He took a picture of the Grammar Table for his
mother before leaving, and then he and his exuberance
were off.

¶

Besides "that that," there aren't a lot of words you can
double up in English like, um, *that*. You can put two instances of "do" in quick succession, but you can't say
this: "I'm going to walk walk to the park."

Doubled words happen in some other languages a lot more than they do in English. For example, in Indonesian, *anak* is child and *anak-anak* is children. When I was studying Arabic, I learned that I could say *shway* to mean "a little" and *shway shway* to emphasize that idea.

Doubled words in English can happen with verbs that act as both helping verbs and action verbs. Here are some examples:

> *But I <u>do do</u> my homework every night, Mommy!*

> *By the time he'd finished one piece of cake, I <u>had had</u> three.*

In both sentences, the first verb in the underlined pair is a helping verb and the second is an action verb.

Here's another doubling example:

> *She gave <u>her her</u> receipt.*

The first "her" is an object pronoun, and the second "her" is a possessive adjective.

Even the mini-word "to" can pile up when you're not looking.

> *You have to know what that's comparable <u>to to</u> perform a proper analysis.*

In this sentence, the first "to" is a preposition, and the second "to" has the meaning "in order to."

None of these sentences are wrong, but there are cases where doubled words sound awkward. I don't care for this last one, and you could easily rewrite it to avoid the double "to."

> *To perform a proper analysis, you have to know what that's comparable to.**

or

> *You have to know what that's comparable to in order to perform a proper analysis.*

I will leave that aesthetic judgment up to you.
Do do be do!

---

* It would be difficult to get that concluding preposition out of that position, and there's no reason for me to try.

Quizlet

••

Identify the function of each doubled word in the sentence below. This one is advanced, so please don't feel bad if you can't do it. However, do pat yourself on the back if you can!

> Yes, I <u>do do</u> the dance <u>that that</u> girl taught me.

Answer: *do #1 = helping verb, do #2 = action verb, that #1 = relative pronoun, that #2 = demonstrative adjective*

47

The Art of Writing with Your Actual Hand

American nostalgia for the days of universal cursive instruction is not universal.

"I once took cursive lessons," a young man in Spokane told me, "and when they stopped, I realized that was the last time I would really ever need to write it except for a formal signature." He did not enjoy it, he said.

When I was a kid, I loved it, but back then there was no computer keyboard competing for my attention, and there was a daily reason to know cursive, because that's how we wrote our homework assignments.

In South Bend, I talked to another young person, a friendly woman in a purple dress, about languages as well as about cursive. She had taken four years of German in high school—voluntarily and intentionally. That impressed me. When she signed a release for the Grammar Table documentary, I saw her tidy signature.

"You have pretty neat handwriting," I said. "It looks like you were taught by someone who maybe was trained in a previous generation, because it's very slanty and flowy."

"I actually switched to cursive in high school," she told me. "I had an issue with people cheating off my answers, and I found out that people who tend to cheat on exams can't read cursive. And so my entire high school career, I would do written tests in cursive."

"They wanted to cheat off of you because they were like, 'This woman takes German, so we know she knows something!'" I said.

In Richmond, Virginia, a grammar enthusiast named Nanette said, "You know what they don't teach anymore these days? Cursive! Our daughter was in a Catholic school, so she got two years of cursive, but a lot of kids now only know enough to sign their name."

"Do you have nice handwriting?" I asked.

"No, it looks awful," said Nanette.

"I have the worst handwriting," said her friend, Colleen. "We were taught cursive in third or fourth grade. And then you had to write everything in cursive all through junior high. I have the literal worst handwriting, though. And you would think I'd have good handwriting, because I had to write in cursive for so long."

"I have good handwriting, but I hate doing cursive, so I print," I said. "I love printing, because to me it just looks tidier. I like the upright letters. Wait, I'm going to show you my handwriting." I began signing my name.

"That's nice," said Nanette. "That's how my aunts write. They all are teachers, and they've got that beautiful cursive handwriting."

"Well, I guess this isn't that great, because right here you really can't tell what's going on," I said, pointing at the last name in my signature.

"I think with your signature you can't judge," said Nanette.

"No," agreed Colleen. "I've had the same signature regardless of what my name is."

"It could be anything!" I said, laughing.

"I've had multiple last names," said Colleen. "No, not multiple; it's not like I've been married thirty times."

"She's not Elizabeth Taylor," Nanette assured me.

"But I didn't have to change my signature when I got married and my name changed, because it's just a loop," Colleen said. "So it works!"

In Starkville, Mississippi, I encountered some concern about the lost art of handwriting. "You know that in some schools they don't even require students to learn cursive?" asked a man about my age.

"Yes, I do know that," I said.

"I was kind of shocked," said the man. "I was very surprised."

"I have mixed feelings about it," I said. "I loved learning it in school, and it creates an intimacy with words, I think. I'm kind of a bionic typist, but when I really want to get ideas for something, I tend to get out a notebook and write by hand. However, I print rather than use cursive, so I'm not a huge cursive fan. I love printing. I have very tidy printing."

"Pretty letters," said the man agreeably, looking at some of the words written on my notepad.

"It's difficult to argue for cursive when you hardly ever use it," I said, "though I've read that it does some brain stuff that might be important for language skill development."

"What about reading things that are out there like the Constitution or the Declaration of Independence?" he asked.

"I know that argument," I said, "but almost no one reads them in the cursive. They tend to read the printed text that's next to them in the museums."

"Yeah," he said. "You're right. I guess just the ability to read letters from your mother or your dad or your grandparents or . . . I don't know."

"Do you have old family letters?" I asked.

"I do," said the man.

"Because I have some and they're hard to read, even though I'm used to reading people's handwriting, because the style of cursive is different," I said.

"Mm-hmm," he said.

"I do have mixed feelings about it," I said. "I think it is a way to connect kids with language. But the specific educational value of it is a scientific question that's outside my area of expertise. I just don't know. From a practical point of view, if I had to choose between having kids learn cursive and having them read twenty more books a year, maybe I would pick the books."

"I see," he said. "Where's the time better spent?"

"I just want the language skill development," I said. "And I don't know the best way to do that, because I mostly focus on grown-up stuff."

¶

"Look at that handwriting," said Jason in Decatur, Alabama. We were still discussing punctuation—and, apparently, still discussing my handwriting as well. "It is so fancy," he added.

"It's beautiful," said Jack.

Jason was smoking another cigarette. "I love handwriting," he said. "I love calligraphy, too."

"Really?" I asked. "I never did anything with that. Did you ever study it?"

"Oh, I have a little bit," said Jason. "I have never been

really good. I just kind of"—he wrote in the air with his hand—"did basics."

"Did you get a calligraphy pen?" I asked.

"Yeah," said Jason. "Yeah. Like a . . . What do they call it?"

Jack said something inaudible, and Jason told him, "Hey, go fuck yourself, nobody asked you."

"*She* did," said Jack.

"Do you have nice stationery?" I asked.

"Yes!" said Jason. "Stationery. That's what it is."

"So you like stationery," I said.

"I do," said Jason.

"Did you like stationery stores growing up?" I asked.

"Yes," said Jason. "My sister is, like, super artistic, and I used to go to Hobby Lobby with her, and she bought all this, like, sculpting stuff and everything, and I saw it and I was like, I love calligraphy, man. It's just such beautiful ways you can write all these words, so yeah, I got me a little calligraphy set—you know, with a fountain pen!"

"Oh, that's fancy," I said. "I have no fountain pen."

"All the inks and everything, yes!" He was getting so excited that Jack and I began laughing. "And it's different tips," he added. "I didn't even know there were different tips!"

"Did you know he was into this?" I asked Jack.

"No, ma'am, I did not," said Jack.

"And I was like, Man, this is so cool!" said Jason.

"No, ma'am," said Jack. "This is news to me."

"I know, man, I'm a nerd," Jason said. "I love calligraphy." He wrote in the air again with his hand as he smoked.

"So you can read cursive easily?" I asked.

"Absolutely," said Jason.

"I don't know whether this is true in Alabama," I said, "but you know that a lot of kids now in the United States don't learn cursive."

"Yeah, they work on computers now," said Jack.

"I am aware of that, and that's a very unfortunate thing," said Jason. "Yeah, because everybody knows typing. But I believe that typing is a very strong skill to have as well. Cursive is important. It absolutely is important, but I think that living in the modern age, people ought to be able to type at least a hundred words a minute."

"You have a very well-developed text-production philosophy," I said.

"Thank you," said Jason. "I appreciate that. I'm not real sure what that means, but I appreciate it anyway."

Quizlet

••

Write the sentence below—which contains all twenty-six letters of the English alphabet—in cursive.

*The quick brown dog jumps over the lazy fox.**

My answer:

The quick brown dog jumps over the lazy fox.

_____

* This sentence normally contains a quick brown fox and a lazy dog, but I reversed the nouns to give the dog a break.

48

School Days

At the Grammar Table, people often like to reminisce about things they did back when they were in school. In Salt Lake City, a man named Douglas who was around my age asked, "Remember diagramming sentences?"

"Yes!" I said, throwing my arms up in enthusiasm. This is what diagramming looks like, and I learned it from Ms. Barbara Beebe during the 1978–79 school year, when I was in eighth grade.

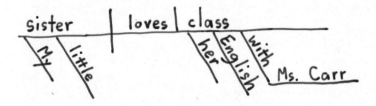

In this system, introduced by Alonzo Reed and Brainerd Kellogg a century before it arrived in my Southern California classroom, you draw a long horizontal line, put the subject on the left of it, the verb to the right of the subject, and any direct object to the right of the verb. You place adjectives, adverbs, and prepositional phrases below the main line under the elements they modify. There's a lot more, but those are some of the basics.

Most people who learn diagramming these days learn a more modern method, but there is lingering nostalgia for the old one, as there often is for the ways of one's childhood.

"I hated it," said Douglas.

"I loved it so much," I said.

"I never figured it out," said Douglas, "but I wondered, why did we ever quit doing that?"

"Maybe because people hated it?" I said.

"And did it really make a difference?" he asked.

"For me it did," I said. "It's central to why I'm sitting here at the table today, because it really captured my imagination. A lot of kids hated it, but I loved it, and I even did it as an adult. I got a sentence-diagramming book and I started up again."

"When I was done with that and I heard that they weren't teaching it anymore, I'm like, Finally!" said Douglas. "Now if you just get rid of the algebra, I'll be fine."

All over the country, people brought up this once-popular instructional tool. Usually they were around my age or older. In South Bend, Indiana, a man asked me, "How do you feel about the fact that schools don't teach sentence diagramming anymore?"

"I think there are other systems you can use to convey similar knowledge," I said, "so I don't feel sad about it. But I loved it."

"You did?" asked the man, who clearly did not.

"For me that was the thing that glued me to language love," I said. "In fact, I just reunited with my diagramming teacher in California a few months ago." (Hi, Ms. Beebe!)

"It kind of goes back maybe to personality types, I think," said the man. "I never liked diagramming. My wife loves it. But she also loves to line things up on the windowsill."

¶

Some school memories linger longer than others. "Do you have any grammar questions?" I asked a pair of women in Santa Fe.

"So many," said the younger woman, who had reddish hair and was probably in her twenties.

"Do you have a *Warriner's*?" the other woman asked me. It turned out she was the younger woman's mother, and her name was Maria. She meant *Warriner's English Grammar and Composition,* a popular English textbook that I used when I was in school.

"I don't have a *Warriner's* here," I said. "I might have one on my shelf at home. Do you teach?"

"No," said Maria. "When I went to my all-girls high school, Ursuline Academy, for the four years, the Ursuline nuns gave us the little *Warriner's* book."

"I went to an all-girls high school!" I told her.

"We had to carry it around to every class," she said. "It was the rule. Any violation of the book, they would just, like, put the number of the violation, 1A—in every class, anything we wrote. If we were writing an essay or a report, the rule was, one error brought your grade down from an A to a B, two errors to a C—so the first weeks of school, we were all devastated. But the rule was you could rewrite it. You would have the corrections there with the numbers, and then they would grade it again."

"That's very systematic," I said. "I'm intrigued by the cross-department coordination."

"The students secretly called it the bible," she said. "So we'd say: 'Do you have a bible?' And sometimes teachers would overhear us and they'd wonder, 'You're carrying around your Bible?' And then it was like, no no no, it's our *Warriner's*!"

"Do you still remember, since you were so exposed to this, what any of the number references stood for?" I asked.

"Gosh, no," she said. "I wish I could."

"I bet some of the teachers remember," I said, "so that on their deathbeds, if a nurse comes to tend to them, they'll be like, That was 2A."

"Oh, yeah," said Maria. "Or 3A. Exactly. I bet you you're right."

"Did you appreciate that grammar focus?" I asked.

"I did," she said.

"Did you also go to a strict school with a grammar bible?" I asked her daughter.

"No, I did not," said the daughter.

"Did you already know about your mother's bible?" I asked.

"No, I didn't," she said. "This is so funny!"

¶

"I love your table," said a man named Vincent in Detroit. "I have a mug someone gave me that says I'M SILENTLY CORRECTING YOUR GRAMMAR."

"Do you walk around with it a lot?" I asked.

"I want to bring it into meetings and then start sipping on it when people say the wrong shit," said Vincent. "But I don't."

"Because you don't want to be mean, right?" I asked.

"I don't want to be that guy," said Vincent. "But I'm silently always hearing the wrong thing."

"What if it's a long presentation and you have to hear the wrong thing seventeen times?" I asked.

"Oh my god," said Vincent. He told me about a teacher he had in elementary school who would give bonus points to students when they heard someone make a grammatical error.

"It could be the principal making an announcement on the PA," he said, "and she'd be like, 'Somebody's ears should be burning. Whose ears are burning?' And if you got the right answer, you got bonus points. And it just kind of stuck with me, so I'm always hearing people speak incorrectly and say the wrong word."

"Did that teacher want you to tell her? Or actually tell the principal?" I asked.

"We did it in the confines of the classroom," said Vincent.

"Okay, because I was going to say, there are certain etiquette issues around that," I said.

"No," said Vincent. "The principal would make an announcement over the PA for the whole school, and the teacher would be waiting anxiously for the announcement to end so she could find out if any of us caught what she caught."

¶

Great teachers leave behind great memories.

"Oh my god," said Kelly, in Toledo. "I had the best

English teacher in ninth grade. That's where I learned grammar, and it's stuck with me."

"What was the teacher's name?" I asked.

"Her name was Mrs. Skoulis," said Kelly.

"Oh!" I said. "It sounds exactly like a teacher's name should sound. Seriously, it's like 'School us.'"

Kelly appeared unimpressed by this observation. She continued, "I learned a lot, but I don't remember what some of these things are called."

"You don't need to," I said. "You incorporate that into your being."

"Right," said Kelly. "I just know how to do it."

"Do you want to give a shout-out to Mrs. Skoulis?" I asked. "Is she still alive?"

"I have no idea," said Kelly. "I feel like she was pretty old back then."

"But twenty-five was pretty old back then," I pointed out.

"No," said Kelly. "She literally was old. And this would have been in the seventies. A teenager's perspective is different, but I'm going to go out on a limb and say she had to be at least in her fifties or sixties at that time."

"Okay," I said. "So she might no longer be with us."

"She might not be," said Kelly.

"Except in our hearts and minds," I said.

"Her legacy lives on!" said Kelly's co-worker.

Quizlet

....

As a special quizlet for nostalgic Reed-Kellogg sentence diagrammers, diagram this sentence:

> Poor Horace left the orchids in the trunk
> of a yellow cab.

Answer:

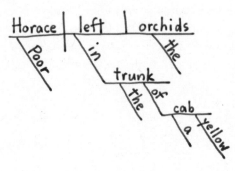

49

Grammar Boogie

Brandt and I were packing up Grammar Table items beneath inky skies in Starkville, Mississippi, discussing whether we should go to New Orleans that night.

"Drive safely if you do," said our new friend Ken, a.k.a. Kyin.

"Why do you say that?" I asked. "Because of the weather?"

"Yes," said Ken. "It's uncharacteristically dark right now. And the skies are really black."

"Okay, thank you for the warning," I said. "Even though we love this, we'd rather not die for it."

"Yeah," said Ken. "I'd hate to know I was the last person to see you."

Because of the Grammar Table, now I know Ken. Before we went to Baker City and many other places, they were dots on a map. Now Baker City is a place that I will always remember, where I met new people and experienced humor and joy. I know the grand old hotel there. I met a local woman whose husband had just recovered from cancer. I met a committed local reporter. I met the people responsible for getting beautiful public sculptures installed all through the town. Brandt and I saw the rambling, creative inside of the home of a gallery owner there. I know something about Baker City, where other members of this human community live and visit, and that is just plain moving to my heart. The world feels simultaneously bigger and smaller.

This type of thing happened all over the country, and people surprised me every step of the way. In Memphis, before we were kicked out of our choice location across the street from the Crosstown mall, I spoke to two security guards, a man and a woman, who were extremely nice to us even as they were doing their job and helping to remove us.

While the man was on the phone speaking to the main office about whether the Grammar Table could stay, I asked the female guard, "Do you have any grammar questions?"

"Oh!" said the guard, whose name was Zelda. "I'm a student of the English language."

"Are you?" I asked, delighted. "Do you want a Grammar Table postcard then?"

"Yes," she said. She took it and looked at it.

"If everybody put their cell phones down and started back opening up their English book—" said Zelda.

"Exactly," said her colleague, who was now off the phone.

"—and learned how to read," said Zelda.

"If I need a substitute, I should just come to you," I said.

"All you got to do is holler," said Zelda.

"Have you always been like this?" I asked.

"Always," she told me. "In elementary school, before I even knew what advanced English was, I was in advanced English. I just love the word, you know. I love reading because you can go all over the world just from a book."

This conversation took place in a barren concrete park next to a parking lot across from a mall. You never know who will surprise you. So while I love grammar, it's not really the end, I suppose, but rather a means.

"You're giving your life to grammar," a reporter in New Orleans said to me.

"I don't know that I'd put it quite that way," I said.

"It's not nice to comma splice?" he asked.

"Oh my gosh," I said. "Grammar rhymes. This could be in *Grammar Table: The Musical*."

"Da-da da da-da da," sang the reporter, doing a little grammar dance, complete with dash hands.

From the Grammar Table to you: Language is a dance we all do together as human beings, and I hope you have enjoyed this dance. Let's keep dancing, together, okay?

Acknowledgments

I am grateful to my parents, who caused those first sound waves to travel into my baby ear canals and bring early understanding and language joy; to my larger family for decades of love, words, and wit; to all the teachers who ever taught me new facts and ideas; to my literary agent and friend, Victoria Skurnick of Levine Greenberg Rostan; to Jim Levine of Levine Greenberg Rostan for his generous help; to my editor Olivia Bartz and publisher Deb Brody, who gave this book a home at Houghton Mifflin Harcourt; to my editor Jessica Vestuto of Houghton Mifflin Harcourt, who nurtured it to completion; to my copy editor, Alison Kerr Miller, who dropped entertaining language tales into her editorial comments; to senior production editor Beth Fuller, who patiently answered my plentiful questions; to all the people from around the world who shared pieces of their language lives with me at the Grammar Table; and to Brandt Johnson, my husband and business partner, who has been making me laugh with his wordplay for twenty-eight excellent years and who, from the moment he first fastened my Grammar Table sign to the table so it would stop flying away, has been my partner in these grammar adventures.

Tabletop Bibliography: What's on the Grammar Table?

The tabletop inventory changes from day to day, but here is a partial list of what has shown up on the Grammar Table.

Style and Usage Guides

The Associated Press Stylebook
The Chicago Manual of Style
Garner's Modern English Usage by Bryan A. Garner
Fowler's Dictionary of Modern English Usage, fourth edition, edited by Jeremy Butterfield
The New York Times Manual of Style and Usage by Allan M. Siegal and William G. Connolly
The Elements of Style, 2005 illustrated edition, by William Strunk Jr. and E. B. White

Dictionaries

Merriam-Webster's Collegiate Dictionary, eleventh edition
The American Heritage Dictionary, fifth edition

Grammar

Essential Grammar for Business: The Foundation of Good Writing by me

Linguistics

The Cambridge Grammar of the English Language by
  Rodney Huddleston and Geoffrey K. Pullum

English as a Foreign Language

Practical English Usage by Michael Swan
*English at Work: Find and Fix Your Mistakes in Business
  English* by me

Other English-Related Books

These change with the seasons, new releases, and my
mood, but I've brought out Benjamin Dreyer's book
*Dreyer's English: An Utterly Correct Guide to Clarity and
Style,* Mary Norris's *Between You and Me: Confessions of
a Comma Queen,* Cecelia Watson's *Semicolon: The Past,
Present, and Future of a Misunderstood Mark,* and Cath-
leen Schine's *The Grammarians: A Novel.*

Books on Other Languages

I typically bring out books on at least two languages other
than English: German, Spanish, Swahili, Persian, Russian, French, Italian, Lakota, Japanese, Portuguese, Chinese, Arabic, Korean, Hindi, Polish, or whatever feels
right on a given day. If your native language is something
other than English, there is an excellent chance I have
brought out a book to represent it on the table.

Index